CLIFF MORGAN
The Autobiography

Beyond the fields
of play

CLIFF MORGAN
The Autobiography

===

Beyond the fields of play

===

CLIFF MORGAN
with
GEOFFREY NICHOLSON

Hodder & Stoughton

First published in Great Britain in 1996 by
Hodder and Stoughton
a division of Hodder Headline PLC

10 9 8 7 6 5 4 3 2 1

British Library Cataloguing in Publication Data

Morgan, Cliff, 1930–
Cliff Morgan
1. Morgan, Cliff, 1930– 2. Rugby football players – Wales –
Biography
I. Title II. Nicholson, Geoffrey, 1929–
763.3'33'092

ISBN 0 340 65741 3

Typeset by Hewer Text Composition Services, Edinburgh
Printed and bound in Great Britain by
Mackays of Chatham PLC, Chatham, Kent

Hodder and Stoughton Ltd
A division of Hodder Headline PLC
338 Euston Road
London NW1 3BH

Contents

Acknowledgements

The author and publishers would like to thank the following for permission to reproduce their copyright photographs: Sport & General, Colorsport, the *Western Mail & Echo*, and the BBC.

1

At a stroke, everything changed

It's hard to pinpoint the moment I became ill. It was probably while I was doing the radio commentary on a Services rugby match in Germany in the middle of March 1972. I had better explain how I came to be there. I'd spent the previous fourteen years – ever since I retired as a player – working for the BBC or ITV, either on the staff or under contract. But at this time I was totally freelance. My bread and butter was doing BBC rugby commentaries and introducing a weekly record programme, 'These You Have Loved', which I adored. Another regular employer was the British Forces Broadcasting Service. They didn't pay very much, probably about £25 a broadcast, but they were a congenial lot and in my position you never said no to anything. It might be the last offer you got.

To BFBS the British Army of the Rhine's rugby cup final was one of the big events of the season. So I found myself at Bad Lippspringe describing the play live to servicemen at home and all around the world. It wasn't the easiest thing I've ever done. The commentary box was a stool and a microphone on the roof of an army lorry parked with its nose right up to the touchline. The players from the Duke of Wellington's Regiment on one side, and the Welsh Guards on the other, were mostly strangers to me, so to identify them I had to keep referring to the numbers on their backs. Already that day I'd done a few other local programmes for BFBS, mostly to do with music. I was in the sun, and I didn't feel terribly well, though I thought it was just some sort of bug I'd picked up.

That may have been the start, or it may have been during the evening meal. I had been driven back to Cologne to stay with the head of the BFBS sports section there. He'd made my visit the excuse for a dinner party, and there was a lot of lively shop talk about Cliff Michelmore and David Jacobs, who'd both begun their careers with the forces station, about remote broadcasting outposts like Belize, and the activities of the British Army stationed among their former enemies in Germany. I still wasn't feeling right, and though I struggled to keep going in the conversation, in the end I had to excuse myself and go up to bed. And that's where it finally happened. Strokes come in different ways to different people. Mine came when I was asleep that night.

I knew nothing about it until I woke up the next morning feeling, well, not exactly giddy, but not quite sane. I tried to lift myself up and found I had no feeling down the left-hand side of my body. I thought I must have slept awkwardly on my left arm and leg, stopping the circulation, and as often happens, they had just 'gone to sleep' for a few minutes. But the feeling didn't come back into them. Then, when I tried to sit up I found I couldn't balance properly. It was the opposite of being drunk: I was OK lying down; it was only on sitting up that I found the room going round. I remember falling to the side, and not knowing what the hell was happening. I was very frightened. I fell and lost consciousness, which was how my hosts found me. They sent for a doctor, and though I drifted in and out of consciousness in the ambulance, when I next woke up properly with a clearer mind, I was lying in a hospital bed. There were tubes in my arms, and drips, and goodness knows what. And before I drifted off again, I saw this woman looking down on me, the most beautiful I'd ever known, or so it seemed to me at the time. It was a nun, one of the nursing sisters who worked in the hospital. And whenever I woke, she always seemed to be there.

Gradually the periods of consciousness lengthened and I took in my surroundings. I was in a bed near the door of a long, narrow ward in Cologne general hospital. And the curious thing was I found myself moving every day or so closer to the window on the right hand side. I was conscious of this, but I couldn't explain it. What I didn't realise was that they were moving dead patients out of the ward, and closing up the gaps. All the same, I was worried because I didn't know what was going on. The doctors were doing masses of tests on me, but they and the nuns spoke only German. I was getting no visitors at this stage and had time to brood. I thought this was the end, and asked why the hell was it me. It was shock more than anything, but it was shock that made me feel – probably because of my chapel background – that I had done something wrong. This was a sort of judgement on me.

For a day or so Nuala, my wife, didn't have a clue what was happening to me. She knew I was doing some work in Germany, but not exactly what it was or where exactly I was supposed to be staying. She began to get concerned when I didn't return, though it was not until BFBS phoned her that she discovered that there was anything wrong with me. Then there was another delay before she came to see me because she had to borrow money from my father to buy an air ticket to Cologne. We didn't have any money in the bank. Once Nuala reached the city, BFBS and the Services looked after her. The Army sent a Roman Catholic padré to meet her at the airport and, although he was confined to a wheelchair after some accident, he cared for her wonderfully, bringing her to the hospital and taking her back to catch her plane home next day. She couldn't stay longer because she had to look after our two children, Catherine and Nicholas, who were just in their teens. I felt extremely lonely when Nuala left and I had to go back to sign language to express myself. But two developments helped to give me a lift.

The news of my illness – I didn't yet know it was a stroke – must have got out, for suddenly people were coming to see me in the hospital. The first visitors I only vaguely remember, but I know there was a cricket team from London which included the Scottish internationals Ian Robertson and Mike Biggar. And among the Service people who arrived was an Army officer, Denis Shuttleworth, who had played scrum-half for England. He was very concerned about me. People from the Royal Navy and the RAF were also trying to see that I was properly looked after. And I learned that Larry Lamb, who had refereed ten internationals in his day, was using his considerable clout on my behalf as Air Commodore G.C. Lamb.

Then, when I was two beds away from the window, they moved me out of this ward and up to the fourth floor to share a small room with a German patient. He'd also had a stroke, but he was well on the way to recovery and was due to go home in five or six days' time. I imagine the hospital put us together because he could speak a few words of English – and, it turned out, Welsh. Thirty years before, he had worked as a prisoner of war on farms around Bridgend, near where I was born, and kept coming out with phrases like 'Iechyd da' (Good health) and 'Bore da' (Good morning) which, even with his strong German accent, made me feel more at home. He was terrific to me. He told me I needed a shave, and since I couldn't use my left hand at all, and wasn't much good with my right, he shaved me every morning. Because I couldn't walk properly, either, he'd half-carry me to the lavatory. He did everything for me. But more than anything he made me feel less isolated and that lifted my spirits.

Worries still kept me awake at night. There were two things especially on my mind. One was, had I fixed to pay the school fees for the kids? The other, at the back of my mind, was what would happen to 'These You Have Loved', which I was due to record on the Thursday evening. I couldn't do it, and I had to get messages to them. As it turned out this was one of the few permanent losses I suffered through my stroke. Richard Baker stood in that week, and then, as my absence lengthened, was asked to take over the programme which was eventually transformed into 'Baker's Dozen' and had an extremely long run. If it couldn't be me, I was happy that it should be Richard. I had also been due to turn out in a charity match in the Scottish borders with Alex 'Moose' Hastie and David Chisholm. Fourteen years after retiring, and nearing forty-two, I was still playing charity rugby almost every week. I must have been mad.

Still, these were only passing concerns. They would have to solve themselves. The long-term anxieties were much harder to come to grips with. What bothered me most was that while I was out in Germany, all the problems were at home. Nothing personal about them, just the question of where the next twenty quid was coming from. We just spent what I earned as a freelance, and now I wasn't earning anything. I didn't know when I'd be able to go back home or if I'd ever work again. The left side of my body was paralysed, my mouth was twisted down and my speech, on which I depended most of all, was badly slurred. Stupidly, I wasn't insured; we didn't bother about anything like that, which was crazy. What I didn't know at the time, I'm glad to say, was that a terrible row was building up about who was going to pay for my treatment. Not the BBC, I wasn't working for them, I was working for the BFBS. But they were arguing about whether it really was their responsibility. Fortunately, the matter was soon taken out of their hands.

When I hear people of my generation talk about the days of the genuine amateur, when players got no money, I think of my stroke. Two weeks after it happened the freemasonry of rugby was at work and I found myself in an ambulance being taken from Cologne to the RAF hospital at Wegberg on the Dutch border. I can't explain exactly how it was arranged, but I know it was Larry Lamb who contacted my wife and got the RAF to look after me. At Wegberg everything that could be done was done for me. What I received was beyond price, for at no cost to me I got the finest medical attention and also, because of rugby,

I had a constant round of visits from the hospital staff which kept my spirits up. I may not have been paid to play rugby, but years later I was more than compensated for that.

Doctors who might not be experts on strokes, but just showed a sympathetic interest in my problems, did a lot to help me through the early stages of my rehabilitation. Two surgeons in particular made certain I was entertained and cared for. One was an Ear, Nose and Throat specialist, known as Jones the Nose, the other an ophthalmic surgeon called Jones the Eyes. They used to pop in and see me when they were on their rounds and between operations, and they kept me ticking over and lifted my spirits, for it was very easy to fall into despair. I had hours and hours on my own in the nights, because I couldn't sleep at all well. I'd nod off and wake up, it was never constant sleep, just a few hours' cat napping.

One of the people who regularly came to see me was the padré who had looked after Nuala. He seemed to arrive when I felt particularly lousy, and what helped was that being disabled himself, he was able to address with unusual candour and understanding the frustration and despair you go through when you have a stroke. Naturally, I wanted to get better, but these talks helped to stiffen my will to recover. A lot of people with strokes give up, and I can understand why.

It was during this spell, too, that I received a letter from Richard Burton who was filming in Budapest; Elizabeth Taylor was there with him. He found out by chance what had happened to me. England were playing a soccer international in the city, and Peter Lorenzo, a successful tabloid football writer who was covering the match, wanted a few words with the great actor. As Richard was walking across the lobby of his hotel to take the lift, Peter, to gain his attention, called across, 'Did you know your friend Cliff Morgan is very ill in hospital in Germany?' Burton grabbed him, and took him up in the lift to get the whole story. Then he wrote me this letter which I still treasure:

> Dewch mas o'r le na (Get out of that place). You will need time for recuperation after this ordeal. Have one of our homes in Gstaad, or Pays de Galles in Geneva. Everything will be provided including sticks and coal! Should you need anything as mundane as money, you have only to ask.
> Cofion (Wishes), Richard
> With love, Elizabeth

That letter gave me a great boost. So did another event shortly afterwards. I was down in Physiotherapy, which was like a gymnasium, and going through further tests when one of the doctors examining me wished me 'Happy Birthday.' It was 7 April, I was forty-two, and I hadn't even remembered. He said that to celebrate that evening I could go up in my wheelchair to the doctors' bar on the top floor and have a pint of beer. That would be marvellous. The only snag was, when I got there they tied my right hand behind my back so that I had to raise the glass to my distorted lips with my practically useless left arm. I recognised that even this celebration was physiotherapy by another name, and I was determined to do it. I'd guess that only a third of the beer went down my throat; the rest I dribbled down my pyjamas and my borrowed dressing gown. All the same it was, for me, a glorious evening. Afterwards one of the sisters produced an x-ray of my head and gave me a white pencil to sign it as a souvenir for the staff. I'd signed a few autographs in my day, but this one was the most macabre. I'd never known I looked like that.

After my fortnight in Cologne I was another three weeks at Wegberg before being repatriated. I was flown by 'casavac', an air ambulance which ran a regular service between the BAOR and home for the benefit of sick servicemen, pregnant wives and now, to complete the RAF's generosity to me, an incapacitated rugby commentator. I was landed at Northwood, and then taken by ambulance to Wexham Park Hospital at Stoke Poges.

This part of it had been organised by David Coleman, the great all-rounder of sports broadcasting. I had first met David twenty years before, in my early days as an international, on Angus McKay's 'Sports Report'. We had later become colleagues on 'Grandstand' and 'Sportsview'. And now through a friend, John Williams, a vascular surgeon at Wexham Park, David had arranged for me to continue my treatment there.

Nobody seemed to know quite what had happened to me. Had my stroke been caused by the odd kicks on the head I had suffered playing rugby? Had I been rushing around too much in my work? John Williams sent me to St Mary's Hospital in Paddington for yet more tests, and the trip in the ambulance turned out to be pretty dramatic. A car cut across our path forcing the driver to swerve into a concrete telegraph post. While the front of the ambulance was a mess, we were unhurt, only shaken. But the police and the ambulance service arrived, and there was the usual enquiry. Then, only a few weeks later, I was with six other patients being taken by ambulance from the hospital to the nearby Farnham Park Rehabilitation Centre when we were involved in another crash. We were all thrown about, and I ended up on the floor. I was trapped by a woman who was lying across my legs, and blood from the nose of Mr Singh, an Indian patient, was dripping on my forehead. The head of the ambulance service turned up once more, noticed me, and said, 'Not bloody you again!' All my other journeys were made by car.

These became shorter when I left hospital and moved in with the lovely Williams family who looked after me day and night. From their home I travelled daily to the centre with Susan Williams and Barbara Coleman, David's wife, who gave the most precious and expensive thing in the world, their time, to act as my chauffeuses. Then, when John Williams thought I was ready to do so, I became a Farnham Park resident, sharing a room with four other men. The rehabilitation process began to accelerate.

Farnham Park is a big, old country house with lovely grounds, which was set up under the National Health Service to help accident victims to recover, as far as possible, their former faculties and well-being. There I met people who'd had a leg amputated, who had suffered car and motorbike crashes. One young man had badly damaged his back by falling into an empty swimming pool. The centre also took a special interest in sports injuries: a Queens Park Rangers footballer was having problems after a cartilage operation, an international javelin thrower, 'Tubs' Baker, was trying to get her elbow to respond properly. Some injuries were far more severe than others, but we were all in the same boat and it brought us closer together.

The routine in the centre was to get up early in the morning, make your bed, then help some neighbour who was more disabled to get ready for the day. One old boy next to me had artificial legs, and hated being helped to get into them. But you'd try and do little bits and pieces for him. Then you'd go down for breakfast, and I must say the food was terrific. The rest of the day you'd move from one group to the next doing different routines.

I was there four months, becoming the longest-serving inmate. In fact because of that, when the old matron left some years later I was asked to go back to make the presentation to her. Yet I was absorbed in what I and everybody else was doing, and the only thing that seemed worryingly long drawn-out was my time away from work. I was incapable of broadcasting, but Angus McKay said the BBC was doing a special radio programme to mark some anniversary of 'Sports Report'. Why didn't I write something which they could use with some rugby commentary I had done? They could pay me for that, so there would be a couple of quid coming in. It was a small thing, but it was the kind of encouragement I needed.

The various courses of treatment that Dr John Williams, who ran the centre, drew up for me consisted of physiotherapy, swimming, occupational therapy, games, long walks through the beautiful landscape of Farnham Park, and, most vital to me, speech therapy. I was desperate to succeed in them all. A woman teacher had the thankless job of getting me to speak properly again. She taught me how to form my lips and use my tongue, which was paralysed on the left-hand side, to get them round words. She would make me say 'ah-ey-ee-oo-ah-oo-uh' dozens of times in front of a mirror until I could do it to her satisfaction. Eventually it paid dividends; communication with other people became easier and my distorted face got back to normal.

This speech training often came after occupational therapy, during which we fitted little bits of metal together. I haven't the faintest idea what they were meant for, though I know we were under contract to some engineering organisation to produce them. I had to do it left-handed since that was the side of my body which was affected. On a typical day, this would be followed in the afternoon by a session in the baths where you had to force yourself to swim hard using both your arms and legs. Next morning it might be a walk through the wood and, since I couldn't do this unaided, I had to use a stick or callipers. But again, slowly, I learned to do without them. One day I remember having to climb up ladders. I'd fall after one rung because I couldn't pull the left leg up. But I'd try again until I managed it. I was determined as hell to get up if I could. The following day the whole process, with a few variations, was repeated.

In the games period I was introduced to volleyball. And what I found I couldn't do was run and catch the ball at the same time. I had no co-ordination. Running and catching a rugby ball were two things I had always delighted in, and I felt the most bitter frustration when, for all my efforts, I couldn't do it. For perhaps the first time, I also felt sorry for those who had never been able to co-ordinate eye and body. How horrible it must be for someone like that. At least I was no longer feeling so sorry for myself. The help we received from the staff was superb, but it was also down to earth. If you gave way to self-pity, you were soon brought back to reality by people who actually cared.

I know it's a truism, but it's only when you're in trouble

that you discover who your real friends are. The frightening thing was the number of people who had asked you to speak at their dinners – not for cash, just a pat on the back – and who simply melted from the scene. It was as if I'd be no use to them in the future. This discovery made it the most revealing time of my life. In sharp contrast were the real people. David and Barbara Coleman, having brought in a television to ease my long nights, visited me practically every day. Peter Jones, the radio commentator, was another regular and full of entertaining stories about what was going on at the BBC; both he and Michael Parkinson brought in champagne and Guinness to make black velvet for the boys. Phil Lewis, head of Events at the BBC, I could always rely on. Rex Willis, my first scrum-half, brought up a trio of old pals from Cardiff – Dr Jack Matthews, Bleddyn Williams, Stan Bowes. And a week never passed by without Henry Cooper calling in.

Henry and I were the first team captains in the television quiz, 'A Question of Sport', which was given a trial run of six programmes and is still there a quarter of a century later. The formula is simple, but what has made it so popular is that the viewer can often answer the question quicker than the sporting celebrities in the studio. I remained with the programme until my stroke, Henry was still there – though we appeared in it together once more while I was at the centre. They sent a photographer down to snap me in the pool for the Picture Board round which opens the show, where the panel has to identify sports personalities snapped in unusual situations. I was wearing a bathing cap and trying to do the breast stroke. As we watched in the common room at Farnham Park, we saw Henry go for picture number six and, when it was revealed, confidently answer, 'Anita Lonsborough.' The boys fell about, so did Henry when he was told the answer. What the lovely Anita thought, I can't imagine.

Henry was already a familiar figure at the centre, and had a marvellous touch with the patients. Some of them seemed almost beyond rehabilitation. One in particular, a young chap who had received severe head injuries in a motorbike crash,

couldn't talk, walk or use his arms properly, and responded
hardly at all to physiotherapy. One afternoon Henry walked
into the gym, said hello to everyone and began chatting with
this boy. And suddenly the boy said, 'Henry,' just like that.
It was not very distinct, but you knew for sure that he had
recognised Henry, and that was the first word he'd spoken.
The physiotherapist who was looking after him burst into tears
of relief; at last she had found something to give him a boost.
And from there on the boy began to make painfully slow but
regular progress. That was a critical moment for me, too. I
found myself intensely moved by what Henry had been able
to achieve through a combination of his own natural decency
and concern and his position as a boxing hero. And I became
convinced that, having enjoyed the privilege of being a sports
star, there was something to help the disabled that I could and
should put my heart into when I had recovered.

Incidentally, I owed another turning point to Henry, who
always left twenty pound notes with the sister so that we
could have a drink at the pub on the hill. This was great for
the morale, and positively therapeutic, since those of us who
found it difficult to walk would push the people who were in
wheelchairs. That way we got support without having to use
the dreaded callipers. Then one particular evening I remember
walking up to the pub and talking over a beer, sharing a laugh,
listening to the problems of other people, and at that moment I
just knew that I was going to get better. That's what I had fought
for in the gym and in the swimming pool, trying to get my arm
over and to use my legs, trying to find my old co-ordination. And
suddenly I felt confident that I would do it. I would still need the
support of my family and my closest friends, but I now knew I
would get it, which was a concern as well as a delight. I knew
somebody was going to be there, but I worried that I was going
to create pressures and become a bore to them. And of course,
being convinced that I would eventually recover didn't relieve
my immediate problems. When would I be able to go back to
work? And how would we manage for money until I did?

Nor could I rid myself of the feeling that my predicament was some sort of punishment for bad behaviour. Being brought up in a close nonconformist family can induce as many feelings of guilt as being raised a Catholic.

2

Freedom of
the Rhondda

If my father had gone to play for Tottenham Hotspur – as they asked him to in 1929 – I would probably have been born a Cockney and gone to school in North London. There's a sobering thought for you. How different life would have been. But my mother was against the move, and in the matriarchal society of the South Wales valleys, that was enough. Like so many apparently hard men who risked their lives daily in the pits, my father left family decisions to the wife. He wouldn't do anything, buy anything, unless my mother agreed. I still think it was, in its way, a sign of strength not weakness, but there's no doubt who was the boss of the household. Nearly a quarter of a century later it was my mother who influenced me not to go north and play Rugby League for Wigan. Even at the age of twenty-two I daren't go against her. Mind, I think she probably got it right. I'd have missed an awful lot if I had gone.

So my parents stayed at home, and on 7 April 1930 – soon after the long miners' strike had come to an end – I was born at 159 Top Trebanog Road, Trebanog, in the Rhondda Valley. It was the third house from the end of a row owned by my grandfather, Isaac Christmas Morgan. What a lovely name. The Welsh are so obvious; he was born on Christmas Day.

Like the rest of the terrace, ours was a solid, stone-built, three-bedroomed house. It opened straight onto the street, but had a tiny front garden just as wide as the three steps which ran down from the front door to the pavement. Years later I remember Cliff Jones, a great Welsh fly-half of the 'thirties, explaining: 'Why the Rhondda produced players who could side-step and weave was that once you went out of your front door you were on the main road. You were watching you didn't get knocked down by a passing bus. Then off the main road you were on the railway line with trains shunting coal, which meant you had to have your wits about you there. Then off the railway line and you were in the river. So all your life you had to develop this nervous awareness of what was going on around you. And that's what produces sharp outside-halves.' He swore this was true, and though I'm not saying it worked in my case, this house remained my home until I left to live and work in Ireland at the age of twenty-four.

I never saw my father play football, he finished two years after I was born. He played as an amateur, winning the Ely Valley Shield with Trebanog Rovers AFC, and must have been very, very good. Everyone said so. And obviously he impressed this scout from London, though whether or not he would have made it at Tottenham, you just don't know, do you? But he never became a professional footballer, he remained a coal-miner.

He started by working in the levels owned by my grandfather, who had himself been a collier. Before open-cast working was developed, the level was the simplest kind of mine – a horizontal tunnel cut into the hillside to follow the coal-seam. Not being a pit, it didn't need lifts and winding gear to take the men down to the coal-face or to raise the coal to the surface. Ponies did that and, unlike the true pit ponies, which just had one annual holiday in the open air, these came to the surface every night.

It was the sort of small-scale operation which could be run as a family business, as my grandfather did. He bought permits to cut levels into two mountains, and employed my father, and my uncles Tave (Octavius) and Will, not only to dig the coal and bring it out but to flog it round the streets. So there were no middle men, and my grandfather became quite wealthy. He was tall and a big man in every sense. He stood out anywhere, but especially in Trebanog, in his astrakhan collar, Anthony Eden hat and silver-topped cane. But it was not until I started playing rugby that I became a favourite of his, and he didn't figure much in my early years.

Eventually, my grandfather's coal-seams were worked out and my father moved to our one local pit, the Cilely colliery. There he stayed until one day in 1947 I came home from school on the bus to find an ambulance outside the house. My father had been walking down through the pit, following behind the journey of coal trams, when the rope snapped and the journey ran backward over him. He suffered a Potts fracture of the ankle, and although he could still get about, that finished him in the coal-mine. He then found a job as local agent for the Refuge Insurance Company, which he did until he retired. It became harder for him towards the end, so my mother took over half his work, walking round the village collecting the subs – not to earn anything for herself but to give Dad a shorter day.

She had been Edna May Thomas when they first met in chapel, the daughter of another miner and the first of nine children, four of whom died below the age of six and all buried in the Rhondda Valley. She had scarcely any formal schooling because, being the eldest child and only daughter, she had to stay home and help to bring up the others. Which wasn't easy on a miner's pay. Her mother, Elizabeth, used to make faggots – beautiful faggots, I've never tasted anything like them since. And her brother would put them in the sidecar of a motorcycle, with a big white container of peas, and sell them around the village. She could never make enough. My mother, too, had to go out from an early age to work in the police station at Porth, scrubbing the cells and feeding the prisoners. She also picked coal from the tips, carrying it home in buckets, to stretch the family income. But from the time she married she never earned a penny. Her life centred on the home and the chapel. And whatever she did for other people – visiting them and cooking them meals when they were sick – she did for nothing. People always went to her for advice because she thought things through. She had a common-sense logic which she had learned, I think, in bringing up a family entirely of brothers.

Welsh mining villages are often depicted as grim and inward-looking, which is not at all as I remember Trebanog. For one thing it was on the top of a hill; Trebanog means 'three hillocks'. On the north side we overlooked the Rhondda, and to the south the Vale of Glamorgan. And if you climbed to the top of our mountain, Mynydd-y-Glyn, which was 1800 feet high, you could see the coast at Barry Island and the Bristol Channel beyond. You even seemed to be above the clouds. Often when we were at infants' school, my cousin Betty and I, we'd set off in bright sunshine, and then as we walked down the steep hill to the valley we'd pass through a film of fog. It was only when we reached school that we'd be back in the light again.

Trebanog wasn't much more than a single L-shaped road. The longer stretch went on down the hill to Porth at one end, and Tonyrefail the other. Then there was a little left arm which took you down to Williamstown and on to Tonypandy, Treorchy and all the historic places in the Rhondda. And the curious thing is that one side of the street was in the Rhondda Urban District Council area, while opposite we were in Llantrisant and Llantwit Fardre Rural District. This meant that someone living only twenty yards away on the other side went to a different school from you.

Right opposite our house was the Baptist chapel, but the one we attended was Carmel English Congregational – the 'English Cong' – not made of the traditional stone and brick, but a curious tin-shed of a building 125 yards down the road. Mind, the only thing English about it was the language in which the services were held. Unlike my father, my mother didn't speak Welsh, a common situation where we lived. Up in Treorchy and some other villages there were little closets of Welsh-speakers, but generally in the Rhondda, because so many people from other parts of Britain had come there to work, the everyday use of the language had almost died out.

I learned my Welsh from my father and from school, but for my mother's sake we didn't speak it at home. We used it very little, too, when we were playing as children. And the sadness to me is that you lose the natural usage when Welsh is not 'the language of the hearth'. Today my Welsh is not good Welsh, it's not pulpit Welsh. It's the Welsh of the mines or the steelworks, ordinary Welsh. And this is where I think the BBC in Wales have made matters worse. They've dismissed the ordinary Welsh that most people speak in the industrial south, and insisted on perfection, with all the correct intonations and mutations. To me these aren't important, because the act of communication is about somebody understanding what you are talking about.

I suppose what had the earliest and most lasting effect on me were my mother and the chapel, though since my mother was a pillar of Welsh nonconformity and a Sunday School teacher, it is sometimes hard to distinguish the influence of one from the other. But it was her rules – on the way you thought and acted, even the way you dressed – that came first. She wasn't a rebel in any way. She may have been a nonconformist by religion, but in all other ways she was a conformist. Everything was right if it was according to tradition. She was meticulous in observing these things. I went into the grammar school during the war when you couldn't get hold of the official school caps with the white rings around them. So what she did was buy tape and sew these rings round my cap herself. It had to be correct. But at the same time, she was very warm, very funny, and also extremely active. She had a beautiful contralto voice and sang, with my father and later with me, in the Porth and District Mixed-Voice Choir which was 116 strong. And this was all done by reading music from tonic sol-fa, not from old notation. I've still got some copies of the *Messiah* and *Twelfth Mass* in tonic sol-fa which we used in the choir. Again, although she had missed so much basic education as a young girl, she was a marvellous teacher and her Sunday School class adored her. She was naturally articulate, and even before she had learned to read properly, she had been taught how to bring up children.

My mother also organised things, and with all of that her life was full and rich.

I'd think her philosopy, which was love and celebration, made a matchless foundation for a good life. Not only for herself but for her family and her neighbours. She had this sense of service which she felt was the rent she paid for living in this community. She was fantastic.

Although she never had very much money to spend, she always managed to put money in the envelope at chapel. It was the first thing she set aside when my father brought home his pay and gave it to her. And do you know, after I left home in 1954, and right up until she died in 1969, she kept putting half-a-crown a week into the collection for my membership of the chapel. And never mentioned it to me. It was my father who told me afterwards, 'Oh, she's been doing it for years, bach.' She just didn't want my name to be dropped from the register.

Whether or not we were short of money, we always had good food. She had learned how to cook from her mother, another great manager who could make wonderful meals very cheaply; I mentioned the faggots. My mother inherited this gift for stretching things. She bought cheap cuts of neck of lamb for a broth which would last for two days. She made beautiful apple tart too, the apples also coming cheaply from the orchard across the road. Then there were gooseberries and rhubarb from our own garden. And as children we gathered wimberries from the mountain; to these my mother always added a few blackcurrants to sharpen up the taste.

Nearly all her cooking was done over an open fire in the black-leaded kitchen grate. It had two rings which swung out above it to support the pots, and an oven at the side where she baked her bread. She also put a heavy iron plate, a bakestone, over the coals for cooking things like Welsh cakes. And this fire was kept burning summer and winter because the only means we had of heating water was to put it in a bucket on top of the grate. We had no bathroom at that time, but in a collier's household you could never afford to be without hot water to fill the tin bath. This was brought into the kitchen at the end of each shift so that my father could soak off the grime from the pit. The kitchen, a cosy place despite the stone floor, was also where we ate every day at a scrub-topped table.

You could tell the days of the week from the food my mother put on that table. There were never any surprises; there couldn't be. Monday was always cold meat left from Sunday lunch, sometimes made into rissoles. And that meat, by the way, would have been cooked on the Saturday night, so that nothing interfered with attendance at chapel on Sunday morning. Tuesdays, Henry Coles, with his horse and cart, brought fish to sell door to door; he used to cut beautiful big cutlets of hake – a very popular fish in those days – so there was hake and chips that night. Wednesday and Thursday it was the broth that I mentioned, made from lamb, onions, carrots and potatoes or whatever else we had in the garden. And so it went on.

This daily routine made it easier for my mother to plan; she always knew what she'd be able to buy with the money she had. But there were seasonal variations. On Friday night in the spring and summer, for instance, we had broad beans with pepper and bread and butter. This was also the time of year when, regularly on Thursdays, Harry Penny brought round fresh Penclawdd cockles. Live cockles which you left in a bucket of salted water overnight to get rid of the grit, and then boiled for Friday supper to eat when they were still steaming. Once a month, too, Mr Penny brought West Wales laverbread, a kind of seaweed which grew like a transparent skin on the rocks along the coast. Before it reached the customer, it was boiled into a sort of mash, and your first strange, salty taste of it was like your first mouthful of beer: you wanted to spit it out. But in much the same way, too, you soon got to enjoy the flavour of laverbread and it became the great monthly treat. My mother fried it without oil in the pan, just the fat from the bacon. No eggs, and no toast, always bread and butter.

In the winter, when there were no cockles to be bought and nothing much was growing in the garden, we'd have whatever vegetables they were selling at the Co-op. They were our evening meal on Fridays. Or just occasionally, fish and chips from the shop. Or maybe thick slices of the streaky, salt bacon which hung in whole sides from the ceiling of my grandfather's wash-house. Then on Saturday my mother did her big shop, and the week's round began again.

Years later, after I had left home, it was my oldest friend, a lorry driver named Don 'The Count' Davies, who brought my mother and father Penclawdd cockles every Friday. Don is a remarkable man, who has always got the most out of life. At sixteen he cheated his age to drive ambulances during the London blitz. Nowadays he acts as a steward at Lansdowne Road as well as the Arms Park and, like his mother, the once celebrated diva Madame Bessie Davies, he travels the world – Moscow for St David's Day, for instance – as Trebanog's roving ambassador.

As a kid, once I was outside the house, the whole of my conscious existence was centred round either chapel or play. On Sunday we went to Carmel three times before going on to Porth for choir practice. It was the one day I wasn't allowed to play with a ball, not that I'd have had much time to. The adults, too, practised their own self-denial; we took Sunday papers, but always left them under the seat to be read on Monday. When I was a little older, there was Christian Endeavour to attend on Monday evenings, prayer meeting on Tuesday, the young people's club on Wednesday, and at various other times I went into chapel to practise on the piano and the organ.

It was in Sunday School that I learned to read tonic sol-fa. And it was there, not in my day school, that I learned to read properly and picked up the principles of good manners and behaviour. Things you don't think about much at the time but which mark you all your life. You always refer back to them. I'm not saying that I didn't often feel frustrated by the chapel's restrictions on how you thought and what you did, but it certainly shaped the climate of my youth. And apart from anything else, I simply enjoyed it.

I used to love people reading aloud at Sunday School. There

was a Mr Ewart Rowlands who would read the text and comment on it as he went along. '"The Lord is *my* shepherd." Not anybody else's. Mine personally.' And from men like that I learned about the timing, the ups and downs of the voice, which you use when you are trying to hold the attention of your listeners. Things which later on became part of the way I earned my living. To someone who was going to be a broadcaster, it was a terrific background.

The first minister I remember in the chapel was Mr Bryant; he had white hair and a white moustache and looked like a heavy Lloyd George. In those days sermons lasted twenty-five minutes, but you didn't notice the time because the preachers had the same gifts as Burton and Olivier. They grabbed people in their hands and they held them. Their language was beautiful, and they took you to heaven if only for five minutes.

But the minister I got to know best was the Rev. E. Wyn Parry. My mother took him in as a lodger when he was a young man of twenty-eight or thirty. He was ordained on the Thursday night, came to live with us immediately afterwards and stayed until he married three or four years later. He was another influence on my life, because he taught you things and showed you things, gave you books and told you stories. He'd written a book himself on Dr Elfed Lewis, who composed the verses of some of the great Welsh hymns, and came from a village called Conwyl Elfed in West Wales. I particularly remember one of Mr Parry's anecdotes about him. At Christmas Elfed had been walking through the snow with his father, who told him to follow in his footsteps to be sure of reaching the front door. From this experience, years later Elfed wrote in Welsh a famous hymn:

> Arglwydd Iesu dysc i'm gerdded,
> Trwy y byd ar ol dy droed.

Or in English, 'Lord Jesus, show me where to walk, Through the world in Thy footsteps.' It's a simple enough story, but Mr Parry had a gift for weaving tales which somehow stuck in your mind.

Another member of the chapel who fascinated me was Clyde,

the one black person in the village. We had two coal stoves to heat the chapel in winter, one on either side, and he had a regular place next to the stove on the right. Clyde was a big, gentle man – in my mind always associated with Paul Robeson – who had come to Trebanog to work in the mines. And although he must have had a surname, he was known to everyone as Clyde the Darkie. It sounds awfully patronising and insensitive now, but it was not said with any nastiness. In fact it was meant with much affection, because Clyde, a simple soul with a great heart, would do anything to help chapel activities. In particular, because he got on well with children, he was always involved with street parties, and each year was put in charge of one of the buses which took the Sunday School to Barry Island for the day.

It's hard to believe that the annual Sunday School and miners' outings to the sea were the only holidays we had as children. The first was always held on the Monday which followed the celebration of our Sunday School anniversary, one of the chapel's big occasions. For this the pulpit would be moved from the centre, where it took pride of place through the rest of the year, and along the back wall of the chapel, the men would nail planks onto a wooden frame to build a platform for our performance. We could only hope that it would be sturdy enough to take the strain of the choir, the soloists, the reciters – and my Uncle Arthur with his baton.

On the Sunday there would be glorious anthems like 'How lovely are Thy dwellings fair'. My mother and her friend May Roberts would sing a duet, 'The old rugged cross'. Meanwhile we kids sat and waited for our turn. One year my contribution was the 'collection piece', recited while the deacons took the silver collection. It ran:

> Thank you very much,
> I know I'm very small,
> I've only come to tell you,
> Jesus loves us all.

There were smiles of pride and relief from the family as, in the velvet jacket my mother had made, I walked back to my place.

Next morning the village was alive before seven o'clock and, hoping that the rain would keep off, we queued for the threepenny pieces which were doled out as pocket money by the Sunday School superintendent. 'Don't spend it all at once.' No, but how could you make it last long enough to cover the Big Dipper, the Water Chute, coconuts and candy floss? Luckily the sands came first, and they were free.

We'd not leave Trebanog until everyone was ready and the five double-deckers were full. By which time many of the kids had started into their sandwiches. Then it was off for an hour's noisy sing-along to Barry Island:

> We're going to the Mansion on the Happy Day Express.
> The letters on the engine are J.E.S.U.S.
> We proudly call the Master, he gladly answers, Yes!
> We're going to the Mansion on the Happy Day Express.

Or it might be:

> Telephone to Glory, O the joy divine,
> I heard the currents moving down the line.
> Built by God the Father, through His Son alone,
> A little talk to Jesus on the royal telephone.

I suppose I never felt chapel to be such a great constraint because otherwise we had a very free life as kids. When you think of it, nowadays you wouldn't let five-year-olds like Betty and me walk a mile and a half out in the country to primary school in the morning and then walk back home in the afternoon. Later on there were so many children going there from the village that we had a taxi service, Patey's Taxis, to take us. Later still there was a regular school bus. But when Betty and I began we simply walked, and nobody imagined that any harm could come to us.

People were far more trusting. Our front door was never locked. My mother would leave the insurance book, and the money to be entered into it, under the cloth on the living room table. And the insurance man would walk into the empty house, take the money and leave the book there. Nothing was ever stolen.

Like most mothers mine shopped for almost everything at the Co-op. The system was that every so often you bought a certain number of Co-op cheques, say £1-worth, and then used them to pay your bills for as long as they lasted. So the cheques were precious, but my mother, without a second thought, would leave them on the front doorstep with the empty bottles to pay for the Co-op milk.

It was one of the few mysteries about my mother that she didn't shop with Mr Rowlands, the secretary of the chapel, who ran a similar and rival general store. I'm sure it wasn't just the Co-op divvy – the customers' share in the profits – that attracted her, though it must have appealed to her frugality. Most likely, as in so many working-class families, she though of the Co-op as the people's shop and was loyal to it as a matter of political principle.

In the 'thirties the streets were safer and children played a lot of games on the pavement. Ropes were hung from lamp posts so that we could swing around them. The girls endlessly played hopscotch – scotch they always called it. Boys as well as girls skipped – the difference being that the boys, to be one up, put in a double turn of the rope to each skip. But we were also allowed to play in the fields – the most important of which was the Relay Field behind our house. It was so called because it had the Relay Shed in it. And that was the centre of broadcasting around the Rhondda. I'll explain. Because people in the valleys always lived in the shadow of some mountain or another, they couldn't be sure of getting radio programmes at home simply because they had stuck an aerial on the roof. Instead they had to rely on one high aerial on the mountainside from which the Rediffusion company relayed the programmes by cable to the houses in the village below. In Trebanog this relay system brought us the BBC Welsh Home Service and the Light Programme.

The rest of the Relay Field was ours to play in, and was the nearest thing we had to a public park. In winter it was coats down as goal posts for a game of football. In summer we flattened and mowed a sort of cricket pitch. Sometimes we also played free-lease, though that was mainly a school yard game. One side would try to capture their opponents by chasing and touching them. While the other side would try to spring the prisoners by running in and touching them without being touched themselves. In fact it was during the releasing bit that you learned to side-step the opposition.

When we got tired of these games, we went up the mountain to dam off the river with rocks and clods and make a swimming pool. We tickled trout, collected hazel nuts and buried them for Christmas, and gathered wimberries. This was mostly for our own mothers, but if we had any left over we'd sell them by the pint to the neighbours.

One bizarre memory I associate with the field is of the summer night when practically the whole of the village gathered round the Relay Shed, which had been specially opened up, to listen to a broadcast from America. It was on 30 August 1937, when Tommy Farr, a Rhondda man from Tonypandy, challenged the great Joe Louis for the world heavyweight title at the Yankee Stadium, New York. The fight commentary wasn't on the stations we got at home; they had already closed down for the night. So these hundreds of people went up the Relay where the transmitter could pick up the American broadcast. I was seven at the time and was taken up there by my father and mother (and what would she want with listening to a boxing match?). As kids we were running around playing while it went on, but I heard enough of the fight, and Tommy Farr's defeat, never to forget it.

There was no television, of course, during my childhood, and you were so busy with playing that you had to make time even to listen to favourite wireless programmes like 'Tommy Trouble' and 'Galw Gary Tryfan'. Adult radio didn't attract me much until I was in the grammar school sixth, and we were told to listen to two series so that we could discuss them in class. They were Alistair Cooke's 'Letter from America', then only a couple of years old, and 'Quite Early One Morning' in which Dylan Thomas read his poetry and talked about life in Wales.

Reading for pleasure also came with moving on to grammar school. It was then I first went down the steep hill to the public library at Cymmer, near Porth. I remember the smell of the books and the walls, as different a smell as the smell of Africa. You felt you were within walls of power, as if you were in parliament.

The first thing I ever read was the Bible. This meant that my language and reading tended to be slightly old-fashioned. I managed to modify it over the years. And although I found it almost as hard to make time for reading as for listening to the radio, I did build up my own small library at home – again thanks to the chapel. After we had collected money for the missionary service, there would be a presentation to the helpers, and in that way I got *David Copperfield*, the plays of Shakespeare, Lamb's *Tales from Shakespeare*, *Pear's Encyclopaedia* and a Welsh dictionary.

Several years later my father bought me a second-hand copy of *Rugger* by two prominent Englishmen, Wakefield and Marshall, and when I took it with me to Tonyrefail Grammar School to show it off, Ned Gribble, the rugby master, added a book by W. J. A Davies, a famous England stand-off of the 'twenties, to my collection. That must have been when I was about fifteen and starting to get really excited about rugby. At twelve cricket was still my favourite thing, and after that, football. I'd seen rugby played at school but I wasn't at all keen to join in. And although Trebanog had its own rugby club, I never even went to watch them as a boy. Nor was I ever to belong to them, simply because I moved straight from school to Cardiff University and the Cardiff club.

I do remember turning out for Trebanog in one holiday match against Penygraig, which made me realise how lucky I had been not to play for them regularly. It was over Christmas 1951. I was starting my second season in the Wales side, and on Saturday 22nd we had played South Africa at the Arms Park. We lost 3–6. That was a hard game, but it no way compared with playing against Penygraig. Oh my God. No way. They were going around saying curious things like, 'I clogged him. Duw, he's not very good is he?' 'Who does he think he is? I don't want to talk about it, but I poked him one.' 'He thinks he's big playing for Wales, but we pulled him down to size.' And that was just a Christmas game. What was it like in a serious match?

We were a pretty close family: difficult not to be, of course, in a place the size of Trebanog. When I was eight or nine my mother's brother, Uncle Arthur, who was a baker's roundsman, and single, came to live with us. He brought his piano with him and occupied our front room. Because the piano was there, I fiddled around with it, and that persuaded my mother, who believed in the power and beauty of music, to send me to Mrs Brand in Porth to be properly taught. With her help I reached Grade 5 and eventually played the piano in chapel. Then because I knew music I joined the orchestra at the grammar school. I didn't have much choice in what I played. A viola was the only instrument left on the floor when everyone had scrounged the rest. It meant learning a different clef, a tenor clef, but I stuck at it for years. The orchestra played during prayers in the morning, which was good fun, and I've had enormous enjoyment out of music ever since. All really due to Uncle Arthur.

He was my mother's brother, and as a small child I think I was closer to her side of the family than to my father's. My mother's mother, Elizabeth Thomas, the one who made the faggots and peas, was very easy to get on with. She had spent her whole life in service, first to her family, making ends meet for her children's sake – her husband being one of those who handed over his diminished pay only after he had been to the pub – and then literally by working as a domestic help. During the later war years she cleaned and polished, washed and ironed, for a young couple who lived in the big house at the foot of the hill only two doors away from her own home. They were Cliff Jones and his wife, Mary – Cliff being the former Wales fly-half with this theory about the street-wise nimbleness of Rhondda rugby players.

At that time my mother's family had just come back from a spell in England. Shortly before the war they joined the steady migration from South Wales to the Midlands to work in the pits at Binley, on the outskirts of Coventry. From there they moved on to the factories at Radford, which soon converted to munitions, and stayed on as long as the bombing let them. One morning my grandparents came up from the air raid shelter to find that their home was no longer there. They returned to Wales, where they eventually retired. And gradually they were joined there by my uncles, who were no longer looking for jobs in the pits. With the trades they had acquired in England, they could get skilled jobs in surface industries.

My father's parents, more affluent and living in a much more imposing house than the rest of us, were prominent figures in the village, though not in my own early life. I wasn't in my grandfather's favour at first because my mother and he had had some private squabble over chapel – to which he didn't belong anyway. One of the differences between them was that she wouldn't allow me to go out in his car on Sunday for seaside jaunts to Llantwit Major, Barry Island or Porthcawl. I had to stay behind to go to chapel.

My grandmother wasn't involved in that dispute. She and my grandfather shared the house but lived separate lives. She was a small, dominant, austere lady who had been a Morgan and a person of consequence in the Rhondda hierarchy even before her marriage. Her family were big iron founders in Porth, and to this day you'll find manhole covers and culverts up and down the valley bearing the name Morgan Foundry. It's like walking on your family history.

At Christmas and Easter she always summoned us – my cousins Betty, Gwyn and Glyn and myself – and gave out presents. But it was like a royal audience. She treated tradesmen in much the same way. Thomas & Evans used to deliver Corona pop around the district from Porth, but only my grandmother summoned the rep to the house to warm his backside by the fire and take her order. The goods were delivered in a Chevrolet van, which seemed only fitting. Even on the rare occasions when she bought from a shop, my grandmother never took apples or grapes, for instance, without trying them first. Nor would she ever choose from the back of the window. It had to be from the front where the best fruit was put to show it off.

My grandfather was also autocratic in his way, though much more sociable. After he gave up the mines he became, I suppose, a kind of entrepreneur before his time. He owned quite a lot of property in and around the village, including the Labour Club in Pontyclun. He invested in some of the initial shares in Dunlop Tyres and BP. And with a passion for motoring, he had bought the first car in the area with pneumatic tyres. Later he owned a two-seater with an open top and a buggy seat at the rear which you pulled back. Then he went on to a black Wolseley – a beautiful car which he polished in his garage after every time he took it out in the rain. It had a partition between the back and front seats, two umbrellas in the back, and a marvellous smell of leather from the upholstery. Eventually my grandfather sold the car to the fire service for some unexplained use in the war.

Money seemed to be attracted to him. In the 1937 Calcutta Stakes, based on the Derby, he drew the only ticket in the whole of Great Britain, a horse called Roberto. The Calcutta had a higher prize than the Irish Sweepstake, and my grandfather got telegrams from Lloyd's of London asking if he wanted to sell shares in it. It might have been better if he had, for Roberto wasn't placed, though just for drawing a horse at all he won a prize of £750.

He loved almost any sport. While the rest of the village was listening to the commentary on the Louis-Farr fight up at the Relay Field, my grandfather was watching it from a ringside seat. He had gone to New York with Jobie Churchill, Tommy Farr's trainer before Ted Broadrib was brought in.

It was only when I started playing rugby for Tonyrefail Grammar School that he began to take any special interest in me. He came to watch a seven-a-side tournament which we won by beating Pontypridd County School in the final – a side which included Glyn Davies, who was to play fly-half for Wales just ahead of me. After matches like that my grandfather began taking me back to his house and putting me in the bath, because he had a proper bathroom not just a zinc tub in front of the fire. He started to care. He died before I played for Wales, but he was proud enough to sit there in the front of the stand, leaning on his silver-topped stick, watching me in schoolboy matches.

He also began to fill my head with scraps of local information, legends and verse. He encouraged me to read our daily paper, the *Western Mail*. He told me tales of boxers like Tommy Thomas who used to train by wrestling with a bull in a field. I'm sure half of it was exaggeration and lies. There were stories about Mabon, organiser of the Cambrian Miners' Association in the Rhondda, and of the great political meetings in the valley, and these were at least half true. And there were the historical curiosities – how Dr William Price of Llantrisant pioneered cremation in Britain by cremating his own son. That was fact. He'd make you sit and listen, even if you didn't want to, for you daren't defy your grandfather or your father.

My grandfather also had a remarkable memory for verse, some of it good, some of it doggerel, and some he wrote himself, like this monologue which he could rattle off by the yard:

> Dai Muffler was a collier bold
> Who worked in pit and level,
> And spite of stories often told
> Was neither saint nor devil.
>
> No linen collar did he wear,
> Like you and me and t'other,
> And though he'd often loudly swear,
> He was a man and a brother.

I met him on Bank Holiday,
As merry as Dan Leno,
Just off to have a holiday,
And what he called a beano.

He hailed me right across the street
And waved at me his cutty,
And out of me took all conceit
With, 'Well, how is it, butty?'

I just consider myself lucky to have touched these little bits and pieces, because scraps of curious information made you go away and learn more. To that extent they have affected my life ever since. I'm equally grateful for having been made to listen to Dylan Thomas and his readings, because I got to love the sound of poetry.

My grandfather had made his will in 1939, before he began to take an interest in me, and while it left my mother and father the house we lived in, it distributed most of his money and property among my father's two brothers and three sisters. Now he obviously wanted me to have a greater benefit from what he had accumulated, but this wasn't to happen.

The evening before my grandfather died, I came home from playing in a match and the village policeman immediately took me down to the Church Village Hospital in his bull-nosed Morris Oxford. My grandfather told his solicitor and my father, who were already at his bedside, that he wanted to change his will on the spot so that 'the boy', as he called me, would have a start in life. My father told him not to bother, he should get well first. So nothing was done. And by the time we reached home, my grandfather had died.

As usual, my mother was so sensible about it. 'What does it matter?' she said. 'We've got the house. We've got a roof over our heads. We're lucky.' She didn't resent it in the least that she didn't have money and possessions. I also came round to thinking that an inheritance might have changed me as an individual and stopped me doing the things that I've done since. So I've never regretted it either.

The odd thing was that, by almost any definition, my grandfather was a capitalist. All the same he was a Labour man, a councillor and chairman of the Labour Club in Cymmer. And because he had employed only his family in the levels, his comparative wealth attracted no animosity in the village. There was resentment about working conditions in the pits, terrible resentment. But none of it came his way.

I don't think I knew a Conservative until I was twenty-six. Parts of the Rhondda, Ferndale in particular, were hotbeds of Communism, stoked by Arthur Horner whose name spelt out to many people all the joys of a revolution. But for the most part it was second nature to be Labour. It hardly needed saying. In chapel, when they were talking about Christ and his love, and retelling the stories of Noah, and the good Samaritan, and the money changers in the temple, everything seemed to have a political touch to it. There was such deprivation in mining, farming and quarrying communities that you couldn't avoid the comparison between religion and politics. Apart from which, it was in chapel that election addresses were given in Trebanog. Holding my mother's and father's hands I'd been taken to them since I was a young child. No argument over whether you wanted to go.

There was a terrific increase in political activity towards the end of the war and the build-up to the 1945 general election. Our MP for Pontypridd, Arthur Pearson, came to our chapel to make speeches. Everybody turned up, even my mother – and she was no more a political animal than one of the chapel seats – and there'd be heckling from the back. Feelings were very strong, and you were always made aware that you had to belong to the party of the people.

By day you had wonderful old cars coming through with big loudspeakers. And people didn't resent them, they liked them, because they were something new. It was like watching the arrival of Lipman, a Jewish tinker who used to come round from time to time to cut window glass and put it in for you, and sharpen you knives and chisels. These comings and goings were occasions.

What you were always certain to hear through the loudspeakers in those days were men with terrific Welsh accents and a powerful way with words. They had all been to college – Nuffield College, Oxford, maybe – and had come back with these rich, rounded, oratorical phrases. They were latterday Lloyd Georges, and I fell under their spell completely.

Even when I went to Cardiff University in 1949 I travelled home at night, and though I knew I would have to leave Trebanog eventually, I was in no hurry to break my ties with parents, friends, chapel, choir which had been the centre of my life. I was never bored or restless there. So in the late autumn of 1952, when I was playing for Cardiff and Wales, I was still at home to receive my first serious offer to go North.

The Rugby League clubs were particularly active trying to recruit Welsh players at that time. A few weeks later they would land their biggest prize so far when Lewis Jones, the high-scoring Wales and Llanelli full-back, one of the finest sporting talents I have ever seen, accepted a then-record £6000 to join Leeds. But at Trebanog they met more than their match – not from me but from my mother. I mention the story here because it illustrates, better than anything, her attitude to life.

If I was at home on a Sunday morning, which I mostly was, my mother always brought me up a tray with the same breakfast – boiled eggs, bread and butter and a cup of tea. This was not to spoil me, but to make sure I was ready in time for chapel. You might have cuts round your eye or been given a kick on your backside or whatever in the game the day before, and you might be thinking, I don't want to get up today. But always you had to get up for chapel.

About nine o'clock on this morning, a Rolls drew up outside our house. And everybody in the street was pulling back their curtains and looking out because they'd never seen a posh car like this turning up in the village. And suddenly my mother came back upstairs and said, 'There's some men from Wigan want to see you.'

'Mam, I shall be professionalised if I even talk to them,' I told her. 'That's the laws of the game.'

'Well,' she said, 'you can't leave them outside the house.' She went downstairs, and when I eventually followed her they were inside having breakfast in the kitchen. She had cooked them bacon, eggs and black pudding.

They had put an open attaché case of money on the table, £5000 in £5 notes. They were white fivers. I'd never seen a white fiver before in my life. That made me dubious. And there was a cheque for £2500 on the top. It was post-dated, which meant I had to play six months for the club before I could cash it.

My mother watched all this, and listened to what Bill Gore, the chairman of Wigan, had to offer, then told me she wanted me to turn Wigan down. She preferred me to go on living at home. She didn't want me to leave. There was the comfort of living in the village. And money . . . ach-y-fi! All very well, but the important thing was education. And it was she who stopped me going to Rugby League, just as she had stopped my father going to Spurs. I couldn't bring myself to go against her. In the end she said they would have to leave now because it was nearly ten to eleven. 'It's been lovely to have you here, but on Sunday morning we go to chapel.'

It was all done with such good grace that the Gore family and my parents kept in touch with Christmas cards every year afterwards. When my mother died, Bill Gore came to South Wales once more to attend her funeral. And five years later his son drove him down to Daddy's funeral. I never signed for Wigan or anywhere else, but I've always had a great respect for the Rugby League since then, and done lots of things for the charities they promote. When I was at the BBC I loved to deal with the Rugby League crowd because they were so honest. Their officials would come to a meeting in Leeds, and in twenty minutes we'd have a chat, shake hands on what we'd agreed, and without ever signing a television contract, they would honour everything.

3

One of
Mr Gribble's boys

In 1941 I passed scholarship, the exclusive rite of passage from Gellidawel Junior School to Tonyrefail Grammar School. It wasn't the 11-plus in those days; it was the scholarship. Fail it, and you would probably go into a central school, leaving at fourteen or fifteen to look for an unskilled manual job or get apprenticed to a trade. Pass, and the limitless opportunities of grammar school – or county school as it was often called in Wales – were opened up to you. You had only to apply yourself from there on and, however poor your background, you could go on to university, become a teacher, doctor, lawyer, engineer – even join the BBC. Most people now would say that selection into sheep and goats at the age of eleven was crude and unfair. But at that time it was accepted as a fact of existence, especially in that nonconformist Welsh tradition which valued the gift of education – guaranteeing a safe, respectable middle life, or so it was supposed – scarcely less than that of religion, which secured the after-life.

At any rate, no doubts about the fairness of the system stopped me feeling thoroughly proud to have passed. That autumn, in my green blazer, and the green cap with three white rings my mother had sewn on, I went up to the big school, which had its motto carved above the main door: 'Nid Dysg Heb Foes' (No Learning Without Culture). I wasn't brilliant at lessons, but I worked at them – the teachers made you – and I ended up in the sixth form doing Botany, Geography and Chemistry for Higher School Certificate, with English as a complementary subject. So in spite of myself I learned things, and I loved every second of it. I don't remember ever having a bad day at school. I learned the viola and played in the school orchestra, took part in concerts and eisteddfodau, joined the school branch of the Urdd Gobaith Cymru, the Welsh League of Youth, and went on their summer camps.

Above all I came under the influence of the great Ned Gribble, who did more than anyone to shape my future in rugby.

Tonyrefail was a fairly young school. It had been put up in brick, in contrast to the usual stone public building of the area, only twelve years or so before I went there. It was on a road which went up into the hills above the town, and not only was the situation open, but so were the two-storey classrooms formed around two grass quadrangles to give them plenty of light. There was nothing heavy or Victorian about the school. All the same it was the biggest building I had ever been into, and I was slightly frightened of it. And though its exterior was modern, its ways were still fairly old-fashioned.

We wrote with steel-nibbed pens, and we had ink monitors whose job was to make sure that everybody's ink-well was filled each morning. There was frequent, though not at all severe, corporal punishment. And our headmaster, Abraham Jenkins, who eventually died at the age of 103, was the kind of person my father always wanted as Prime Minister, somebody you could look up to. He was absent-minded but a disciplinarian, interested less in freedom than accountability. He wanted pupils to learn the basic things, and on the occasions when he took a class, usually to fill in for an absent teacher, he drummed the subject thoroughly into you. He set this tone for the whole school, and that was the climate of our youth.

I suppose the classroom teacher who most impressed me was

Sidney Gabe – Mr Gabe to us – who was the Physics master. He taught with a rod of iron, though not literally. As punishment in the Physics lab, he'd crack you across the backside with a wooden one-metre rule, and you'd see pieces flying off the edge of it. He must have got through hundreds of these rulers in his time. It certainly made things stick in your mind. I still remember the formula for velocity, and Fletcher's Trolley – and a whole lot of things which I have never found any use for in my adult life.

Apart from whacking facts into you, Mr Gabe had a fine talent for spotting questions which were likely to come up in our exams, School Certificate and Higher. That often saved us. And he could also be remarkably graphic in explaining difficult points. As the master in charge of cricket, he would talk about the way the ball spun, and he'd work it out for you with diagrams and formulae on the blackboard. The only man I ever met with a similar knack was H.B. Toft, Bert Toft, a great England hooker turned rugby writer, a considerable scholar and, for a short time, my employer, as I'll explain later. Coming back from a match, Bert would get out his writing pad and prove, for instance, with arrows and triangles, that you can't possibly put the ball into a scrum at 'a reasonable speed'. In practice it had to go in fast. Or that a player could disguise a forward pass simply by accelerating, instead of checking, as he gave out the ball. So on those points rugby law was a bit of an ass. He also claimed that rugby was different from all other games, since you didn't play towards a goal. The approach was on a broad front right across the field.

I went to Tonyrefail as a fanatical soccer enthusiast, but as I grew up I couldn't escape the influence of rugby either at home or at school. Like every other South Wales boy I had been brought up on the story of the try the All Blacks *didn't* score at Cardiff Arms Park in 1905. The Scottish referee, John Dallas, was quite convinced that Bob Deans, the New Zealand centre, had been pulled down short of the Welsh line and had illegally wriggled across it. He therefore disallowed the try. Deans contested this decision to the end. Reportedly, with his last breath, he said: 'I did score at Cardiff.' Rhys Gabe, the Welsh centre who claimed to have tackled him, just as vehemently asserted that Deans did not. Shortly before he died he insisted to me in an interview that he had stopped Deans with six to twelve inches to go: 'If he was over the line, as he claimed, why did he try to struggle forward?' Impossible to say now who was telling the truth. And what does it matter? All I knew, and all I needed to know at Tonyrefail, was that Rhys Gabe, the Welsh hero, was our Physics master's uncle.

Not that our Mr Gabe had anything to do with rugby in the school, except occasionally to supervise the team off the field when they travelled away. The training, the selection and the conduct of the team on the field was the sole preserve of Ned Gribble, who taught woodwork and metalwork and was the master in charge of games. Since football was frowned on in the school, and Grib didn't believe there was another game but rugby created by God, for the best part of the school year games simply meant rugby. In the summer there was cricket on a matting wicket, and tennis, and I played both for the school teams later on, but they were just a holiday from the serious business of winter.

I know that woodwork masters aren't generally very high in the pecking order at school, but Grib was an exception. He was a big man; he had presence; he was a gale of humanity. If he walked into the staff room everybody knew he was there. Intellectually he might not have ranked as highly as Mr Williams the Welsh, Mr Evans the English, or Miss Henry who taught everything and was my form mistress. But he dominated your life if you played sport, and even the more academic teachers accepted the strength of his personality. The strange thing was that if Mr Gribble sent for you – which was more likely to happen when you reached the sixth form, and you could well be in the middle of an experiment in the Chemistry lab – no teacher would ever say, 'No, you can't go to see him now.'

He was on the Welsh Secondary Schools Rugby Union and managed the first Wales schoolboy team to visit South Africa after the war. Clive Rowlands was in it. Everybody in the game in Wales knew him. It was partly the name. You don't easily forget a name like Ned Gribble. But it was just as much his conviction and authority. He set standards of behaviour. If somebody did something dubious in a game, for instance, he'd say, 'Right, cool your heels for five minutes on the touch line.' In that way he operated a sin bin in rugby at Tonyrefail long before it had been generally heard of or given a name. He wouldn't let you go to a match unless you were wearing your school tie and a jacket, and you couldn't be scruffy anywhere. When you had meals after the game, sausage and mash or whatever, you had to sit properly to be served at the table. He was very insistent on good manners, believing that rugby was a reflection of what you were and how you lived. He used to illustrate this with his curious theory that if you stammered in life, you stammered on the rugby field.

I didn't play rugby properly until I was sixteen. There were three hour-long games lessons every week, and we used to practise and play a miniature form of rugby in each of these. But there was only the one school team, so you had to wait until you were in the senior school before you could try to qualify for that. So I went on playing soccer with a tennis ball endlessly in the school yard, kicking it against the wall to get round people. At twelve it was still my ambition to be a footballer, which was understandable because every little village had its soccer team. In particular I wanted to be like Stan Thomas, a plumber who played on the right wing for Williamstown, the next village to mine. He was a beautiful player. We used to call him Stan the Bouncing Ball. I always wanted to be just like him.

Because of that background I used to try things in rugby like drop-kicking the ball, making it bounce up and down, and kicking it through instead of passing it, all things that Grib severely disapproved of. 'Soccer Joe!' he'd shout at me, and it became my nickname. I got to know all the soccer players by collecting cigarette cards, and I used to take these sets to school to show the boys. If Grib caught sight of them, it would be 'Soccer Joe' again. He hated soccer.

I never got to hate soccer. I love the game still. But gradually, under Grib's influence, rugby began to take over. His message had an almost missionary quality. Rugby was the only game that taught you all the basic principles of conduct, he'd say. Through it you learned to suffer defeat, and handle it gracefully. More important, you learned to deal with success in a dignified way, which was even harder.

Grib's approach to the game was clear-cut and based on a small number of enduring principles. He was as adamant as hell on one thing, that the rugby ball was shaped like it was for handling. And he taught me that the books were all wrong about catching a ball with two hands. What you did was catch the ball with one hand only, using the other hand to secure it. If you did that, you were swaying the right way to pass the ball on. Even as you took it, it was going in the right direction. He was a great one for securing possession, which was the forwards' job, but once the ball was available in any broken play, it was there to be passed. He'd shout, 'Hands, hands, hands!' from the side of the field, and he never compromised over that. He also insisted that everybody in the team should handle the ball, forwards as well as backs. Gower Jenkins, a front-row forward at Tonyrefail who played for Wales as a schoolboy, could run and handle like a threequarter as a result of this teaching. And Grib insisted that whether you were playing in a school game or in an international against whoever – New Zealand, Australia or South Africa – handling and running was the right approach. And that's the style the Japanese and Italians have adopted today. They're playing beautiful football with the ball in their hands.

He knew that you had to be tough in the tackle, but he physically taught you how to do it safely. He showed you where to meet your opponent's body, explained why you should wait instead of going in head-on. He was still saying the same things twenty-five years later. I remember Grib being in the stand in 1967 when Danny Hearn, the England centre, played in Dublin. Afterwards he said of Hearn, 'Nobody can tackle like that, going straight in with your head. You've got to tackle with your shoulder, wait for them and take them on the side.' Early in the following season Danny was playing for a combined Midlands/South-East side against the All Blacks at Leicester, when he suffered the terrible injury which left him permanently paralysed. It was all the result of a crash tackle he made on the New Zealand five-eighths, MacRae. I was doing the commentary on the game, and can never forget the impact of the tackle or the gradual realisation by the crowd that Danny wasn't going to get up from it.

What Grib didn't like was unnecessary confrontation. This might sound naive today, when players are so fond of knocking each other over, so creating a gap where there should have been someone standing on his feet. Grib wouldn't have all this. Believing in toughness was not a licence to knock people over to make a space. That was too easy. He wanted to see you run round your opponent or side-step him. He used to put a line of sticks down the field and make you run along them alternately side-stepping to left and right. But what he put greatest stress on was passing the ball. This was because the ball can travel faster in a pass than any man in the world is able to run. And to make the contest even more uneven, Grib taught us how to spin the ball as we passed.

While the hands were most important, Grib insisted that I must be able to kick with both feet, too. The ball was then a big, leather thing, heavy as hell, but he laid down that if you were naturally right-footed, you had to learn to kick it with your left foot. And the way you did this was to wear only one boot, the one you were going to kick with. In the end I could kick as easily with my left foot as my right.

All the same, there was a limited time and place for kicking, as I learned painfully on the Monday after the school had played at Maesteg. Grib hadn't come with us. He missed away games from time to time. Being on the selection committee of the Welsh Schools Union he had to watch other players or attend meetings.

It was Mr Slocombe, a Maths teacher, who was in charge of us. By that I mean in charge of getting us to Maesteg in good order and good time, ensuring that we behaved ourselves at the table and so on. He wasn't a coach, and couldn't have told you whether it was a good game or a bad game or whether or not you'd done well. He just happened to be the duty teacher that morning.

Maesteg hadn't been beaten for two seasons, and to put it simply, they kicked a penalty goal and I dropped a goal, which meant we won 4–3. I enjoyed dropping goals and could now do so with either foot. We used to practise drop-kicking the ball from the corner flag as if we were taking corners at soccer, swinging the ball in between the posts. I loved it as much in those days as I've grown to hate it since.

I thought Grib would be delighted that we had won the game and taken Maesteg's record. So, as I was doing some practical work in the lab on Monday morning, I wasn't surprised when a little boy from the second form came up and said, 'Mr Gribble wants to see Cliff Morgan.' So, with an Excuse me, sir, I went across to the workshop where Grib was banging away with a hammer at his furnace. I can see it now. Grib wearing some boy's school cap on his head, as he usually did for metalwork. He said to me, 'What about Saturday, did you enjoy Saturday?' So I replied, 'Yes, sir,' thinking that he was going to say, Well done, it was terrific. Instead he said, 'I understand from very, very good sources that if you'd let the ball go we'd have got a try and five points, not the four with your arrogant, selfish foot. I've decided to drop you from the school team for the next fortnight.'

He kept to his word. I didn't play in the next two matches. But, you know, the strange thing is that after the lesson of Maesteg, I never dropped a goal in all my international matches and Lions tours. Maybe it was part of the ammunition I should have had. It might have made me a better player. I know there were times when a drop-kick at goal was the only sensible move open to me. But I listened and reacted to everything Grib said, and something in the back of my mind said, Don't drop a goal.

But the Maesteg game was still several years ahead. In the junior years we – the girls as well as the boys – used to go and support the school team on a Saturday morning. Sometimes we went by bus if they were playing somewhere like Pentre Grammar School at the top of the Rhondda. You didn't have to do it, but you knew it was expected. Afterwards you were free to go back to your village and your first love, football. But meanwhile you were drawn to rugby, too, by finding heroes among the boys ahead of you. Selwyn Collins – I wanted to be like him because he was a beautiful rugby player. And Trevor Jones, the captain of the team – you practically touched your cap to him. He went on to Aberystwyth University, and became a big shot in agriculture in South Wales. The whole atmosphere of our rugby then was created by admiration for the most exciting players you saw at school or in your village – but only occasionally, if you were lucky, at a senior match. The process is much the same today, but with the great difference that nowadays kids are less likely to have local heroes. They copy the sports stars they see day by day on television. Having been a hero-worshipper at school has made me all the more aware of the influence that international players have over kids. It's a responsibility that lots of them, who just play for the money, don't begin to understand.

The process was well understood, and encouraged, at Tonyrefail. After morning prayers the headmaster would make his various announcements. But Monday morning was special because, between the hymns, he would report on the previous Saturday's game, and whether we'd won or lost. Since I played the viola with the school orchestra, I would be sitting behind him. And later, when I got into the rugby team, he would turn round and nod his head if I had scored a try.

Closer to home I had the example of Cliff Jones, the majestic fly-half who played for Cambridge University and Cardiff and won thirteen Welsh caps in the period 1934–38, which was roughly when I was in infants' school. He still lived nearby but was pretty rich by our standards; he was a barrister, and his father had a fruit distribution company at Porth, the biggest in the Rhondda. As I mentioned, my maternal grandmother was in service in his house. Since I had never seen him play rugby, Cliff Jones couldn't be a hero to me in the way that Selwyn Collins and Trevor Jones were. But I was well aware of him as a local legend, the most brilliant fly-half of the 'thirties, small, quick-witted, elusive and successful.

I met him first when I was about fourteen. I had gone for a walk with my father on the Waun, the high moorland above the village where people often took their picnic sandwiches in summer to give themselves a cheap outing. We were standing looking at the view when we saw a man coming round the hill on a horse. My father recognised him as Cliff Jones and, as he rode up, called out, 'Hello Mr Jones, this is my boy. His name is Cliff as well.' Jones got down from his horse, shook my hand and, full of the old nonsense, asked me, 'What are you doing now? Are you playing rugby?' I wasn't yet, but he went on chatting for a while – he was a very quick talker – before he said cheerio and rode off. As we walked back my father told me wonderful tales about him, and especially about the Saturday before Christmas in 1935 when Cliff Jones and Wilf Wooller and the Welsh team had beaten the All Blacks in Cardiff. To meet him now on the Waun was a chance event that would go on haunting my imagination. And though I didn't know what I wanted to do, I wanted to be like him.

A year or so later I visited his house, but though I met his wife, Mary, he was not at home. My grandmother had asked her, as servants do, whether she could take me in to see 'the room'. This was part-study, part-library but also a trophy room, almost a monument to his playing days. There on display were photographs of the three Varsity match teams he had played in, his light blue Cambridge blazer, cap and scarf, an Army cap and a Welsh cap, portraits and action photographs and all the memorabilia of his playing days. Looking around reinforced the impression he had made on me when I met him on the Waun. I didn't covet a trophy room for myself. Just as well, since I gave away pretty well all my souvenirs to better causes than nostalgia. But the sight of that Welsh cap did have a lasting impact. I thought, I'd love to have one of those.

Meanwhile, I hadn't even got into the school team. It's strange, really. We were a small school and a mixed school, which meant there were only 160 boys from the first to the sixth form. And since the team was confined to the senior boys, Grib effectively had only twenty or so pupils from which to pick it every Saturday. All the same, you had to work hard for your place, and Grib still left you in no doubt that you were privileged to represent the school.

For I don't remember how long – months anyway – I used to carry my bag as one of about four travelling reserves. In it were the shorts my mother had ironed, clean socks, clean boots. I'd invariably come back with the kit dirty because I had lent it to someone, and my mother would soak it and rewash it without complaint, while I went out to play football. I used to wonder if I'd ever make the grade.

When Grib decided that I was ready to play for the team, I just naturally, instinctively played with the ball in two hands, and ran, because that was the only way I knew how to play. But it wasn't as a fly-half that he picked me. Grib started me off as a hooker, because I was little, and hookers in those days were small fellows. In the front row you got rough and you got tough as you learned the job.

Next he played me on the wing, then in the centre, and only at last moved me to the position I really wanted, fly-half. Years later I asked him why he had done all this switching around. He said, 'So that you would understand when you got to fly-half how lousy it was to stand on the wing and not get the ball on a bloody cold day.' He drummed it into you, until it became second nature to let the ball go and get the wing running. He was probably right. It may sound naive these days, but everything hinged on getting the ball to the wing. If I now try to picture a school match, I see that sevens final against Pontypridd, and our wing, Peter Cook, who was also a great tackler, running in to score from the half-way line. That sevens tournament, which came in my last year in school, was typical of Grib. Sevens was pretty new to Wales at that time, but Grib calculated that even a moderately successful rugby school like Tonyrefail could beat the others if it hosted the event and took it seriously. And he made sure it passed off with no controversy by inviting all the first-class referees from around the Rhondda and the Vale of Glamorgan to officiate.

For a while I still played football after my morning rugby match. But by the age of sixteen I had to give it up, except for school yard soccer, of course, because rugby was taking over my life. It was in my blood. Grib had put it there. We didn't only play a match on Saturday, we often went on to watch one. When we went down to Canton High School in Cardiff, for instance, our game was always arranged to coincide with a decent fixture at the Arms Park. So in those post-war years, as the first major teams returned to play there, I saw some marvellous sides, including the New Zealand Expeditionary Force with great men like Freddie Allen and Charlie Saxton. Then on Monday Grib would talk to us about the game we had been watching, always wanting to make us aware of rugby's subtleties and possibilities.

Apart from the three games lessons we all had, if you were in the school team you had extra sessions at lunchtime. They mostly consisted of five-a-side or six-a-side games played not on the field but in the fifteen-yard strip between the goal-line and the dead-ball line. In that cramped area you had to pass as quickly as you could and twist and turn out of trouble. The All Blacks do a lot of their training in confined spaces, and it was typical of Grib that he should be ahead of his time in this. He was the same in his attitude towards tactics, teaching you to read the game and see where you were going.

This lunchtime training wasn't compulsory, yet practically everybody turned up for it, and there were certain perks attached to it. For the rest of the school there were first and second sittings for lunch, and we would not only miss both but would have to get through our meal quickly. Bertha Davies, the cook, understood this. If you were 'one of Mr Gribble's boys' you never had to queue. Miss Davies would find special bits of food for you and she'd make you chips. Mr Gribble's boys were in clover. Another bonus we enjoyed was being able to go and talk to Grib in the woodwork room or the metalwork room, while the kids in the first form were making their book-ends or steel chisels. He revelled in conversation, and after he'd talked about the game we had seen on Saturday, he'd tell us who else we ought to go and watch and what we could learn from them.

I played for the Welsh Secondary Schools in my final year at Tonyrefail when I was eighteen. I don't think I'd have got into the side if Grib hadn't been on the committee, because the competition was fierce in those days. I played in masses of trials – the first when I was sixteen and had just got into the school team. And two years later there was a trial at Pontypool Park which was to have unexpected consequences. To be exact it was just the first half of a trial; when we changed ends an outside-half from Cardiff High School came on and took my jersey. It was a freezing cold day, and pouring with rain, but I was left on the touchline without any other top to wear. The dressing rooms were locked, so I couldn't get to my clothes. I just had to sit there shivering until my father, who had travelled there with me, came down from the stand, took off his overcoat and put it over my shoulders. He also produced a flask of tea, which warmed me up a bit. But after that I had a spell of illness and didn't play for some months, which meant missing a crucial part of the season. I suppose I shouldn't have gone back to rugby as soon as I did, but in the middle of that 1948–49 season I won the first of my two Welsh Schoolboy caps. It was only later, when I went for my National Service medical, that the doctors discovered a shadow on one of my lungs and I was rejected. At the time I felt more grateful than concerned, and since then I've never suffered any after-effects.

In the January at Newport the Welsh Secondary Schools

XV, which included two future Wales and British Lions forwards, Bryn Meredith and Russell Robins, played against Bob Oakes's Yorkshire Public Schools, which was just called Yorkshire in most of the papers. It was a terrific game and after it I got probably the best notice – by Dromio in the *Newport Argus* – that I've ever received. 'What a joy it is,' he began, 'to see in the Rugby field a youngster who reveals a genius for the game. Some lads are born to play football. Without conscious thought, without instruction, they dodge, swerve, sidestep, and are dazzlingly effective in individual attack. Such a lad was C. Morgan of Tonyrefail.' If only all reports were as flattering (though he did go on to imply that I was a bit selfish on the field). I'm not sure, mind, what Grib, after all his efforts, would have made of 'without instruction'.

J.E. 'Johnny' Williams, who was to play with me on the 1955 Lions tour of South Africa, was in that Yorkshire schools side. And in my second game, against England Schools at Cardiff, the opposition included Ted Woodward, who would go on to play for Wasps and win fifteen senior caps. We 'narrowly' beat England 30–3, but the only thing Grib was concerned about afterwards was whether we had played the game well, whether it had looked right for the public. He wanted it to look classy, to have style. Anything that was dubious he didn't like at all.

It was in my last year at school, too, that I got my first smell of playing with the big boys. I was asked at a few hours' notice to turn out for Cardiff. Well, it wasn't the official club side, exactly, but it had most of the famous Cardiff players in it – Bill Tamplin, the captain, and Des O'Brien, who was captain of Ireland, Jackie Matthews, Bleddyn Williams. How it happened was that Les Hayward, who played in the front row for Cardiff, had joined the staff as gym master. One afternoon he came round to the class I was in and said, 'I want you to play for Rex Willis's team in Porthcawl tonight.' It was called Rex Willis's team because his sister lived in Porthcawl and the match was in support of some local good cause. I had to get permission to leave school and go home to collect some kit, and then Les, who was also playing, of course, drove me over to Porthcawl. I'd never met any of these people before, though in a couple of years they were to be close friends. It was also the first time I played outside Rex Willis, who would become what I always called my better half. It was as a result of playing at Porthcawl that Les – whom I still met regularly at London Welsh Male Voice Choir practice until his death in May 1996 – took me down to the Cardiff team trials the following season.

It wasn't all rugby at school. I got Matric, and chose to do science for Higher – A-level as it is now – with the idea that I'd later study Medicine. Without being outstanding at work, I did reasonably well. I loved doing dissections of earthworms, frogs, dogfish and so on, and sections and drawings of plants in botany. Microscopes and other pieces of lab equipment were highly romantic to me. I suppose I might have made a decent village doctor if I'd qualified and, having had these early ambitions, I'm pleased that my son, Nick, is now an orthopaedic surgeon. But I didn't have the application to follow it through. Life was full of so many other distractions.

In school we had a branch of the Urdd Gobaith Cymru, and I'd introduce their concerts, play the piano for them, organise sing-songs and dances. And there I learned a great deal from a fellow who called himself Tommy Tumble, a youth organiser from Tumble in West Wales whose real name was Tommy Schofield. I saw the way he handled people in a room, in a conference, or at one of the youth camps by the sea in Llangranog. He was one of those people with perfect timing, like Bob Hope or Sophie Tucker. I suppose I was a bit of a show-off. I wanted to be there and do my bit, which is how I learned to do certain things, like talking to an audience. It gave you the confidence not to feel embarrassed when you stood up in public to say, 'Good evening,' even if what you went on to say was not particularly important. Once you had said, 'Good evening,' the rest was easy.

Taking part in eisteddfodau – as nearly every schoolchild in Wales does – has the same effect of making you lose your self-consciousness in front of an audience. It helps explain

why the English are natural spectators while the Welsh are
natural performers. Even when they are being spectators. Our
big event was the St David's Day inter-house eisteddfod, when
the girls went into the hall wearing daffodils, and the boys
wore full-grown leeks which they later had to eat. We stank
for days. I was in Tŷ Haran, and in my final year I conducted
the house choir. I also took part in the choral whistling and the
choral verse-speaking competitions. The competition between
the houses was intense. You had to win, and it prepared you
for the world outside by teaching you that life was always a
bloody competition. Those eisteddfodau, with all their cheering
and shouting and chanting, made you edgy and keen. And we
thought, rightly or wrongly, that it was part of the business
of the education system to teach you that you had to learn a
part, perform it as best you could, take knocks, and compete. It
was old-fashioned, but that's how we were brought up. I loved
it, I loved the eisteddfod, I loved the piano, the sound of the
orchestra, the choir singing. And knowing that you were the
best, even if sometimes you didn't win.

By that time I had also joined my mother and father in the
Porth and District Choir, whose Sunday evening practice I had
been attending as a non-singing member for longer than I could
remember. It was part of the weekly ritual that after evening
chapel four or five friends would gather at our house for a slice
of cold meat, and then we'd all go down the hill by bus or on
foot to another chapel at Cymmer, near Porth. There, as a baby,
I'd be sat in a chair as a captive audience, and as an older boy I'd
listen enviously. By the age of fourteen I knew by heart all the
tenor, bass, soprano and contralto parts in the *Messiah*, *Elijah*
and almost every sacred classic in the choral repertoire; and
while hymn-singing was in English in our chapel, here it was
usually in Welsh. By seventeen I was ready to take my place as
second tenor to my father's tenor. I stood next to John Thomas,
who used to tap shoes in the village – he was a cobbler in other
words – and whose brother was the great Rhondda novelist and
story-teller, Gwyn Thomas.

Now I had to attend practice on two other evenings, one with the full choir, the other with the tenors and basses. I loved every minute of it. And so did everyone else. If Stanley Williams, the conductor, took the basses through their part in practice, and they sang it especially well, the rest of the choir would burst into clapping. Talk about teamwork. There was as much mutual support in the Porth choir as I ever found in any rugby team. And more fun and laughter on their trips away than on many rugby tours. I remember one particular trip when we took the Campbell steamer across the Bristol Channel to Weston-super-Mare. And on the way back, since Stanley wasn't with us, I conducted the choir in 'Dyn a Anned o Wraig' (Man who is Born of Woman), a wonderful Welsh anthem, with all the passengers gathering round us on the deck. And somebody made the remark: 'Their singing is to the Welsh what sight is to the eye.'

Twice we won the mixed choir prize in the National Eisteddfod – at Dolgellau in 1949 and Aberystwyth, 1951. And when the buses arrived back in Porth at one or two in the morning there'd be hundreds of people in the streets waiting to cheer us home. We also put on splendid Christmas concerts, and since my father at various times was chairman, secretary and treasurer of the choir, I've still got receipts from Isobel Baillie, Kathleen Ferrier and the Polish bass, Marian Nowakowski: 'Three guineas for singing 2 nights of the *Elijah* in Porth with the Porth and District Choir and an efficient orchestra, leader Mr Challinor.' Those events were the highlights of my days.

Now, of course, I was mooching off after practice with Cynlais Evans, my closest friend, to Bracci's, the Italian café, where we'd talk for hours. I was also going into Porth to see *Goodbye Mr Chips* and *Laura* at the Central picture house, always hoping that there would be a girl-friend to share one of the double seats in the back row. Up to then we'd had a pretty cat-and-dog relationship with the girls who made up half the school.

We used to change for games at one end of the gymnasium, the girls at the other. But one day when we were out on the field, and the gym teacher was absent, the girls got into our dressing room, filled our shoes with water, tied our clothes together, and switched them all around. We came back in and it was chaos. Next morning in prayers the headmaster, Abraham Jenkins, took us through the usual hymn-singing and then looked down over his glasses and said, 'Will all those girls who were concerned in that incident in the boys' changing room yesterday stand up and come forward.' The whole of forms five and six stood up and came to the front. 'You dirty little girls, playing with boys' underwear!' was all he could find to say. He walked out of assembly, and no more was heard of it. But by the age of watching Hollywood films we had begun to feel more romantic towards the girls.

I was in love with two in particular. One was Shirley White, who was very beautiful, a girl you wanted to be with. I was always crazy about her but too shy to talk to her except to say hello. It was only when I wrote an article about my schooldays in the *South Wales Echo* that an aunt of hers sent a letter to say that she was then living in Rome, where her husband was in the embassy, and her two children were doctors. The other girl, with whom I had a long affair at school, was Mary Locke. She later married a local boy who became a doctor and when he qualified they moved to Sheffield. I did keep in touch with her from time to time; in fact I used to send her my rugby ties which she would unpick and then sew together to make patchwork eiderdowns. It made me wonder how it would have changed my life to marry somebody from school. But I was far from ready to make up my mind on matters like that. I was still making my way in the rugby world.

I went straight from Tonyrefail to Cardiff University, and because of rugby I neglected my work. I was playing for the Biological Society against the Engineers, say, on a Wednesday; for Cardiff seconds, or with luck the firsts, on a Saturday; and lots of other games beside. I didn't totally waste my first year. I got 100 per cent in Practical Chemistry. But I did badly in Botany and was asked to go back early to re-sit the exam the following September. Until the week before, I had every intention of doing so. But the exam happened to clash with a chance of playing for Cardiff, and I chose rugby without a second thought. As a result I was asked to leave university before the start of my second year.

I suppose I was stupid. I'd thoroughly enjoyed college. It was a privileged life, even if you had no money; during the day we lived on bowls of pea soup with a fourpenny loaf divided between four of us. But that hardly seemed to matter. The ex-servicemen had brought a great atmosphere of casualness to the university. They'd be playing the piano, double-bass and clarinet in refectory as we ate, and I was very sad to leave it all behind. I also felt I had badly let down my family and myself.

I might have coped better if I had been older myself; most of those ex-servicemen got their degrees. Or if there had been someone there to tell me, 'You're not doing this right.' On the other hand, perhaps I had done it right. I can't imagine that I would have had a better life if I had turned up for that exam. Most of the good things which later happened to me stemmed from that one rash decision. But I couldn't appreciate that in September 1950. I had no idea what to do, where to look for a job. And I had to work off this feeling of being a failure.

4

Rugby with a Cardiff accent

Even before that invitation to play in Rex Willis's XV at Porthcawl in 1949, I had never really doubted which club I would join when I left school. It had to be Cardiff. There were no local alternatives. Pontypridd and Treorchy had clubs, of course, but at that time they weren't playing first-class rugby. Neath wanted me to play for them, but Ned Gribble said, 'Cardiff's the place for you, because they've got Bleddyn Williams, Jackie Matthews, Rex Willis, all those sorts of players there.' And as usual Grib was right. It was playing as the link between the incomparable Rex at scrum-half and two centres of that class that helped me to develop my game and brought me my first cap.

Shortly after the Porthcawl match I had received another message from Cardiff through our gym teacher, Les Hayward. Would I stand by as a reserve for a Wednesday evening match at the Arms Park? No need to ask twice. Given a day's notice this time, I went to the ground straight from Tonyrefail Grammar School, wearing my school cap and carrying my father's soccer bag, one of those old-fashioned Gladstone bags in which doctors used to carry their stethoscopes and so on. But when I presented myself at the players' entrance, all that Jack, the doorman, said was, 'Schoolboys round the back.'

I said, 'No, I'm supposed to be playing here.' And I had to wait at the door while someone went to the office of the Cardiff secretary, Brice Jenkins, to see if I really was a player. Well, I was and I wasn't. Eventually they let me in, though I didn't get a game. I had only been asked there in case Billy Cleaver couldn't turn up. When he did, I just hung around without talking to anybody.

This experience didn't put me off. If anything it made me all the keener to join Cardiff, and I applied for a trial. There I had the advantage of playing with Goronwy Morgan, the scrum-half I had partnered in the Welsh Secondary Schools side. He was from Seven Sisters, a mining village like my own but in the Dulais Valley to the north of Neath. In fact his father and mine had become great friends as they went round the circuit of schoolboy trials and internationals. After the trial the club accepted both Goronwy and me, and so in the first half of that season, which coincided with my one and only year at university, we continued playing frequently together in the second team. Before that, to be eligible to play, we had to join the Cardiff Athletic Club. This cost £1 a year, which, as ever, my mother found for me.

I soon realised that I was in a very competitive situation: the newest and youngest of five outside-halves at the club. Billy Cleaver had already been capped by Wales, and would play in all their major matches that season. Then there were Derek Illes, a hell of a good player, Dr St John Rees, who later became Medical Officer for the Rhondda, and Alun Thomas, who had joined Cardiff from Swansea. So in a way I was lucky to hold my place in the Rags, as the seconds were known, let alone get picked for Cardiff itself whenever Billy cried off.

That happened first in the October. On the Thursday I had a call at college to say that Billy wasn't able to play against Cambridge University at Grange Road on the Saturday afternoon or at Northampton on the Monday, the two games

Soccer was my father's first love. Here he captains the victorious Trebanog
Rovers. Uncle Tave is seated extreme left and my grandfather, Isaac
Morgan, outside whose house the picture is taken, stands third from the
right.

Soul of the community, the chapel. My father and mother are third and
fourth from the left in the first row at this cymanfa ganu in Porth. I was
probably pumping the organ.

A Sunday School outing to Barry
Island in the summer of 1934
(above). I am the small boy being
restrained by my mother, with my
father to her left. Behind are my
Uncle Arthur and Grandmother
Thomas.

Mrs Morgan's baby in the velvet
jacket she made me and, at this
stage in life, still clutching a football.

A wartime family picture (my father
has his ARP badge in his
buttonhole) and I am wearing the
Fair Isle pullover my mother knitted
for me.

Ned Gribble who converted me to rugby at Tonyrefail and to whom I owe
so much. In 1949 he saw the fruits of his coaching when Gower Jenkins, left,
and I won our Welsh Secondary Schools caps.

The team that beat the English Secondary Schools at Cardiff Arms Park.
Bryn Meredith, third from the right in the back row, would become the
greatest hooker of all time, but here he was a prop. Russell Robins was
captain and went on to become a marvellous international back-row
forward. Glyn John from Maesteg is to his left. Sitting in the front with me
is Goronwy Morgan from Seven Sisters.

The Porth and District Mixed-Voice Choir who won the chief choral prize at the Rhyl eisteddfod. I am third from the right in the back row. My father, a great second tenor, is between the third and fourth white-bloused ladies from the left.

The new manager of Wire Ropes Wicklow gaining some shop-floor experience.

Nuala's formidable grandmother who recognised a ball-playing pauper when she saw one, with Pamela, Sheila and Nuala.

Line up for the very first 'A Question of Sport'. Supporting quiz master David Vine are, from the left, Morgan, Lillian Board, Tom Finney, George Best, Henry Cooper (my fellow team captain) and Ray Illingworth. Devised in 1970 and given a six-programme trial run, it is still going strong twenty-six years later.

The last programme being made at the old BBC North Manchester studio prompted some demolition squad help from the team leaders, Cooper and Morgan, while Debbie Johnsey, Malcolm Macdonald, John H. Stracey and Gareth Edwards look on.

Alun Williams tests me on the questions for 'Make Your Mark', a series of weekly knock-out quiz programmes between Welsh rugby and soccer clubs.

On the set of *Villain* to interview Richard Burton, with the film's director Michael Tuchner. Richard always said he would rather have played once for Wales than played Hamlet.

In Cardiff just before transmission of Welsh 'Sports Parade'. From the left, David Coleman, producer Dewi Griffiths, Bill Adams, 'Grandstand' floor manager, my invaluable secretary, Avis Prior, and me.

Members of SPARKS launching boating holidays for the physically disabled. Celebrities on the terrace of the Palace of Westminster include, standing left, Ed Stewart and Douglas Bader and, second from right, Alec Bedser, with Tim Brooke-Taylor and me in front.

Finding a dry corner on a wild day to interview HRH the Princess Royal while making a documentary on Riding for the Disabled, of which she is Patron.

Conducting the Scarlets at Stradey.   Nuala in Jazzland.

I was there – with Lord Tonypandy and Max Boyce at a tribute dinner given me by the Variety Club of Great Britain.

being treated as a mini-tour from which the club would return on Tuesday. Could I stand in for him? It meant missing lectures, but that hardly crossed my mind. I could catch up later.

In the Cambridge University side that winter were six present or future internationals including Arthur Dorward, the Scottish scrum-half, and two fellow countrymen, Glyn Davies, my old opponent when he was stand-off for Pontypridd Grammar School, and John Gwilliam, the Welsh back-row forward and captain. These were the great days of Oxbridge rugby, and I was only sorry that I wasn't playing in it. But you needed three distinctions in Higher to be accepted by either university, which stopped a lot of rugby players getting blues. Still at least I had the consolation of playing on the winning side against them both.

Porthcawl had been for fun, but in those first eighty minutes at Grange Road I had not only to graduate from junior to senior rugby, but to adapt my game so as not to embarrass the hardened internationals who depended on me. I suppose I was still performing like a schoolboy: you know, I'd run a bit and only then let the ball go. But you simply can't do that in senior rugby. If it's going to be a fast ball to the wing, you have to take it on one foot and pass it on the other. Jack got clobbered five times in the first five passes I sent him, until finally he said, 'I don't want the ball a bloody hour-and-a-half late.' And Bleddyn talked with you right through every game I played with him. In the match at Northampton on the Monday, which we also won, I remember him telling me: 'I can't beat Jeff Butterfield on the outside, he's too quick for me. I'll take it short and early.'

In this way Bleddyn taught you what you had to watch out for; he knew the game and was a marvellous tactician. What may be forgotten, he was also a beautiful kicker of the ball. When you saw the way he leaned into the kick so that his body came over the ball, it was like watching the swing of a great golfer or a great football striker drive through the ball. These two centres were tough people, but they played entertaining rugby. Bleddyn, after all, scored forty-four tries in a season in the centre – and made another fifty for the wing as well. Rex, Jack,

Bleddyn: I really felt fortunate to have dropped into company like this. I don't think I was over-awed by them, and they wouldn't have wanted me to be. I know that at Northampton I had the cheek to say, since Cardiff's regular kicker, Bill Tamplin, wasn't playing, 'I'll kick your goals for you.' And I did land a couple, too. The only ones I ever kicked for Cardiff.

By chance the first home game I played for Cardiff was against Oxford University, who also had some terrific players like Brian Boobbyer in the centre and Murray Hofmeyr at stand-off – both of them England caps, even though Hofmeyr, who was picked at full-back, was a South African. Brian Mark was my scrum-half. The occasion sticks in the mind for the memory of how underwhelmed the Arms Park crowd were to see us. Brice Jenkins was on the loudspeaker before the game, making the club announcements in his heavy Cardiff drawl. This mongrel seaport accent which has developed in the most cosmopolitan settlement west of the Usk is strange to the ears even of Welshmen. Or perhaps especially of Welshmen. And this afternoon his message wasn't well received.

'In the Cardiff XV there are two changes from your pro-gramme. At number seven, delete W.R. Willis and insert B. Mark.' There was a groan and mild booing from the crowd. 'And at number six, delete W.B. Cleaver and insert C.I. Morgan.' Another groan. I thought what a welcome that was to the Arms Park. I understood it eventually. The Cardiff crowd took for granted the greatness of Willis and Cleaver. When they were missing, their disappointment was just as intense as if they had gone to the theatre expecting to see a leading actor and found he'd been replaced by his understudy.

I still played most of my rugby for the Rags, but I got the occasional call when, say, Billy cried off against Llanelli on a Monday evening at Stradey Park, which isn't a pleasant thing to contemplate if you're an outside-half. But I took all the opportunities that were offered – who wouldn't? – and they came even more regularly towards the end of the season. With the international championship over, Billy, who had played for Wales at full-back and centre, as well as his preferred position at stand-off, was selected as a utility player by the 1950 Lions leaving for Australia and New Zealand (Willis, Williams, Matthews and Cliff Davies were also picked from Cardiff). And in those days, when the team travelled each way by ocean liner, this particular tour stretched to the best part of seven months. That meant a long absence from club rugby, and I was moved up to take Billy's place. By the end of April 1950 I had played more games for the first team than for the Rags – fifteen in all, which earned me my Cardiff cap. It was far more than I could have hoped for in my first season.

I had always felt a sentimental attachment to the Cardiff club. In 1945 I had stood in the queue there to watch the New Zealand Services team. I had seen Dickie Guest, a wing for Waterloo, drop a goal from the half-way line. Marking him on the Welsh side, I remember, was Les Williams, who afterwards went North to Rugby League. I'd been to internationals there with my father, and club games with the school team. And a year before I had seen Jackie Matthews, who hadn't seen me, and bumped into me on the pavement. This was something to boast about at school. With all these memories of Cardiff and the Arms Park, I would have been satisfied, when I paid my first sub to the Athletic, just to run out once that season in the blue and black jersey. Instead, eight months later, here I was next in line to a much honoured player who might retire from the game at any time.

Of course, everything was new to me that first year – spending my days at university and in the big city, walking through the Gwyn Nicholls Gates at the Arms Park, and up the stairs into the dressing room. It wasn't beautifully set out like modern dressing rooms. There were showers but only two baths, the ordinary domestic kind, between the whole lot of us. I suppose the room was clean, but it was pretty dim and rough, and one big table in the middle served for everything. It was where you dumped your kit, where they left the mugs of tea for when you came off the field, and where you'd stretch out waiting for a rub-down from the masseur. I suppose I was naive and easily pleased, but I loved it. I loved walking into the room and smelling the place, the Wintergreen oil and the stale clothes. I remember those smells like yesterday. They're more vivid to me than sight. And for all its dinginess, there was something about the room that made you feel not just important, but special.

At lunchtimes I used to walk up to the Arms Park from college to practise passing with Rex Willis – him passing the ball to me especially. And the person who was invariably there with his Scotch terrier was Wilfred Wooller, the big Wales and Cardiff centre of the 'thirties who was still captain and secretary of the Glamorgan county cricket side. He lived in the flats overlooking the Arms Park. He could never resist giving advice. 'That's not the way to take a pass,' he'd say, and then he'd demonstrate the right way. And as far as technique was concerned, I probably learned as much from Wilf as from the regular training sessions on Tuesday and Thursday nights.

Rex, however, gave me even more. He had a remarkable record at scrum-half. He'd risen through the ranks in little more than a season, starting at Llandaff, a junior club in the suburbs of Cardiff, then moving onward and upward to Cardiff and Wales. And in the course of the following summer he would end up a British Lion. I suppose as a fly-half the one player you depend on more than any other is your scrum-half. And at that crucial point, when I was trying to prove that I was the valid successor to Billy Cleaver, I had the good fortune to find myself playing with Rex.

To me he was an exciting figure. He was posh, drove fast cars, had long hair, and looked an unlikely scrum-half. But he also had big shoulders, a strong frame, and was prepared to defend you against all opposition. I never recall him giving me the ball when it wasn't a good ball for the outside-half to receive. He never passed it on just to get out of trouble himself. And it was for that unselfishness that I called him my better half. He was one of the Cardiff players who made it worthwhile to play, because he was always serving you. Today people don't like being servants, but Rex didn't mind in the least being in what many consider the less glamorous of the two half-back positions. He took enormous pride in giving his outside-half an immaculate service.

The speed of his reactions was unbelievable, but in other respects he wasn't a natural. He was a self-made player who had to work hard to acquire his skills. He got to know the game by listening to the great forwards surrounding him, and to backs as perceptive as Bleddyn Williams, who taught him how to read the play. In turn Rex – along with Bleddyn, Jack and Wilf – made me by polishing up what I had already learnt from Ned Gribble.

Not that I was short of further advice from Ned, either. He frequently dropped into the house at Trebanog, and had a great influence on my parents' attitudes to what I should be doing. He was also a regular in the Cardiff club. Some years after I left school he was on a double-decker bus which overturned, and as a result of his injuries he had to have a leg amputated. Some people say he never fully recovered from the shock, but I remember him at the club most Saturday evenings in the 'fifties. He had his own special corner and held court there, and because people valued what he had to say on players and teams, he always found an audience. I loved the man for his whole approach to rugby, and I wasn't alone. When he died in the 'sixties, and I came down from London to be a bearer at his funeral, I found that all the other bearers were Mr Gribble's boys, too.

We had regular club training of course, but there wasn't much shape to it. We used to put on any old gear we could find, wear spikes to stretch our legs and make us go faster, and then run up and down the field passing the ball and going through a few uncomplicated drills. While it kept us limbered up, it added very little to our knowledge of the game. But there was an extra reason for looking forward to training nights – especially if you were a student with hardly any money. Cardiff provided us with a meal, of sorts. When we came back in the dressing room there was always a big box of kippers waiting for us. We cooked them one at a time in front of the electric fire, and ate them with our hands. As far as I know they were delivered on Brice Jenkins's instructions and the practice was unique to Cardiff. I got a taste for kippers in the end, I could tell a good one from a bad one. But there was no brown bread; we weren't that sophisticated. These free fish suppers went on for only another couple of years, after which you were lucky to get a cup of tea or a glass of beer on training nights.

The other bonus for a student was that on Saturday after the game you and the opposing team would be given a marvellous meal and offered all the beer you could drink. In my case this was little or none. It was tea or milk in those days, then the bus to Trebanog. Later on, though, even my mother took to keeping a little drink in the house so that if, say, Dr Matthews and his wife drove me home after a match, I could offer them something. I wasn't expected to take a drink myself.

The start of the 1950–51 season brought the end of my career at university and of Billy Cleaver's in first-class rugby. He retired soon after returning from the Lions tour, and I was picked to replace him. What helped my cause was that Alun Thomas had gone to play in the centre. Alun was undoubtedly a class performer, but the Cardiff selectors decided that he was a better centre than stand-off – just as the Irish did in the case of another highly talented back, Mike Gibson. At any rate I got the stand-off's job and became a permanent fixture in that position until I moved to Ireland in 1954.

Playing for Cardiff you always felt that you were part of rugby history, and in 1951 it meant even more to be there when the club celebrated its seventy-fifth anniversary with a match against the returning Lions. Afterwards there was a dinner at the City Hall at which stories were told of past players and administrators and songs were sung about everyone in the club. It was pure nostalgia, but that's what appealed to me. I took a romantic view of being part of a club with a great past which was respected wherever rugby was played. And I was equally romantic about the game itself. What I loved about it was that you fought hard to beat the other side on the field, but later on, got together with them to celebrate the battle. In that way everyone got to know everyone else in rugby, and by talking to different generations of players in the clubhouse you learned the history of the game.

If my own generation failed the game, it may have been in not passing on the stories of the past as our elders had done. Once, when trying to fix up a meeting place in Cardiff with a current Welsh international, I discovered that he didn't know where on earth in the city to find the Gwyn Nicholls Memorial Gates (which, perhaps I'd better explain, stand at the main entrance to Cardiff Arms Park). Nor had he any idea who Gwyn Nicholls was. And things are little better over the other side of the Dyke. When I was leaving a reception for the 1991 World Cup, held at the Rugby Club round the corner from the BBC, I introduced one of the England players to Jeff Butterfield. 'Did he ever play?' the young chap asked as we got beyond the doors. Bloody hell, Butterfield; yes, he played a bit. An England international for seven consecutive seasons in the 'fifties, and holder of a record number of caps in the centre before the proliferation of international matches made records that much easier to set.

Many things contribute to making a club great. Age is one of them, though not the most reliable: clubs come and go. Who now remembers Marlborough Nomads or the Mohicans, both founder members of the Rugby Union in 1871? Great players, obviously, are another. But even they can't make their mark without public support and strong administrators. Fortunately, wherever Cardiff played there was always a huge crowd because a travelling circus of Cardiff supporters – not always coming from Cardiff – would pack the touchlines at Penzance and Newlyn, or the stand at Coventry if they managed to get a seat in it. You could always rely on a body of spectators who were on your side, and it meant a lot to us. In turn we had to keep them entertained. That was the principle that Bleddyn, a great influence on Cardiff during my years there, used to work on. We had got to enjoy ourselves so that people who had paid all this money to watch us would enjoy themselves too.

According to current theory, that isn't the way to go about it, but not knowing any better, that's what we tried to do. And we even won a few matches in doing it.

The club was also lucky in its administrators. Brice Jenkins, the secretary, and the first person I met there, was typical of his kind in those days, watching every penny that was spent, every ball that was bought. As a civil servant, he was meticulous in his work, and disciplined in his relationship with the players in much the way he must have been towards his office staff. You certainly couldn't do just what you liked, or even wear what you liked, about the club. But I soon came to respect him because he had these unshakable standards of decency in the game. He dropped his guard, too, when he got to know you and was more than generous with funds in anything that touched on the honour and reputation of Cardiff. And nothing touched it more acutely than our rivalry with Newport.

We played Newport twice at home and twice away every season, and despite the repetition, each match would turn out to have the biggest gate in South Wales. At the Arms Park we would get crowds that wouldn't have shamed an international, and although Rodney Parade hadn't our capacity, unless you reached the ground by midday, you wouldn't get in for the 2.30 kick-off. Because Brice Jenkins thought it was worth ten points to us, he insisted that we had brand-new gear – shorts, jerseys and stockings – every time we played Newport, and a new ball whenever we played them at home. Mind, it wasn't all that extravagant since you get through a lot of kit in a season, and the old stuff would be handed down to the second team or used in training. Apart from which, the gate money that these matches brought in contributed an awful lot to rebuilding the Cardiff clubhouse.

If we beat Newport four times in the season, anyone who had played in all four matches was awarded a blazer badge with the Cardiff emblem and the date on it. We did get the grand slam in 1952, and just before the presentation of the badges, Brice came up to me and said, 'Clifford, I've made a bit of a mess of this, I'm one badge short. Arthur Hull totally slipped my mind.' Arthur was a great forward from the Rhondda, a loyal, sentimental man who would have been terribly hurt to think he had been overlooked. I said – and it was easier for me since I knew I wasn't forgotten – 'Brice, why don't you give me an envelope with something stuffed in it to make it look right. You can let me have my badge later.' Forty-four years, and many reminders later, I'm still waiting for my badge.

Brice could be penny-pinching in small matters, but he was extravagant in others. In 1953, after Cardiff beat New Zealand, he decided that everyone who had played in the match should be given his own photograph of the winning team. He took Rex and me aside and said, 'Come and help me choose the frames.' But when we got to the shop he didn't take the least notice of our opinions. I think he just wanted us there as witnesses. He said, 'What do you think of this one? This is the one I think we should have.' And when Rex said, 'That's damned expensive Brice, too expensive for frames,' he produced one of his favourite phrases in his thick Cardiff accent, 'Not at all Rexy, I don't want to spoil the ship for a ha'porth of tar.'

It was the same when Cardiff went away. We travelled third class on the train, but that didn't matter because when there were eight of you in the carriage you'd have so much fun you didn't notice the journey. But when the team stayed overnight in London it was always at the Manderville, a very posh West End hotel. And when we were taken to the theatre, or sometimes the cinema, on the Friday night, it was always in the best seats. We saw *Annie Get Your Gun* and *Oklahoma*, and Agatha Christie's *The Mousetrap* at the Savoy theatre just before it started its record run at the Ambassadors. It was Brice's idea that we should be given the best, since the club expected the best out of us on the pitch.

Another guardian of tradition was Hubert Johnson, who had taken over as chairman after returning from war service with the RAF, and had patiently created the club's rugby museum. It took him donkey's years to prepare – I can't say complete, since it's still being added to. I only know that I had long stopped playing rugby and was working in television when we put on a programme, which included the Irish poet, Louis MacNeice, to launch the museum. Hubert had kept mementoes of all the major touring sides and clubs that visited Cardiff. And the one thing he was particularly proud of was a springbok head given him by Frank Mellish, manager of the 1951 South African side. Cardiff had lost to them, but Mellish acknowledged that it was such a desperately close game that it could have gone either way. Hubert also had the whistle which the Neath referee, Albert Freethy, blew in anger at Twickenham in 1925 before sending off the All Blacks forward, Cyril Brownlie, for kicking another player. The incident became notorious because many New Zealanders thought Freethy had punished the wrong man; still, he'd applied the laws as he saw them, and the same whistle has been used to signal the kick-off of recent World Cup finals.

Another person who also kept up, or in some cases laid down, the traditions of the club was Babs Filer. She had joined the staff as a sixteen- or seventeen-year-old girl, had run the bar, which was also a skittle alley, and had ended up as steward of the whole club. In fact she *was* the club; everyone who ever came there knew Babs. She enjoyed all the characters in the game, adored Cliff Davies who used to sing in the bar, and Maldwyn James, the hooker and another tenor; she loved to hear the piano going, and join in the sing-songs. She couldn't do enough for the players, providing thick slices of ham and jars of pickles to keep us going. In particular she looked after you if you were young, telling you not to do that, to do this instead.

When I was first introduced to Babs we shook hands and I said, 'Hello Miss Filer.' 'My name is Babs,' she replied, 'and you can call me Babs if you like.' Which sorted that out. But she was very serious about showing respect where she felt it was due. She told me not to call Haydn Tanner, Haydn. He was Mr Tanner. In the same way Jack Matthews should be Dr Matthews. I broke that second commandment pretty soon, but it was a long time before I used Mr Tanner's Christian name, and in those stricter days it was helpful to be reminded not to be familiar too quickly. Babs was fairly tough, too. People who behaved badly did it only once, and there were no drunken mauls in the club in Cardiff. She was important to us, and I find that I remember Babs vividly – more vividly than most things there.

What also made Cardiff a great club, of course, was the quality of the players and of the sides we played. We were living in that narrow ninety-two-mile stretch of coastal plain and valley where all the first-class rugby in Wales is played. And that concentration of the national game in an area smaller than Kent, far from making life easier, made it that much more intense. You couldn't walk down the street in Cardiff without being stopped. Not because you were a star, but simply because people recognised you as a Cardiff player and wanted to tell you what they thought of the last match or the next. Later, if it happened when I went shopping with Nuala, my wife, she'd say, 'I'll see you later,' and walk off. I'd have to go looking for her afterwards. She didn't like these interruptions. But because I was lucky enough to play for Cardiff, and these were our supporters, I knew I had to talk to them. And even if I'd have preferred to be left to myself, I don't think I ever resented it as an intrusion. I heard such wonderful stories this way.

It was amazing how many tough, skilful clubs there were only an hour or so away from Cardiff. Newport, Pontypool, Llanelli, Swansea – you couldn't differentiate between them in those days. And Bridgend, Neath, Aberavon, Ebbw Vale, Pontypridd couldn't be taken for granted either. The Newport games, though, are what I best remember, in part for Bill Tamplin's remarkable ability to kick goals at Rodney Parade, but even more for the duels between the two international wing-threequarters, their Ken Jones and our Haydn Morris. I could never say that Haydn, though very quick, was the better of them; he wasn't. But he, too, always seemed to score at Newport. That had much to do with Bleddyn. Something you don't often see today is a centre carrying the ball with two hands and with a mere move of the shoulder beating the opposition to create a gap. Bleddyn had this gift to perfection. In my mind's eye, I can see him leaning inward and pulling Ken in that extra half yard, then slinging out a beautiful pass to Haydn Morris. He had to stretch to catch the ball, but with Ken lured out of position, he had a clear run of fifty yards to score a thrilling try. I remember, in 1954, Haydn scoring two gorgeous tries, but again through no fault of Ken. It was Bleddyn making that extra yard, which took me back to what Ned Gribble said at Tonyrefail: 'A class player is the one who can make a yard for his colleague.'

I remember just as vividly a terrific game in which Newport beat us at the Arms Park in front of 47,600 people. Roy Burnett, Twinkle-Toes Burnett we used to call him, was playing at fly-half for them. And that afternoon he ran around me twice, with John Lane scoring a fantastic try from one of his breaks. Then just about half-time we were bombarded by hailstones and had to run for cover, and as soon as the weather cleared up Newport scored another try. That was it. Yet it's a good memory, for the Newport side was playing exceptional rugby at that time with Burnett at the peak of his form. We were contenders all through the years for a place in the Welsh side, and though Roy got only one cap – against England in 1953 – we became, and remain, great friends.

There wasn't that same fierce sibling rivalry when we played English clubs, even though they were always keen to beat us just because we were Cardiff. The pecking order then was very different, too. You always knew you had been in a match when you had played against Coventry or Northampton, while Bath were a decent side but not the force they have become. We always played them on the day of the last international championship match. In my first year I was at Bath as replacement for Billy Cleaver who was at the Arms Park helping to beat France and win the Grand Slam. Also in the Cardiff side, surprisingly, was Bleddyn Williams. He had missed the whole of the championship after breaking his leg, and shouldn't have been on the field now. He had come out of plaster only the week before. Despite that he was in line for the Lions' summer tour if he proved his fitness. He doubted that he could, but I, being pretty cocky in those days, told him not to worry. All he had to do was take it steady through most of the game, and then score in the final minute. Well, he did the first part, and towards the end I checked with the ref how many minutes were left. We were cutting it fine, but at the next scrum I was determined to beat the Bath wing-forward. That worked perfectly, I slipped the ball out to Bleddyn and he scored beneath the posts. Next morning we read the headline we wanted: 'Williams Perfectly Fit For Tour'.

I wouldn't have fancied my chances of doing that against either of those Midlands clubs. As it happened I watched my first rugby match with my father not in Wales but at Coundon Road when we were visiting my grandparents: Coventry versus the Met Police, who were captained by Arthur Rees, later Chief Constable of Staffordshire. In my time Coventry had the England international fly-half, Ivor Preece, and a great pack of forwards; and the atmosphere at the dark little ground, with the crowd almost on top of you, was unbelievable.

Northampton were perhaps an even stronger side, with two massive second-row forwards, Hamp and Hawkes, and really polished players like Dickie Jeeps, Jeff Butterfield and Johnny Hyde behind them. One particular defeat in an evening fixture at Franklin's Gardens I still think of as the best club game I ever played in. There was so much running, so much tackling, so much everything in it – and with beautiful, beautiful tries, two from Bleddyn, three from Jeff. It was a privilege to play in just to see Bleddyn, who was our captain, sell a dummy, pull the ball back and dive over for a try, making them look stupid . . . and then, ten minutes later, to see Butterfield reply in kind, running around and making his own gap to score.

Another club I enjoyed visiting was the Wasps at Sudbury. It was partly because they played good, competitive rugby, and I had got to know their wing, Ted Woodward, after playing against him in one schools international. But there was also the attraction of opposites: Wasps were unlike any club in Wales.

On a Saturday they would have thirteen teams playing, six of them at home, five on outside pitches and the firsts playing us on the main field. Off the changing room there was one big communal bath, and you'd often have to jump in after 150 players had already used it. There was a two-inch layer of mud at the bottom. Just as well, or you'd have cut your feet on the concrete floor. We always drew a big crowd of Welsh people from London, and the singing in the clubhouse afterwards was marvellous.

Visiting the Harlequins was totally different. Many saw us, without any real justification, as representing our two countries, and we drew a big crowd by English club standards. So instead of playing at the Quins' own club ground – not the Stoop, which came later, but another field in the Twickenham area – we played at Twickenham itself. This was going to the other extreme; it was far too cavernous for club matches. But then we were invited by the Quins to play in the country's first floodlit match, which turned out to be a marvellous experience. It was at the White City, of all places, with a running track and a greyhound track circling the pitch. But it was such a novelty that everyone who was Welsh or wanted to be Welsh was in the stadium. You could feel the theatrical excitement all around, even if you couldn't see the spectators.

The series continued for several years, and I played in all the games. But I especially remember the first because there was a man playing outside-half for Harlequins called Ricky Bartlett, a hell of a good player, who was hard to spot in the floodlights. He wasn't busy like a Welsh fly-half, darting here and there. He was smooth and beautifully in control of his game. And because he was so good, I managed to slip outside him only once in the whole game. But that once Gordon Wells came up on my left shoulder, and when I popped him the ball he ran seventy yards to score the winning try under the posts. That night instead of the usual sing-song in the club house we all went off with Richard Burton, Stanley Baker and Donald Houston to the Blue Angel night club and went on singing and chatting there for hours.

I'll tell you how keen Richard was on rugby. I went down to a film set to interview him for 'Sports Report', and he talked about the 1950 Wales game at Twickenham. 'I wasn't at the match,' he said, 'but if you check my memory you'll find that Lewis Jones was on one wing and Cliff Davies played in the front row. I was very aware of that match.' He was playing Hamlet in a matinée at the Old Vic at the time, which as it happened was just when transistor radios had come in. Several of the actors had them in their dressing rooms, and as they came on stage Polonius, or Laertes or Ophelia would hold up so many fingers to keep him up to date with the score. 'And even now, Cliff bach, if you give me a couple of drinks, I'll swear that I was there, watching, in the crowd.' And he did say, which I didn't quite believe, that he would rather play one match at wing-forward for Wales than ever to play Hamlet.

He'd tell marvellous tales of the time when he did play rugby. It was very rough. When you were packing down against teams from dead-end valleys you'd swear that their forwards had razor blades on their faces. And when you took a bus to an away game the driver would keep the engine running in case you needed to make a quick getaway. He also swore there was a woman in Aberavon called Annie Mort who 'in shoes that were sensible, dropped goals from the half-way line before every home game to entertain the crowd.'

Some opponents we met only on our short tours. I went on my first Easter tour to Cornwall in 1950, and Haydn Tanner, close to retirement, was due to be in the party too. So were Billy Cleaver and Rex Willis, and I was thrilled to think that if they played together, which was probable, I would be teamed with the great Tanner. Alas, he cried off with an abscess on his tooth, and the opportunity passed. So far my only encounter with him had been when I was lying on the dressing room table waiting for a massage – I'd been kicked on the thigh, which had raised a big lump – when Tanner came through the door with just a towel round his middle. 'Off you get,' said the trainer, 'it's Mr Tanner.' So I had to go back and wait in the queue. Mind, I did once spend a night in his house, sharing the bed with his dog, a big alsatian. The following week they announced the Welsh team, and I was in it. Haydn still swears it was only through sleeping with his dog that I got a Welsh cap.

It's a shame that the Cornish tour, and all the tours like it, have practically disappeared from the calendar, at least of the big clubs. On the way down we played either Devonport Services, or Plymouth Albion, then Penzance and Newlyn, and after that either Redruth or St Ives. The game in Devon wasn't too hard, but once you got into Cornwall it was really tough. They flew at you in the tackle. It was a rude awakening, like playing Gloucester at Gloucester. There were massive crowds, or what they thought were massive, and they'd all come to see Cardiff being beaten. Afterwards it was marvellous. We'd go to the Tinners Arms, and there the perfect harmony of the singing, among men who couldn't understand all the dots but blended their voices by instinct, reminded you how close the Cornish are to the Welsh. I wouldn't have missed the experience for anything.

Around that time of year, too, came a whole series of charity matches, like the one I first played in at Porthcawl, when practically the whole Cardiff team would turn out as So-and-so's XV to raise funds for a chapel or village hall or some unlucky player who'd been badly injured. At St Illtyd's School we'd be Des O'Brien's XV; at Magor, Bill Tamplin's; at Kenfig Hill, Cliff Davies's. You were told there was a bus leaving the gates at the Arms Park at 11.30 on the morning. Then you might have to drive through Gloucester (no Severn Bridge then) to reach Bridgwater in Somerset. You'd play the match, have a great party afterwards, and get back to Cardiff about four in the morning. And these weren't easy matches. You might not be hard on the opponents because they were a local side, but since you were Cardiff they wanted the glory of knocking the stuffing out of you. You'd get a week of that sort of thing, all playing, no training, and than have to meet Llanelli or Pontypool on the Saturday. You paid your own expenses, had a good time and never thought twice about it. You played because your pals asked you to.

And that was it, of course. What, more than anything, gave Cardiff its special place was the quality of the players in the club and their loyalty to each other.

I've said a lot about Bleddyn and Jack Matthews, but not about the way they worked together. At that time clubs and countries liked to build complementary partnerships in the centre, and our two formed the most effective of their day. Bleddyn could side-step, dummy, do all the subtle things, while Jack was more straightforward – a strong runner and tackler, quick off the mark, capable of bursting through the middle and making gaps. A terrific combination. The only pair which might have rivalled them was Northampton's Jeff Butterfield and Phil Davies of Harlequins in the centre for England. Butterfield had Bleddyn's qualities, while Davies was like Jack: big, strong, whack through the middle. Unfortunately, they came together after Jack had dropped out of international rugby, though Bleddyn played against them several times with other partners. Not a lot to choose between them, perhaps, but I think because they played together week in, week out, the Cardiff pair probably had a better understanding.

Another man who made a lasting impression on me in my earliest years at Cardiff, when standards were being set for you to aim for, was the full-back, Frank Trott. I had watched him play in the Services match at Swansea in 1945 with Tanner and Willie Davies at half-back and two great Rugby League wingers, Sid Williams and Alan Edwards, in the side. Now here I was playing in front of this seasoned campaigner, and we became great friends. Frank wouldn't do dramatic things. He didn't kick far down the touchline and wasn't a phenomenal goal-kicker, but he had great anticipation and was beautifully safe. You knew that no-one would ever get past him.

Another veteran and past international I admired was a lock-forward, Bill Tamplin, a deadly accurate place-kicker – with the toe, not round the corner. He was a police sergeant, and touching him was like touching a piece of steel. You wouldn't think he had muscles that could actually move. He had great contests with everybody, but especially Hamp and Hawkes, the Northampton second row, and the marvellous thing was you didn't need a referee to control their battles; they did it themselves. They'd punch each other at the beginning and ask, 'Now, do you want to play rugby, or do you want to do this?'

One time I was having a drink with Hawkes after the match when Hamp came up with his eye closed, black and flat. He'd trodden on Tamp's foot to stop him jumping in the line-out, and though nothing was said on either side, next thing, Tamp clobbered him. According to Hawkes, the punch didn't move more than four inches, but that settled it. They played by the rules – well, more or less – for the rest of the game.

The last two Cardiff players I have to mention had only two caps between them, neither of them belonging to A.D.S. (Stan) Bowes. He had played for the Royal Navy, and for Cardiff against New Zealand. He was captain of the Rags, and always full of the joys of winter. 'Stanley, watch your language!' Brice Jenkins would say to him, and Stan would make even that sacrifice because Cardiff was his whole life. 'Cardiff's me city, Tiger Bay's me parish, and Shirley Bassey's me queen,' was his great phrase.

Stan just loved playing. He wasn't the greatest prop-forward west of Moscow but all the players he came up against, like Snow White of New Zealand and the Northampton and Coventry boys, knew Stan was around. Not just because he was such a hard, tough scrummager but because he was a character. I would have loved him to win a Welsh cap, and even more, to become a Barbarian. That's what he really wanted and nearly achieved, but the then-secretary, Jack Haig-Smith, who was frightfully autocratic, decided that Stanley hadn't behaved well on the Saturday night and should be dropped from the side to play Swansea on the Monday. After that he never did play for the Baa-Baas. That saddened me because he was a better Barbarian, a more decent, honest individual, than many who were accepted into the club. He *was* noisy, he loved his pints and he sometimes misbehaved. But I always admired the way he took care of the young players and the devotion he showed to the club.

I once went with Stan to play for Bleddyn Williams's team at Rydal School in North Wales, and when we got into the dressing room, the jerseys put out for us were in black and amber, Newport's colours. Stan looked at them and said, 'I'm not having black and amber next to my bloody skin!' And he put on a Cardiff jersey underneath. That's how much he loved Cardiff. You had to understand him. The Baa-Baas didn't, but players round the world did. When he died, Snow White flew to Stan's funeral from New Zealand. Because the flight was delayed, he arrived late. But he came to Stan's funeral.

The player who won the two caps was totally different. This was C.D. Williams, a wing-forward always known by his first two initials. He'd been up at Oxford and played in Cardiff's famous game against New Zealand in 1953, but whenever he walked into the dressing room, Stan Bowes would ask, 'You college bastards on holiday again?' That was because they often dropped Stan when the college students came back. But C.D. Williams was a pretty exceptional case. He got a terrific degree, had been a scratch golfer since he was at school, never seemed to score less than 100 at cricket, and played in the Glamorgan match at the end of the season. At the same time he appeared not to make any effort at sport or in his academic life. He relied on natural ability to get him through.

That sort of approach doesn't greatly appeal to national selectors. He was first choice for Cardiff, because he was fast off the mark and a deadly tackler. He also had a talent which is much stressed by coaches nowadays – though more often apparent in Rugby League than in Rugby Union – he was a forward who could handle the ball. But that was not enough to convince the Big Five, who tend to look for serious application. Besides, C.D. was comparatively small. Still, he did eventually play for Wales, getting his first cap in Paris, 1955. The explanation was that Clem Thomas had to cry off late in the week, and the selectors realised that C.D. was probably the only other back-row forward in Wales who owned a passport.

The following season he won a second cap, also against France, and completed his international career by scoring the winning try at the Arms Park. If there were some misgivings about that try, which I'll come back to in Chapter 6, there were none about C.D.'s all-round abilities. I used to enjoy playing with him because he gave you confidence at half-back. You could make a break without worrying over whether you'd get tackled. If you were, then you knew that C.D. would be there backing up, ready to take the ball from you. Years later I used to watch Dai Morris of Wales doing as much for Barry John and Gareth Edwards. I know how it must have felt, for having C.D. at my elbow was a great reassurance when I wanted to take a half chance.

He was slightly extravagant, wild – all the things that you associate with back-row forwards. And that was a great lesson to me. Whatever other people said, you could let yourself go and have fun and still play rugby seriously as he had done. Which was something I was able to put to the test in Ireland after my first five years at Cardiff.

5

First cap

In 1951, when the Welsh selectors finally made up their minds exactly who would play against Ireland at the Arms Park, the team was put out on the 6.30 pm news of the Welsh Home Service. This was on Monday, 5 March, only five days before the match. At that moment I was travelling home by bus, a packed double-decker which went from Cardiff to Trebanog, then on up the Rhondda Valley, so I was one of the last to know that I was about to win my first cap. My mother was one of the first. She was in the kitchen listening to the wireless as she scrubbed the floor under the sink. Hearing her baby's name, she began to jump up, forgot there was a basin above her, and knocked herself out. When my father came in from the glasshouse, she was still dazed both by the blow and the news that her son was going to play for Wales.

The selectors had settled on ten names the week before, but left open five positions, including fly-half, to be filled by A.N. Other. They were going through another of their periodic bouts of indecision, though perhaps with good reason this time. Wales had won the championship the previous winter, started the new season with a comfortable 23–5 victory over England at St Helens, and then crumpled to a 0–19 defeat at Murrayfield,

their heaviest for twenty-six years. Coming home from work –
at that time I was a management trainee at the Electricity Board
in Cardiff – I knew they must be announcing the rest of the team
that evening. I'm certainly not saying I was indifferent to what
they decided. I knew they'd been watching me, and there had
been a lot of newspaper talk about my prospects. But I wasn't
at all optimistic about finding my name on their list.

These days players who are picked for their first international
aren't allowed to play club rugby, or any rugby, in the preceding
week. I didn't have that option. Since I wasn't among the first
ten selected, I had turned out on the Saturday for Cardiff against
Newport, one of the hardest games of the year. As it happened,
that meant playing opposite Roy Burnett; and, if you believed
what you read in the papers, this was a battle over who would
play for Wales. Not that we were the only contenders; Carwyn
James was playing marvellously for Llanelli, and there was a
lot of uncertainty over the selection. Roy was a lovely lad and
a smashing outside-half; he could play every style of rugby,
and had beautiful feet as well. After the game I was even less
confident that I'd be in the Welsh side.

The first I knew of my selection was when I came down from
the top floor of the bus at Trebanog and found dozens and dozens
of people standing around the bus stop. They didn't know what
time I was coming home, but they were waiting all the same,
just to show how proud they were to have an international in
the village. Then the bus driver, who had been been talking to
people through his window, got out of his cab and, ignoring
the passengers who were waiting to be taken to the top of the
Rhondda, came round the back to shake my hand. Gradually
everybody seemed to turn out, and as I walked to my house I
saw that they had hung bunting across the street, and banners
saying, 'Well done Cliff'. How they managed it in half an hour
I'll never know.

I didn't do anything special to celebrate on the Monday night.
There was one pub in the village, but I had never been in there,
even though my mother was friendly with the people who ran

it. There was no drink in the house, of course, and anyway I wasn't drinking in those days. The Saturday before, when I was playing for a sing-song in the Newport clubhouse, I'd had a pint of milk on top of the piano. It was just a fairly normal evening. I went next door to see my uncles and my aunties, and people were knocking at our front door to wish me luck. Many of them came in, but it was just tea in the middle room – my mother must have made forty cups that evening – and pieces of home-made cake and Swiss roll. I felt a sense of pride, but because we didn't have a telephone, I couldn't share it with anybody outside the village.

I'll never forget that Ned Gribble was one of the first to turn up and begin laying down the rules of international rugby. One significant thing he said was, 'What you will find is that the game will almost lose you. It will be so quick that you will start wondering whether you can keep up with it. The whistle will blow for half-time, and you won't even know you've played the first half.' It was true. The first half passed so quickly in Cardiff that I thought I'd been playing for no more than twenty minutes. The noise in your ears on the day was deafening, exactly as he said it would be. And the pace of international rugby was that touch faster than in a club game.

It was a small difference, he explained, and it was the only difference between the two. But the tiny spark of movement, the speed of reaction in your body and upstairs in your head, had to be that much greater. And it was those who were faster and slicker in movement, those with a brain which could work out middle moves – they were the people who succeeded in international rugby. That's what Grib told me that night, and it proved to be the simple truth. It was that essential difference I'd have to cope with.

Grib also talked about Jack Kyle, my opposite number in the Irish team, and then at the height of his remarkable powers. I wasn't frightened of going on the field against Kyle, but I was aware that he was something very different. Aware that he had been through it all, knew it all, and that at the same time he was a decent, lovely man who wouldn't do anything dubious against you. And that wasn't something you could say about everybody. But he was still unreal to me, more a legend than a flesh-and-blood player, and so Grib talked about how to combat him. The one thing Wales needed to do, he said, was to get the ball out to Ken Jones, because Jones not only had Olympic speed, but that superb little body swerve of his away from trouble. 'Get the ball out there as fast as you can.' I suppose that's what we tried to do, but failed because of the genius of Jack Kyle.

On the bus to work on Tuesday morning a lot of people spoke to me about getting picked for Wales. But the funny thing is, because the *Western Mail* didn't reach the village until later in the morning, it was only when I got to Cardiff that I found out what the full team was and what the papers were saying about it. I remember that the *Western Mail* headline read: 'Little Cliff and Big Ben get first caps'. Big Ben was Ben Edwards, the Newport lock who had been brought in as a place-kicker and won his only cap in this match. I was little Cliff partly in contrast to Ben, but also to distinguish me from the front-row forward, Cliff Davies, a British Lion from Kenfig Hill. My first international was to be his last, but we were team-mates at Cardiff and I knew him to be a tremendous ally. It was a great comfort to know he was in the side.

I was now twenty, and I suppose my selection was something of a surprise, because there were older and probably better players around at the time. I don't know for sure, I've never asked, but I probably got a cap that day because of my half-back partnership with Rex Willis at the Cardiff club. Willis had followed Haydn Tanner into the Welsh side the season before, and his fly-half partner that winter, for Cardiff and Wales, had been Billy Cleaver. Now Cleaver had retired, and I was presumably the closest thing available to replace him.

It's a little sad that the stand-off I displaced was Glyn Davies, the boy from Pontypridd County School I played opposite in that sevens final. A precocious talent, he was still at school when he was picked by Wales in the Victory internationals

of 1946. He won his first official cap in 1946–47, when the
international championship restarted after the war. He was now
on National Service and still twenty months away from going
up to Cambridge where he would take three blues. During the
winter of 1947–48 he won five caps (Australia were on tour),
and in the following season three. He was then dropped in
favour of Billy Cleaver, and though he returned in 1950–51,
he lost his place for good after the Scottish defeat.

When I think of it now, he was probably the most naturally
gifted player that I remember at outside-half. He could side-step
sharply off his left foot and his right. He had beautiful hands;
but he also had lovely feet, and that counted for even more. It's
where your feet are placed that makes the difference to how
you catch a ball. He looked so elegant, his movements were so
crisp, he could kick a ball and he made a break with such poise.
He was just a terrific all-round player. Above all I admired his
precision, and if I wanted to be like anybody, it was Glyn.

He was twenty-two, only about two years older than I was,
when his international career ended. Glyn's sister, Brenda,
married the opera singer, Geraint Evans, and years later I
often talked to him about Glyn. I don't think that Glyn
himself was too concerned about losing his place in the side.
He went on to play for Newport, but his mind wasn't totally
focussed on rugby. He began to work in the wine business in
France, and made a great success of that. Unfortunately, his
life, too, was cut short. He died far too young, before he
was fifty.

On the Wednesday I got my invitation to play for Wales from
Eric Evans, the secretary of the Welsh Rugby Union. It was an
amazing bit of work. Most people would imagine that you
would get a beautifully embossed card headed 'International:
Wales v Ireland: You are invited . . .' and so on. But this
was like a piece of paper you'd whip off a lavatory roll.
The kind of stencilled pro-forma that might be put up in a
factory or an army barracks. Typed at the top was 'Welsh
Rugby Union, Craigwen, Rumney Hill, Cardiff. 2nd March,

1951.' That date was on there because it was a general release.
Underneath it said:

Dear Sir,
Ireland v Wales – 10th March.
   You have been selected to play/reserve [reserve was
crossed out] in the above match for which the instructions are:–
Friday March 9th
   4 p.m. You are to report at Cardiff Arms Park with your
kit, for practice.
Saturday March 10th
   12.30 p.m. You are to report at Queen's Hotel Cardiff
for Lunch.
   2.40 p.m. The team will be photographed.
   3.00 p.m. Match.
   6.00 p.m. Dinner at Queen's Hotel Cardiff.
   [And this next bit is interesting]
   Please let me know by return of post whether you can
attend, and what your travelling expenses, for both the
Practice and the Match, will be.
   You are to wear the white-topped stockings you wore
against Scotland. [I hadn't played against Scotland, this
was my first cap] Please don't forget to bring them, as
stockings have become very scarce.
   Are you going to wear your own White Shorts, or do
you wish to borrow a pair of the Union's?
   Yours faithfully,
   Eric Evans,
   Secretary.

I treasure it still, for all the ridiculous things it says. The high
point of your rugby career, your first cap, and you get a lunatic
message like that. And notice how everything is timed to make
certain that you don't stay overnight in a hotel at their expense.
Friday night you went home after practice and came back next
morning on the bus. After the game, too, the dinner was laid

on at six in order that it was over by eight. At that time, even
if you lived in West Wales, you could still get home by train.
You know, in all the eight years I played for Wales I never ever
stayed in a hotel before or after a home match.

I remember writing back to the Rugby Union that night:

Dear Mr Evans,
    Thank you very much for your kind invitation, I am
happy to say I will turn up for practice and the game.
    Yours sincerely . . .

Friday I reported for practice as required, coming straight from
work to the Arms Park and from there going out by coach to the
Glamorgan Wanderers' ground. The staggering things about the
practice were, first, that since we had met at four in the afternoon,
it was already getting a bit dark when we ran out on the field.
Then, although you were playing for Wales, there was no coach
and no pattern to the training. It was just running around. And
though the selectors talked to us in the dressing room, they had
no match plan. When I go to training sessions these days to
watch the players, there's a clinical attitude. Everyone knows
what everyone else is doing. We were just like children playing
a game together for fun.

I hadn't met most of the people in the Welsh team until the
day before the international. I knew Rex Willis, of course, and
Bleddyn Williams and Cliff Davies from my own club. I vaguely
knew John Gwilliam, the captain, from playing against him at
Newport. But I didn't know very many of the others and even
on the Friday the only conversation was about the opposition,
in particular about Jack Kyle. 'Oh, Jack, a great chap he is,
we were together on the Lions tour a year ago,' said Bleddyn
Williams. But much as we wanted to beat Kyle and Ireland, we
didn't have any set strategy for doing it. In a way that suited me
because I was an instinctive player; I just did the best I could. But
as a training session it was a laugh. After it was over, we simply
came back to Cardiff, jumped on a bus and went home.

Next morning I was back on the bus. Luckily for me it used

to stop outside the house and toot in the morning to hurry me up. It was full this morning, being an international day, and all around they were talking about my first cap without recognising me. One conversation was unbelievable. One man asked, 'How the 'ell will he cope with them big fellows, McCarthy, McKay and O'Brien? 'E's only a titch – too bloody small. I know 'im well, see 'im regular. Bet you 'e's not more than ten stone.'

'Don't talk daft, he's more than that, mun. Saw 'im at a do last week, got big shoulders, I reckon 'e's eleven stone if 'e's an ounce.'

And so the argument on my poundage continued. Suddenly the more aggressive of the two turned to me for an opinion. 'You're standing there saying nothing. What do you think Morgan weighs?'

'Twelve stone,' I offered with confidence.

'Bloody rubbish!'

'I'll tell you he is,' I said.

He turned to his captive audience: 'Would you credit it?' he asked. 'It's always the same. Them who knows bugger all about it do always argue.'

That absurd conversation on the double-decker bus will remain with me as one of the big memories. And that's because once I got off that bus in Cardiff, walked from the bus station down Quay Street to the Arms Park, and passed through the Gwyn Nicholls Memorial Gate, I knew I was part of something rare and special, the great tradition of Welsh rugby. This was my first international for Wales, and the great Jack Kyle's twenty-first for Ireland.

The Arms Park was still suffering from the war-time bombing. Two land mines had dropped on the ground, leaving a big hole in the stand and messing up the drainage in front of it. As a result, a wide area of the field was always muddy, even on the hottest day. And that was to have a considerable effect on this game. The mess was neatly summed up in a cartoon by Walker in the *South Wales Echo*. It showed an American visitor looking at this devastation, the broken stand and mud like a Flanders battlefield, and talking with the groundsman who tells him, 'The last game played here was England against Wales.' 'Boy,' says the American, 'it must have been one hell of a game.'

Another consequence of the bombing was that after leaving the dressing room, there was no short trot through the tunnel to get on the field. We had to walk among the crowd and round the river end to make our entrance on the half-way line. I thought it made it all the more thrilling. Then, as I walked alongside Rex Willis, I felt a hand on my shoulder and it was Jack Kyle himself, this marvellous Irish and British Lions fly-half who was already a hero to me. He just looked at me and said, 'Have a great game today, Cliffie, good luck,' in that Northern Ireland accent of his. I couldn't believe it, not before a game. But then as I grew older I came to know exactly what he meant. You felt for opponents who were playing their first internationals. You found you really did want them to do well and not to make a mess of things. So that was a great lesson for me, to learn a certain awareness of the other people around me. It wasn't just a matter of you becoming an international and playing for Wales, it was more a shared experience of coming together. That's what Jack proved for me that day.

Two years before I had gone to Penarth with my father to watch Kyle play in the Barbarian game. 'Now there's a player that you ought to be like,' my father had said. He was so beautifully balanced, and had this gift of lulling opposition into a false sense of security. You'd think he was doing nothing, and yet in an instant he'd pull the ball back, and there he was in a position to score or make a try. I was to discover that the hard way at the Arms Park.

My first lesson, though, came from the great Irish back row of McCarthy, McKay and O'Brien. Their number eight forward, Des O'Brien, played with us for Cardiff. So when the Welsh team was announced, I got a telegram from him saying, 'Congratulations Cliff, bach, is your life insured?' That was his greeting, sent with love and affection, but I really knew what he meant. I was a bit of a coward and didn't like dropping on the ball at the feet of the forwards. But in the opening couple of minutes I knew I had to fall on it, and my vivid memory is of being rucked right back through the Irish scrum. I was on the floor, the ball was in Irish hands, and I didn't even get any credit for my valour. As Grib, whose eye was on everything I did, said afterwards, 'You were still sitting on the floor looking bemused. You should never have been taken unawares like that.'

It was Jack Kyle who taught me my second lesson, equally hurtful, though mainly to my pride this time. I was running up quickly on him, and he was letting the ball go or kicking it forward, and I suppose I was getting a bit too cocky. Because the ball was going out to the centre so often, I started to ignore him. I began moving wider to try to cover the centres and wings and so on. Suddenly I rushed up, and Jack had given the ball to Noel Henderson alongside him and then, under my nose, had taken it back, broken on the inside and scored a try. That was how I learned that you never take anything or anybody for granted in rugby. And especially in an international, your mind mustn't stray for ten seconds. Once it does, you could lose the match by letting through the only try.

It was with immense relief that I saw big Ben Edwards, now lamentably dead, kick a huge penalty goal from near the half-way line. Since tries and penalties were both worth three points at that time, the scores were level, and so they stayed. Ireland, who had already beaten France, England and Scotland, regained the championship they had won in 1948 and 1949. But at least we had denied them the Triple Crown as they had so often done to us.

There was another moment when I thought it was I who had set up a try that could win the match. But once again Jack Kyle came to Ireland's rescue. For some reason I only had one clean break in that match. I went through near our own 25-yard line, and got the ball out to Ken Jones on the wing, just as Grib had hoped I would. The try was on, I thought, as I was thumped over, and lying on the ground, I saw Ken running clear. But suddenly, just as he got near the half-way line, he hit that muddy, smelly patch where the drains had been destroyed, and started to go back yards in his run. Meanwhile Kyle, with that wisdom which enabled him instantly to take in every factor of the game, ran infield and around the mud. He caught Ken about five yards from the try line, and saved the day. Those details are God knows how many years old, but they stand out like beacons to me. Lessons in why you should do this, why you shouldn't do that, in the way you should think about a game.

I was disappointed not to win, as much as anything for my father's sake. He never missed an international game I played in, and he was there for the first. As players we could claim two grandstand tickets. One you got for nothing, the next seat in the row you had to pay for. My Uncle Len always took that one. My mother never came because we couldn't get tickets. Maybe she wouldn't have wanted to see her baby being bumped around, but the chance never came up, so I never asked her.

Later I wondered whether I wasn't lucky *not* to win my first game. To lose or come near to defeat teaches you an awful lot. In my second international we lost to France, in the third, South Africa beat us, so my first three games consisted of a draw and two defeats. We then went on to a Grand Slam the following season, but I think that early experience set me on a different road. I discovered that it didn't matter in the end whether you won or lost, as long as you tried to play good rugby, enjoy yourself and make pals. That probably sounds naive to this generation, but I know it did me a lot of good to understand the possibilities of defeat and to try to overcome them.

I'm also thankful that my international career overlapped with Cliff Davies's, even if it was for only this one match. I went on playing with him at the Cardiff club a little longer, but to play in an international with Clifton Davies was something else. If you imagine his typical Saturday – coming off night shift in the pit, walking home for a bath and breakfast, walking another half-mile or so to the main road to catch the express bus into Cardiff and playing in the front row for Wales that afternoon – then Cliff, too, would cut an improbable figure in today's professional game. And I must say that rugby is all the duller for the loss of the kind of player that Cliff represents.

Cliff was a great prop forward, one of the tireless 'mules of Kenfig Hill'. But beyond that he was a marvellous storyteller, singer, entertainer and a very droll man with a gift for inventing phrases that still stick in your mind forty years on. Often he didn't realise just how funny he was being. He wasn't educated in the formal sense, but his education came from an ability to listen and converse with people, from reading books and working in the pit every day. He was a part-time undertaker as well, and used to tell us unbelievable tales about funerals he'd arranged.

When we were on away trips Cliff wasn't one of those people who liked sitting around in the bar, playing cards or endlessly discussing rugby. He preferred to sing or have a proper conversation about something. Cliff used to remind me of one of those minstrels in the Middle Ages who went around the big country houses entertaining the company. Known among us as the Bard of Kenfig Hill, he was always coming out with these little lines of verse he'd written to amuse us:

> Me and Tamp do love our wives,
> And we will love 'em all our lives.

Tamp was Bill Tamplin, who had played at lock for Wales just after the war, and one evening he said to Cliff, just to get him going, 'Tell me, how's business these days in the undertaking world?'

Cliff said, 'Well, middling, Tamp, not bad.'

'How much are you charging for a coffin these days?'

'Oh nothing special, fourteen guineas,' said Cliff.

'Damn, that's a bit steep. That's a bit expensive. What do you mean, fourteen guineas? I saw one advertised in the paper, twelve pounds ten, and a pleasure to lie in.'

And Cliff Davies came out with the immortal line: 'Well Tamp, take that one if you like. But let me warn you now, pitch pine it'll be, and your arse'll be through it in six months.'

Cliff was intensely loyal to Kenfig Hill. It was his home, the people he loved were there. And it was all he ever wanted. It was one street, a chapel, houses, a pub, a bit like Trebanog. Unlike Trebanog it also had a legend about an ancient city lost beneath the waters of Kenfig Pool. We were chatting one night in the International Bar at Twickenham, Cliff, Hywel Davies from the BBC, and me, when Cliff said: 'Hywel, why don't you bring that archaeologist fellow, Morty Wheeler, that's right, Sir Mortimer Wheeler, down to Kenfig Hill? Mind you, he'd find it a very ticklish area.'

The Kenfig Hill story that is really central to the Cliff Davies folklore, though, belongs to the 1950 Lions tour of New Zealand and Australia. Cliff, the miner, had overcome whatever prejudice there might have been from the ex-public school and university section of the party, and one night as the trip drew towards its close he was feeling a little sentimental about parting from old opponents who had become his friends. They were all talking about holidays they wanted to take when Cliff said: 'Can't offer you much, boys, but tell you what, when the tour is over, come down to Kenfig Hill for a holiday. You know, there's more history attached to Kenfig Hill than any other city in the world.'

At which the tall, elegant Peter Kininmonth, captain of Oxford and Scotland, was heard to snigger slightly. And Cliff, like a flash, added, 'Well, barring Jerusalem.'

I also remember him telling the tale of a young nonconformist minister who came to the village. He was ordained in the chapel on the Thursday night. On the Saturday, he played his first game for the local rugby team. And Sunday morning all the boys went to chapel to give him their support in his first sermon. Coming out, somebody asked Cliff Davies, 'What do you think of the new preacher?' He thought a moment then said, 'Well, I've got to admit he's powerful in prayer, but he's bloody hopeless in the lineout.'

He could surprise you as well as amuse you. In 1950, when he was in London getting ready to leave on the Lions tour, he wanted to get some more shirts to take with him. So he said to

Bleddyn Williams and Jack Matthews, 'Come along with me to this shop where my uncle is the boss.'

It turned out to be the big Oxford Street store, John Lewis, where Cliff asked for his uncle. Jack assumed the uncle must be working in the shirt department or something. But no, the next thing they were conducted to a lift, taken up to the top floor and ushered into this room, as long as a rugby field, where Cliff's uncle was sitting at a baronial desk in the distance. He was the big boss of the shop. A great fuss was made, followed by, 'Cliff, what can we do for you?'

'Some shirts,' he said.

The uncle pushed a buzzer. In came the shirt buyer. 'I want a dozen shirts for my nephew.'

'Certainly, sir.' He turned to Cliff and said, 'Now, could I take your collar size?'

'Nineteen and a half,' said Cliff, and this bloke went as pale as a Buddhist monk. They didn't have any shirts that size in the shop. And because Cliff was leaving in two days' time, they had to make them overnight. Probably Cliff, the miner from Kenfig Hill, was the only Lion in the party wearing hand-made shirts.

He was extraordinary, Cliff. Caradog Prichard, the great Welsh poet and writer, winner of bardic chairs, once translated into Welsh something that I'd written for a book on Welsh rugby. About Cliff I said – and it sounds wonderful in Caradog's translation, though the English version hasn't quite that ring – 'He was a singer, and he was a poet, and to me, represented all that's good and right and proper in our game.' But it's how I still think of him. Cliff stood like a candle in a dark room, and you knew that he represented what you wanted out of rugby.

So that is how I remember my first international, and that extraordinary two days in Cardiff. Hearing the crowd singing as we came out at the Arms Park. Playing against the greatest fly-half I'd ever seen, Jack Kyle. Playing in the same Welsh team as Cliff Davies, representing Wales myself and taking pride in the three feathers on my breast. You knew you would die in that jersey for Wales . . . and then there was also the little matter of the expenses.

An hour or so after the final whistle, we walked across to the Queen's Hotel for dinner. Outside the dining room Eric Evans, Secretary of the Welsh Rugby Union, sat at a card table paying out players' travelling expenses for the Friday training session and the match. He had previously been secretary of the Welsh Schools Rugby Union, so I knew him quite well from when I had played as a schoolboy for Wales.

I queued up behind Ben, who was collecting his four fares to and from Newport. Then I went next to the table and Eric Evans asked, 'Name?' That's funny, I thought. He didn't know me when I'd been playing for Wales that afternoon.

'Morgan, sir.'

'Expenses?'

'Five shillings, sir.' Eric had in front of him a school exercise book with a black cover. He flicked over the pages as if he was reading a bad novel, and suddenly slammed the book shut, banged the table, looked up at me and said, 'You are a liar and a cheat. It's two and fourpence return from Trebanog to Cardiff. That's four and eight!' With that he gave me half a crown, a two shilling piece and two pennies in an envelope. Later my father stuck it into my scrap book to keep. I never touched the money in it.

I thought what a stupid thing this is, and I told my parents about it when I went home that night on the late bus. They were both still in the kitchen, my mother in her nightie waiting to go to bed, but wanting to see her baby after the game. When I mentioned the expenses, my father said, 'Oh, what a nonsense!' But not my mother. She said, 'Well, Mr Evans was right, wasn't he? It wasn't five shillings, it was four and eightpence.' And it comes to mind all the time. I was trying to cheat. So I have always tried to remember the rest of what she added: 'He was right. Don't cheat. It's not worth it.' Nothing like a mother for fundamentals.

6

Gwlad, Gwlad

My debut for Wales – a draw which was to be followed by two defeats – didn't do much to demonstrate that I was the answer to Welsh prayers. The 3–6 defeat by South Africa at the Arms Park three days before Christmas 1951 was particularly disappointing. Having already lost to London Counties, the Springboks no longer had an 'Invincibles' label hanging like an albatross round their necks, and were beginning to play more freely. But we felt we could and should have beaten them. After that match I got some stick for, of all things, kicking too much, but we had this theory that the way to reduce the effectiveness of their back row was to have them constantly turning on their heels to field short punts and grubber kicks. It didn't work; they read our minds (their full-back, Johnny Buchler, in particular) and much of the time we were simply feeding them the ball. In the end, with a try apiece, from 'Chum' Ochse for them and Bleddyn Williams for us, there was only one score in it: a dropped goal from the Springbok fly-half, Hannes Brewis. But though the verdict was close, we felt we had let ourselves down. Nobody was ready to forecast that in the New Year, which was less than a fortnight away, Wales would win their second Triple Crown and Grand Slam in three years.

One rare advantage we had was that the selectors, ignoring the South African result, stuck with the same team for the championship. At least, as far as illnesses and injuries let them. We settled down together, began winning, and by the end of March the local press were talking of another 'golden era'. The Welsh do exaggerate – I've done it myself – and our results didn't compare with the twelve years up to 1911, when the term was first applied to a Welsh team. Nor, for that matter, with the later period of Gareth Edwards, Barry John, Phil Bennett, J.P.R., beginning in 1969 and continuing through the 'seventies. It's curious that in each of those spells Wales achieved an identical record: six championship titles and another shared, six Triple Crowns and three Grand Slams. Ours was more modest. In a shorter period, 1950–56, Wales won two Triple Crowns and Grand Slams, one further championship outright (in 1956, despite losing in Dublin), and we shared the title twice. Even so, after the depression years between the wars, when so many good players went North to earn a living from their rugby skills, this was an undoubted revival. We won three times as many matches as we lost and raised Welsh expectations of a probable victory each time we went on the field. We took too many chances ever to be a safe bet.

My international career didn't quite coincide with this post-war golden era. I was still at university and qualifying for a Cardiff cap in 1950 when Wales won their first Grand Slam since 1911. I came in mid-way through the 1951 season, and remained in the Welsh side until 29 March 1958, by which time we had twice conceded the championship to England. In those eight seasons I missed just three games and won twenty-nine caps, which left me holding the Welsh stand-off record for thirty-seven years. It was on 16 March 1996 that Neil Jenkins broke the record when he won his thirtieth cap against France. There is always some small twinge of disappointment in seeing one's record overtaken, but I have never envied modern players their opportunity to play in so many more internationals than we did. We had our four championship games each winter, a visit from either New Zealand, South Africa or Australia every other year or so, and the chance, perhaps twice in a decent international career, of being selected for a Lions tour. Added to that we had a crowded and far more varied club programme than present national leagues allow. It was enough for players who worked at their jobs or professions right up to the eve of the match. If ours was another Welsh golden age, in my mind it had less to do with our results than with the fact that we conjured attractive rugby out of highly individual players. We had off days, but we didn't often repeat the mistake we had made against the Springboks.

At Twickenham the following January I knew for the first time how it felt to be in a winning Welsh side. This was the ground's last pay-at-the-gate international against Wales; it was all-ticket from there on. The turnstiles closed after letting in 73,000 people, leaving many thousands more in the street. There were high hopes among the Welsh camp-followers, but we made them suffer before we set their minds at rest.

Apart from our forwards, who got a lot of the ball that day, and our captain, John Gwilliam, who had this erratic pass from the lineout, flinging it out so that it turned up any bloody where, two people stand out for me in that match. They were Ken Jones on the right wing and Lewis Jones on the left. Lewis was immobilised early in the match by a pulled muscle in the side. It was something we had never heard of, but had been caused, they said, by the cold wind cutting across him as he ran. Whatever, we went six points down as England exploited our weakness. Ted Woodward, his opposite number, made one try for Albert Agar by kicking past Lewis, who couldn't turn and cover, and he scored another himself while Lewis was off the field being treated for his injury.

Luckily, we were able to pull back five points before the interval from a movement which began just outside our line. Rex Willis had the unselfish habit of moving away from nasty positions before he fed me the ball, and he did so now. Don White, the England back-row forward, who on merit should have captained the Lions team in South Africa, was breaking very fast and hitting lumps out of me. So what Rex did was hold the ball from this scrum near the line, and as White came for me I ran around him without the ball. Then came Rex's pass behind White's back, and I was able to race up the middle of the field where I made a scissors move with Ken on the half-way line. Ken was a Welsh and three A's champion, as well as a sprint semi-finalist in the London Olympics of 1948. His speed did the rest, and Malcolm Thomas converted. It worked so well that two matches later in Dublin, where we won the Triple Crown, we did it again and Ken scored an almost identical try.

Meanwhile Lewis Jones was back on the field, though really only to make up the numbers, because no replacements were allowed at that time. He was still to play an essential part in the winning try. There was a scrum thirty yards out from the England goal-line, and I remember Lewis limping into the threequarter line outside me and taking the pass. It was all he could do, but all he needed to do. He took an opponent out of the game, and then let the ball go, sending a beautiful pass to the centres and so out to Ken Jones who scored another try. At the time you felt certain that Lewis Jones would have a terrific career. Which he did, though unfortunately – for us, not him – it wasn't in Rugby Union. In the October he signed for the Leeds Rugby League club, leaving the Welsh team without a wing-threequarter, without a full-back, without a centre, because he was a great player in any of those positions.

We were full of it after the match. Having eventually reached the dressing room, we started singing away in parties, and eventually I was whisked off to the big bar by the Treorchy Male Voice Choir and a big crowd of Welsh people. I stood on the counter conducting the singing, and got so caught up in my role that I missed the team bus back to town for the match dinner. Luckily, I got a lift in from a policeman, and what I recall best about the occasion was that Lewis Jones wore his grandfather's suit, or so he said; it was certainly a bit green around the lapels. We all had to buy dinner jackets to wear after the England match, which a lot of people didn't like. But I did, because you all looked the same, whether you were Lord Wakefield, or Wakers as he was then, or the son of a coal miner. It was like wearing a school uniform. You all assumed the same status.

So there it was, my first game at Twickenham, and the most significant I had played so far. I must admit there was something, almost an intimacy, about the place in those days. The stands didn't stretch all the way round, and the wind came through the gaps at each end like hurricane Esther. It swirled through the ground affecting the way you kicked and the way you played generally. It might take you twenty minutes to get to know its tricks and learn to push the ball along the floor instead of punting it high. The wind patterns are no longer the same, though what I miss more in the extraordinary concrete bowl they've now built are the big, old-fashioned clocks, one on either side, ticking away right through the match.

The one thing that spoiled the day for me, and made me feel a little less romantic about international rugby, was the Welsh Rugby Union's treatment of Jack Matthews. Bleddyn had been forced to cry off from the match with 'flu, and Jack was called up on the Friday as a reserve. He had dropped out of the Welsh team at the end of the previous season, though he continued to play for Cardiff, and was now concentrating on his work as a GP in Cardiff. Assuming that he was going to play, he travelled up to London overnight on the sleeper, got picked up at Paddington in the morning and reported to our hotel at Richmond. It was only when we got to Twickenham that he found out he wasn't playing. The selectors had decided to play Alun Thomas in the centre instead of him. Even worse, in a way, they didn't even give him a ticket to watch the match. It was an Englishman who came to his rescue, a naval man, Surgeon-Captain L.E. 'Ginger' Osborne, who had been manager of the 1950 Lions. He had a spare ticket, and they sat together in the stand.

I remember him coming into the dressing room and asking the selectors angrily, 'Why the hell did you send for me, when you've got a man, Alun Thomas, here already?' He was furious, and because he was a fairly tough character, and as a doctor used to being treated with a bit of respect, he really told them some home truths. But selectors were a law to themselves in those days and extremely inconsiderate. They didn't feel they had to explain or apologise. And I suppose we went along with it. Unlike players today, we were afraid of speaking out of turn in case we were dropped from the side. The war wasn't long over, and it was still a case of 'Good morning, sir,' with a touch of the forelock. At the age of twenty-one it was a revelation to hear Dr Jack Matthews stand up to them. Being a Welsh international was suddenly more complicated than I had imagined.

The Twickenham game had a terrific effect on our confidence for the rest of the season, and 56,000 people, a record crowd for the Arms Park, came to see us play against Scotland. It was not a great game, but we beat them 11–0, some recompense for the 19–0 'Murrayfield Massacre' of 1951 which cost Glyn Davies his place at stand-off and brought me my first cap in his place. Ken Jones, as ever, scored our one try. The move began at a lineout with Alun Thomas, our blind-side wing, coming into the threequarter line to take my reverse pass, open a gap and make the final, long delivery to Ken. But I remember the game more for the injury to Rex Willis early in the second half. Although his jaw was broken in two places, Rex insisted on playing out the game. Immediately afterwards he went to the Chepstow plastic surgery unit and had to miss the rest of the championship.

John Gwilliam, a former Cambridge blue, now a school-master, remained our captain that season. He had strict views on this role and, because his manner was so schoolmasterish, you listened to whatever he said. At that time the Welsh side was an extraordinary combination of labourers, policemen, students and teachers, but he pulled them together as a team. And although his tapping back from the lineout could be a bit of a trial, in other ways he was an effective forward and full of ideas. In March he led us on to Lansdowne Road, so often in the past the graveyard for Welsh hopes of a Triple Crown. But not this time. It staged one of the great games of that era, and for Wales a 14–3 victory and their last Triple Crown until the mid-sixties.

With Rex injured, I played outside Roy Burnett's regular partner at Newport, W.A. Williams. He also answered to Billy, but like J.P.R. Williams after him, he was better known by his initials; unless you are blessed with a Christian name like Bleddyn, it's the price you have to pay for being born in a country with no great variety of surnames. After a spell in the selectors' dog-house, Clem Thomas was reinstated in the back row, which sharpened it up a lot. Alun Thomas, who had played against England but not Scotland, was back in place of Bleddyn. Otherwise this was the basic team that Wales had settled on this season, and what's curious is that we played just the same way in Dublin as we had in our other away match at Twickenham. Even down to reproducing that first try against England.

We were on our own line when W.A., not as mercurial as Rex, but a strong, sound player, sent me the sort of fast, flat pass that you need to get out of trouble. As I took it, Jim McCarthy, the Irish back-row forward whose job was to arrive with ball and either nail me or make me hurry my pass, wasn't there. Jack Kyle, too, still one of my great heroes, was going slightly away from me. I came inside him with one little short step, and he missed me by, I suppose, half a yard. Next thing I was tearing up the field towards the Irish line, and on the half-way line I could feel the presence and, out of the corner of my eye, glimpse the red jersey of Ken Jones. Alun Thomas and Malcolm Thomas, our centres, had been baulked, but Ken had run infield from the right wing. And as he came round on my left we did a scissors on their ten-yard line. Phipps, a very fast wing, was in pursuit, but he had no chance against Ken, who just went and went and went until he finally dived over in the corner.

The scissors is a marvellous move when you get it just right, which many British players don't do nowadays. They tend to flick the ball blindly to the other player, and it goes down. We were taught – mainly by Bleddyn, who was a perfectionist – to turn our bodies totally in our scissors, and to see the ball into somebody else's hands. And then, of course, if you didn't let go in a scissors you sold the most effective dummy in the world. You half-turned your body towards the opposing player, you checked for the release of the ball, then you held it and went on in that split second when he wasn't quite sure who had it. The bamboozle was all in the timing of that pass or dummy, and what enabled you to get that right was that you carried the ball in two hands. You didn't have to search for it to pass. Unlike lots of mid-field players as we near the year 2000, who tuck the ball into their bodies not to lose it when they knock people over, we held it out ready to pass or to deceive. Two hands with the ball, that was Bleddyn's teaching, and that season I wasn't the only Welsh back influenced by it.

That try was the second in the match. The first and the last were scored by forwards, Clem Thomas putting Rees Stephens over, then Roy John doing the same for Clem. Ireland's only score was a penalty so, in the end, it was easier than we'd anticipated. Not that we'd thought much about it anyway. I don't believe we had made any tactical preparations for the game, and this really applied for as long as I played rugby. The only thing I remember was some chat about the strengths of the opposition. We'd say, 'Kyle is good, got to be on to him at once. Their back row is very quick off the scrum. Their lineout jumping is pretty hot, would we do better if we threw in short, to number three, say?' But these were very simple tactical things. A scissors movement was something created on the spur of the moment. We didn't plan it, any more than we planned to knock people over in the middle of the field to create second-phase, or third, or fiftieth, possession. There were none of those complications. And while we were aware that they had good lineout forwards, it didn't worry us unduly, because we firmly believed that Rees Stephens and Roy John were even better.

Roy John was phenomenal; he leaped like a salmon coming up out of the river. He seemed to stop in mid-air, catch the ball, and turn and deliver it carefully to the scrum-half as though it was something fragile. Of course, he used to jump into a wedge, that is two other forwards who protected him and blocked any opponent who tried to come through on him, which was legal in those days. Then the laws were changed and the lineout became an unruly mess. I think the game should allow the wedge again. If it's your lineout, it's your advantage, and you should get the ball. We were able to make use of this because we had players who could do things with any clean possession they got, and who were ready to take chances, just as Ken and I had done with that scissors. It was the kind of game the team loved to play and the crowd loved to watch. So that match in Dublin has very happy memories for me, even though, as I discovered later, at a certain point during the play I had broken my leg.

I felt the pain after I had gone through a gap and then turned sharply as I was running. I didn't pay much attention to it on the field. In the tension of the game you can often forget about pain. But back in the dressing room I was in agony. I was lying in the bath when Sammy Walker, former Irish and British Lions captain and now BBC rugby commentator, came in and said his producer, the great Angus McKay, wanted me to go up to the commentary position at the top of the stand and be interviewed by Eamonn Andrews. 'Listen, I can't walk properly,' I said. 'I honestly don't feel like it. There's something wrong with my leg.' He went back and reported to Angus who told him, 'Get someone down there to carry him up.' So that's what they did, and Eamonn asked me about Jack Kyle and about Ken's try in the corner and then what would I remember most about this Triple Crown win over Ireland. I'd been doing a few broadcasts over the last year, and suddenly some advice I'd had from Hywel Davies, head of the BBC in Wales, came to mind: 'Don't be obvious, say something that will surprise them.' So I said to Eamonn: 'My father lost his teeth, and he wasn't even playing.' And it was true; I'd just been talking to him outside the dressing room. I'd given him my one complimentary ticket, and it was an awful seat right up in the corner of the stand next to Mrs John, Roy John's mother. At least it was an awful seat until Ken Jones scored his try in the corner just below them. They saw it perfectly. Dad jumped up and shouted and spat his top set of teeth fifteen rows in front of him. He never did get them back. And that was the story I told.

Afterwards I remember Ray Lewis, our physiotherapist, rubbing oil in my leg like hell and saying, 'I don't know what it is, but it's best to keep the leg warm.' Then followed the most extraordinary night. I struggled into my dinner suit, and after the official meal, still not knowing what I had done, I was carried on Lewis Jones's back to the dances. There were two of them, at Cleary's and the Metropole on either side of O'Connell Street, the main street of Dublin. I sat out the dances. Lewis plonked me on a seat with a beer and things. And the euphoria carried me through the evening and the following week. When I got back to Trebanog my mother said something that struck me as very acute: 'You're no longer ours. You belong to everyone now.' And it was true. You couldn't lead the same sort of life ever again. Everybody, on the bus and in the street, felt entitled to a few moments of your attention.

I still didn't know what was the matter with me. According to the papers I was suffering from a badly pulled calf muscle, which I suppose is what the Welsh officials must have told them. I went limping back to work the next week; nobody ever checked on injuries in those days. And then I turned out for Cardiff against Leicester on the Saturday. I suppose I wanted to prove my fitness. The opposite happened. Shortly before the interval, and after a particular burst of running, the pain became unbearable. I went off the field and was taken to hospital, where I should have gone a week before. But in a period when there were no replacements only the seriously wounded left the field. It was at the hospital, after an x-ray, that they found I'd broken the fibula in my right leg. The surgeon who discovered it later used my x-ray, plus a shot of me running and turning, to show his students how a stress fracture could be caused by the weight coming down on your leg as it bent under you.

That was the end of my season. I couldn't be considered for

the Grand Slam match against France at the St Helen's ground, Swansea. Alun Thomas, who played at centre for Cardiff but had previously been the Swansea outside-half, took over from me and dropped a goal. Lewis Jones kicked two penalties. And for the first time that season Wales failed to put together a try. The great French wing, Michel Pomathios, crossed the Welsh line, and Jean Prat converted the try, but the only good it did was to their self-esteem, for we won 9–5. The unfairness of rugby in that era, when tries and penalties were both worth three points, was that in terms of skill and effort it was easier to win games by kicking goals than by crossing your opponents' line. I went to watch, and it's funny how selfish you feel in that situation. I wanted Wales to win, and yet I didn't want Alun to play too well at outside-half. Then he dropped a goal, which wasn't at all surprising; he was a class act was Alun Thomas. Yet although I wasn't picked for the opening match the following season – they said that Rex and I hadn't proved our fitness in time – it wasn't Alun who was picked against England at the Arms Park. It was Roy Burnett with W.A. playing inside him. The selectors always had a preference for a club partnership at half-back when they could find one.

Even if it was at my expense, I was reluctantly pleased for Roy to get a cap. He was a smashing player – good judgement, great acceleration, a beautiful kick. And although we competed like hell on the field, I admired him as a person and felt he was worth his place in the Welsh side. The truth is that of half-a-dozen Welsh fly-halves playing at that time – Roy from Newport, Carwyn James at Llanelli, Cliff Ashton at Aberavon, Viv Callow at Maesteg, Benny Jones at Ebbw Vale and myself – it wouldn't have mattered tuppence which of us played for Wales. At the same time I was pretty sure I'd get another chance. I was still only twenty-two, and while it may have been difficult to get into the Welsh side, once you were accepted as a reasonably decent player, it was even more difficult to get out of it.

Rex and I played for Cardiff at Bath that day, and that's where we learned that England had beaten Wales, who'd been favourites, 3–8. Afterwards we got the train back to Cardiff, and we were walking back down the street together from the station to the clubhouse, it must have been about nine o'clock at night, when we met three of the so-called Big Five, the Welsh selectors. And all of them said, 'Where were you two today? We voted for you to play, you know.' Which must have been the first time that three selectors had ever been out-voted by the other two. I don't know whether or not it would have made the slightest difference if we'd played, but the incident told me something about the small-mindedness of the selectors. They were already making their excuses; they didn't want to admit they were wrong. As they often were.

In the 'fifties the selectors – the 'rugby onions' as Cliff Davies used to call them – were nothing like as knowledgeable as they are now. Ex-players mostly, they gave up their time to sit on committees and wander around the country, but they still didn't know all the current players personally. Nor was there any pattern to their thinking about the Welsh team and how it should be made up. In one particular trial match at Abertillery, the two number eights were Sid Judd of Cardiff and Eric Finney of Ebbw Vale. I'll always remember a Welsh selector walking into the dressing room and saying to Sid, 'Eric, you will have to lead the pack today.' That sort of mistaken identity would be unthinkable today. And even at the time, though it only rarely affected me directly, I felt there was a weakness in the system.

Against England the backs had generally played poorly, or so they told me, but because the selectors always needed scapegoats, it was the two halves who were dropped, never to play for Wales again. Rex and I were brought back into the side to meet Scotland, and there were several other changes. The most influential, probably, was Bleddyn taking over the captaincy from John Gwilliam. There were two new caps, Russell Robins in Gwilliam's place in the back row and Courtney Meredith at prop, though neither man would become a regular until the following season. Clem Thomas returned after missing the England game, and Alun Thomas was preferred to Malcolm

Thomas in the centre. Whatever the general effect of these changes, we scored three tries to beat Scotland 12–0, two of them coming from Bleddyn who celebrated the captaincy with the finest game he ever played for Wales. It was our first victory at Murrayfield since 1947.

I loved playing in Scotland, for they opened up spaces and there seemed to be plenty of room to play. Another thing was they always had school children down on the touchline, where rows of seats were set aside for them. They got big crowds at Murrayfield, 70,000 that year, and the adults were just a blur. But from the field you could see the children's faces, and you were always aware of them cheering and supporting Scotland. They were terrific. That was one vivid memory, the other was of Bleddyn scoring his two marvellous tries and making another for Ken Jones, using all that mastery he had in side-stepping, dummying, drawing a man out of the defence, passing the ball with such precision that the wing could accelerate onto it, pick it out of the air and race on to score. And for a man just coming up to his thirtieth birthday, Bleddyn seemed uncommonly quick in the two stabbing runs that carried him over the last twenty-five and thirty yards for his own tries. There was something about Bleddyn that day that set him apart. I was in awe of him.

Rex Willis was injured again in that match, this time damaging his shoulder, but he soldiered on until we were twelve points up before he went off the field. Then he left me to carry on at scrum-half for the last quarter of a match already won, and to play out the rest of the season with a new half-back partner, Trevor Lloyd of Maesteg.

We went on to beat Ireland and France, but that was no good to us since we'd already lost the chance of keeping the Triple Crown; we would finish runners-up to England in the championship. Perhaps that's why I have no very vivid memories of either match. It was really our forwards who beat Ireland, Clem Thomas and Sid Judd keeping Kyle in check, and then Roy John, Rees Stephens and Gwilliam peeling away from the lineout to send in our left wing, Gareth Griffiths, for a try. Pedlow also scored a try for the Irish, but Terry Davies converted ours, and so we won 5–3.

The French match is even more shadowy. I played three times for Wales at Stade Colombes, and all that comes back out of the mists of 1953 is what a dreadful place it was to play. You came out of the dressing rooms, which always looked tatty, and up through a tunnel behind the posts. Around the pitch was a running track, which meant the crowd was a long way away from you. My one strong recollection of the place dates from my first visit, two years before, when Pomathios was coming down the touchline at top speed and Jack Matthews took off from five or six yards away, caught him whack on the side, and sent him into the cinder track. Pomathios grazed his face, his arm, and his long legs, because in those days the French used to wear tiny red socks and very short shorts. It was like a burn mark down his side, and he came back on the field screaming, 'Matthews, Matthews! Oh my God, why has thou forsaken us?' And Jack said, 'If he comes down again, I'll put him back in there again.'

Mind, playing against France, we always knew that they were better athletes than we were. They all seemed to be tanned and living a hard outdoor life in the Pyrenees – a different sort of animal. For me they were the best rugby players in the world on their day, though when they were off their day they could do the daftest sort of things. I suppose the first time you played against people like Jean Prat you knew you were in a game, because they understood rugby. Jean Prat came out and tackled you, and he really meant it. Yet they were marvellous until they had to make decisions. They were the same in rugby as in politics. When they reached the crucial stage they got it wrong.

Mind, we couldn't talk. Things went just as wrong for us the following season when we met England at Twickenham. We were fancied to win, having beaten the All Blacks at Cardiff only a month before. But though Rex Willis was back, Bleddyn, who had captained us, was still lame from an injury he had suffered and had to cry off. Troubles built up on the field too.

Our full-back, Gerwyn Williams, dislocated his shoulder as he tried to stop Ted Woodward scoring England's first try; he had the shoulder reset and came back on the field, but could only play one-armed. Billy Williams, one of our props, was kicked in the face and missed part of the game. And twenty minutes from the end Rex was concussed and eventually had to go off for good.

Rees Stephens, who was now the captain, told me to take Rex's place. It wasn't for the first time, but in Scotland we'd been leading comfortably, and I got away with it. This time was different. We were under pressure, England were three points up, and I didn't want to go to scrum-half because I didn't know anything about playing there. I was used to being the receiver of the ball and, so I hoped, the tactical master of the situation. I didn't have any technique for passing the ball from the scrum. It was a lunatic thing to play me there. It would have been much better for a forward to go to scrum-half, someone who dished it out to you and left you at least a yard to think and dictate the game. But Rees said, 'Get to scrum-half,' so I did. He also moved Alun Thomas to stand-off and Clem Thomas out to the wing.

I was just about to put the ball into the scrum for the first time when there was this voice from the depths of the front row. It was Dai Davies, the hooker: 'The other side, you silly sod.' So I ran round to put it in the other side. The referee, an Irishman called Captain Dowling, blew his whistle. 'He told me to put it in the other side,' I explained, to which he said, 'You nominated to put it in this side; this is the side you put it in.' It was becoming farcical. I tried to argue, 'No, Dai said I should put it in the other side.' At which point the referee had the last word: 'Any more from you, and you're off.' So I put it in the wrong side, and I felt uncomfortable for the rest of the match, which we lost 9–6. It was the first time Wales had lost at Twickenham since just before the war.

So again our Triple Crown campaign was over almost before it began; that prize fell to England, though by beating everybody else that season, we did share the championship with England

and France. Our final game, against Scotland, was postponed from the end of January, when grounds were frozen solid, and played out of sequence in warm sunlight on 10 April. It was also the last match Wales ever played at St Helen's, which was sad in many ways. It was where Wales had met England in their first home international in 1882, and many of the great folk memories of Welsh rugby were stirred by the events there. But I also knew that a crowd capacity of only 50,000, with most of them standing on uncovered terraces, no longer made economic sense. And I had my own experience of the awkward shape of the ground. Particularly when you're at fly-half, you hardly ever look where you're kicking for touch. You aim your kick by sensing the presence of the crowd along the touchline. You could do this on the stand side at St Helen's, since the crowd ran parallel with the pitch. But on the far side of the field the line of spectators moved away from you at an angle of about forty degrees – or so it felt – so as not to encroach on the cricket pitch at the end. If you tried to kick along the touchline you lost your bearings.

The last international at St Helen's created one bit of history that day. Ken Jones's thirty-fifth cap made another. This equalled the record of Dickie Owen, Swansea and Wales scrum-half and inventor of the reverse pass, set in the early years of the century. Ken was made captain of the side for the first and last time, and we decided that to mark the occasion he had to score a try. We tried everything, and failed. We won pretty easily, 15–3. Two forwards, Bryn Meredith and Rhys Williams, scored tries. Ray Williams, on the other wing, scored a try. And funnily enough, so did I, the first of only three I scored while playing for Wales. We would set it all up, try to bring Ken into the movement, but someone or something would intervene. In one case Ken, who had the safest hands, even dropped a pass. Everything went wrong that day. It was a shame because I can't think of any winger I've watched or played with over the years who gave me such a thrill as he moved with the ball. He was electric. As we came off I said, 'We tried to give you a try, Jonesy.' And he just said, 'Yes.' In fact although Ken went on to set a new record of forty-four caps, he never did score again for Wales. But he remained a great defensive wing, and just his presence on the field was worth a lot to Wales.

After changing, Rex and I walked back across the field with Ken to the Swansea clubhouse – really a cricket pavilion – where we'd board the bus to take us to the dinner at the Langland Bay Hotel. We had our little bags with us and Ivor Jones, one of the Welsh selectors, a great back-row forward who had mesmerised New Zealand when he toured there before the war, came over to us. Ivor always knew someone he wanted to give a jersey to. A rugby club, a charity, a sick child. This time he said to Rex, 'I've got two small boys in hospital, I need two jerseys to give them.' And I remember pulling mine out of the bag and Rex pulling his out, and handing them over. Which explains why I haven't got a jersey left, or a pair of boots, or a stocking, hardly anything. I've still got one Welsh cap, one Cardiff cap, nothing else. But what can you do when you're told that two little boys in hospital would like them?

By 1954–55 I was living, working and playing my club rugby in Ireland but coming back for odd games with Cardiff, the Welsh trials and the championship, which we shared with France. Again, we won three of our four matches, and the one we lost was surprisingly against Scotland, who'd been no great threat in the previous few seasons. In the Irish match at the Arms Park I scored my second try for Wales and, by running up eighteen points in the last twenty minutes, we won 21–3 what had been, for the first hour, a very close game. At the end of that winter I brought my spell in Ireland to an end and went off to South Africa with the British Lions, events I describe in my next two chapters.

After the Lions tour I was too sated with rugby to play much before Christmas, but in the New Year I was made captain of Wales for the 1956 championship. Captains didn't have any great influence in my day because the selectors kept switching the job around; I know I played under nine of them. Now it was my turn. I used to give the players a dressing room talk before the match. There was no brilliant tactical thinking involved; it was all fire and brimstone. I used to talk about the pride of being Welsh, all that sort of emotional rubbish. Whether or not my sermons had any effect – and my guess is not – we won the championship outright in 1956 in spite of one defeat. This doesn't often happen, but England, Ireland and France won two and lost two to share second place. And the Scots won only once.

Rex Willis had retired at the end of the 1954–55 season, having guided me through fourteen of the seventeen matches I had played so far for Wales, and heaven knows how many games for Cardiff. I badly missed him, but my new scrum-half was Onllwyn Brace, who had built up a great reputation while still at Oxford as the unorthodox Celtic ideas man in a successful partnership with the staider Anglo-Saxon, M.J.K. Smith. Wales began the championship well, scoring two tries at Twickenham to beat England 8–3, and three tries against Scotland at the Arms Park where the grass had been blackened by the braziers kept burning all night to partially defrost the pitch. Here we won 9–3, and I scored my third and last try for Wales, with Brace running flat on the open side from a scrum and then throwing me a twelve-yard reverse pass on the blind side. I still had to get through a small mob of Scots, but with the advantage of surprise I made it.

The match we lost was in Dublin, having travelled there by plane for the very first time. We were overrun by the Irish pack, going down 11–3, and the best thing about the day was the speech which the Welsh president, Freddie Phillips of Crynant, made after the match dinner. Freddie was a master of the malapropism, and we used to collect and treasure the best examples. 'That must be the rule, and I am amdamnant on this,' was one we enjoyed. Another time, after the W.R.U. Hon. Treasurer, Kenneth Harris, had announced a new non-interest loan scheme for clubs wanting to improve their grounds, Freddie got up and said: 'Thank you Mr Harris. I will now clarify for everyone. When Mr Harris is talking about these grounds and these buildings, he is not talking about dialect buildings on adjourning grounds.' Now in Dublin he rose and said: 'I was very happy to be at the match as head of the Welsh party, as it were, and prouder still that for the first time in history, the Welsh team have fled.'

Wales were extremely lucky to win their final match at the Arms Park. France were three points up with only ten minutes to go when someone hoofed the ball across the French goal-line at the Taff end of the ground. C.D. Williams, the Cardiff back-row forward, chased after it and touched it down as it went across the dead-ball line. C.D. will tell you to this day that it was a try, and who can blame him. But practically everyone else who was close by would swear that the ball had already run dead. It must have been touched down inches from the Taff. Still, the English referee, Dr Peter Cooper, blew for a try. Garfield Owen converted from in front of the posts. And so we won the match 5–3 and, with it, the championship.

I was dropped as captain after that, I don't know quite why. Perhaps the selectors didn't either, for over the next two seasons, which brought my international career to a close, we were captained first by Malcolm Thomas, then Rees Stephens and finally Clem Thomas. Although we had great continuity in team selection in this period, we had, as I said, no continuity in captaincy. I think this must have been linked to the absence of any long-term strategy for the team such as Carwyn James provided for the 1971 Lions and Geoff Cook in the late 'eighties for England. The team was picked from players who had done well for their clubs, and in some cases played regularly with each other. They were never picked to counter the particular strengths of the opponents. We had a few ideas of our own on that and would put them into practice. But having no thoughts to share with us, the selectors didn't see the need for a strong captain who would say, 'This is how we're going to play it.'

The truth is that I played mostly off the top of my head. I played it as it happened. This would be unacceptable these days but I don't think was wrong for the 'fifties. In fact, although spontaneity may be out of fashion, it's a quality you can't afford to lose at any time. Take Mike Gibson, a fabulous centre-threequarter. Although he played terrific matches at stand-off for Cambridge, for the 1968 Lions and once for Ireland, I still felt he thought too much about playing outside-half. In that split-second when he started to think, the time to act had often gone. By playing instinctively, you went and you did it. At a time when there was no percentage thinking or rugby-speak, and when an up-and-under was called a Garryowen not an 'executive high ball' – what's the difference supposed to be between a high ball and an executive high ball? – it was the players with immediate reactions who made a success of the game.

We didn't even have any lineout codes. I don't honestly believe that half of us would ever have remembered what 27–26–52 was. There was a short lineout or a long one. And what the wing used to do in internationals was throw the ball where the scrum-half was standing. If it was close to his own line he threw short to number two or three. Elsewhere, it was to the middle or the back of the line. And he didn't propel it like a torpedo, he lobbed it in with two hands. The game was so much less sophisticated. I feel sorry for young people who have to think so much about the game. We never had to.

All the same I remember one time when I thought the opposite. I felt Ray Prosser, the Pontypool prop, coming up inside me and I passed him the ball. He was still going forward and it hit him on the head and fell to the floor. I said, 'Pross, you've got to think.' And Pross's reply was, 'You can't expect us pack to think and shove.' It became a catch-phrase among the Welsh players.

That was at Stade Colombes in March 1957, and if I had to choose one game from my last two years in the Welsh side, that would be it. They scored three tries but we scored four to win 19–13, the last Welsh victory in Paris until 1971. We took no titles in the championship for those two years: in 1957 we won two and lost two; the next year we drew with England, won the next two games, but for the first time ever at the Arms Park we lost to France. On the whole we played perfectly decent rugby, but the second golden era was over and only Colombes stands out as a really thrilling echo of its best years. I played, and lost, my first game there on 7 April 1951, and since this was before the championship fixtures were rotated, we invariably met France in Paris on hard grounds and warm spring days. That suited me; I liked firm going. But so did the French, and to beat them in a classic, high-scoring game in those Bermudan conditions was the thrill of the season.

It was no accident that three of our four tries came from the pack, and two of these from front-row forwards: Ray Prosser, who held on to the ball this time, and Bryn Meredith, the hooker. John Faull, the Swansea number eight, and Geoff Howells, the Llanelli winger, made up the number. For match after match at this period we had a solid front row. In the early days it featured Stoker Williams of Swansea, then later came the greatest prop of them all, as any of the boys will tell you, Courtney Meredith from Neath. He was very good looking, but a tough, hard forward, and to scrummage against him was murderous apparently. He was a British Lion and played in that front row with Bryn Meredith, who for me is still the best hooker. And when I talk of hooking, I don't just mean getting the ball back, but playing it in the loose, handling and kicking. He could do everything with the ball. And once Ray Prosser had arrived in the front row, that was the backbone of our team. It was like the Pontypool front row which provided stability for the Welsh team in the 'sixties and 'seventies. You always felt that they were going to win everything that was going.

Over the same period we had back-row forwards like Rory O'Connor. A week before the international, if Cardiff played Aberavon, he would be coming off the scrum and knocking lumps out of you. You were still glad to have him on your side at the Arms Park. I suppose it was back-row forwards I knew most about as opponents, though funnily enough, what held good in club games didn't always apply in internationals. Take Swansea's Clem Thomas. I never had much difficulty playing against him in club games, but playing with him for Wales you knew you were in the presence of a great player. Brian Sparks of Neath was the very opposite. I never had a really good club game against him, yet he wasn't in Clem's class as an international forward. Sid Judd, who died lamentably young from leukemia, was another phenomenal worker; so, too, Russell Robins, not the biggest and heaviest of number eights, but a beautiful ball-player. Rhys Williams, too, was a colossus, especially in the lineout, where critically he won the last five on their throw as well as ours. Those of us in the backs used to think, well, they'll do all the donkey work so that we can make the breaks and get the glory. No wonder they thought there was no justice in the world.

Inevitably people compare 'golden eras'. To me the 'fifties was a terrific period for those with talent, who played the game without putting too much thought into it. And I suppose I have to concede that the Welsh teams of the 'sixties and 'seventies, the John Dawes era, produced better rugby than we did. This was because they had a plan, which originated with Dawes when he was captain of London Welsh, and which he carried with him as captain of Wales and the Lions. It was a very simple one: the players had to go out and enjoy playing their rugby. If you watched London Welsh in those early days, they loved it. But then Dawes had at his fingertips all the talent in the world. He had J.P.R. Williams at full-back – hard and tough and fearless. Gerald Davies was on one wing, not the biggest of men, but he could side-step, slink past, out-sprint almost anyone. There was Dawes himself in the centre, a marvellous distributor of passes, a real ring-master. Then from Cardiff, Wales could call on Gareth Edwards and Barry John, and later, from Llanelli, Phil Bennett. Now what team in the world wouldn't pick those players at half-back to control and guide the destiny of any game?

I've always said that of all the players I've known during fifty-odd years' involvement with the game, regardless of where they came from or where they played on the field, Edwards stood out head and shoulders above the rest. Not only was he a great gymnast, he had all the physical attributes, not least a strong pair of shoulders and a strong neck. And he was fast. His one weakness when he went to South Africa in 1968 was his passing, which was less than brilliant. So on that tour he went out every morning to work on this side of his game, and ended up a great passer of the ball – especially to Barry John with whom he had a marvellous understanding. Barry would say, 'Throw it high, I'll collect it, chuck it anywhere, I'll catch it.' And he did. What Edwards also had, and it's one thing which I believe is essential to great sportsmen – footballers, like the incomparable Pele of Brazil, cricketers, whatever – was 250 degree vision. Even if he was looking straight ahead, he could sense when there were players on either side, what they were doing, chasing him, supporting him. And a final point. If you look at the record of his tries, you'll see he regularly scored – or created a score – just before half-time. And then, as the opposing team was trying to recover from the shock of that score, he'd add another one as soon as play restarted. Which is class, which is really screwing them down.

The side we had in the 'fifties might have matched them physically up front, but I don't think we'd have coped with them playing at their best. While we just relied on individuals to add extra touches to a pretty basic pattern of play, they had a plan, they had style, they were thinking about the game. The results they achieved put a smile back on Welsh faces, didn't they? There was a magical feeling, as though they had brought back something to our rugby that Wales could be proud of. As you watched them, there were moments which took your breath away. This couldn't be happening because the book says it can't be done, yet they were making it happen. They became public property. Everybody seemed to be on Christian name terms with them. You wouldn't believe how many Gareths there are in Wales today, all in their late twenties.

People argue still whether they could have coped with the England side of the mid-'nineties. In my opinion, they would have more than matched up. You've only got to ask yourself where are there individual players in the same class as Edwards,

John, Bennett, Gerald Davies, J.P.R? Maybe the forwards would find it a bit difficult to adjust to the fashion for second- and third-phase possession. To them, if you won outright possession you didn't willingly give it away. They might have had problems, but with a Mervyn Davies at number eight, they'd have overcome them. You can find big, strong players, but you can't replace class and style.

Clive Rowlands, Welsh coach during part of that era, has a famous tale about Dai Morris, a colliery blacksmith and for me a terrific back-row forward for his half-backs. He gave Gareth, Barry and Phil the confidence to take half chances because if they failed he'd always be on hand to pick up the loose ball. Dai also loved racing; he had a horse of his own which he kept on top of a hill overlooking the Rhondda Valley. He was in the dressing room before the England game when Clive came back in for a few final words. He felt he hadn't yet managed to put the right spirit into the team, and wanted another go.

They were all sitting around, Barry John as usual looking out the window, not being too concerned, and Dai Morris with his elbows on his knees, his hands clasped over his ears. 'Boys, look at Dai Morris now,' said Clive. 'His concentration on this game against England. In five minutes' time you'll be going out, I want you all to concentrate on the game like Dai's doing.' And Dai said, 'Shut up man, Clive, I'm trying to listen to the 2.15 from Catterick.' I just loved that attitude, which ran through the team and was expressed in the play of Barry John especially. It wasn't arrogance but he used to think, I can beat this fellow, so let's get on with it, play the game and enjoy ourselves. And it thrilled me to think that this apparently carefree team, having done great things for Wales, formed the nucleus of the 1971 Lions party which achieved even more in New Zealand. It had a joy in expressing the qualities that it had been given by God as, I believe, all qualities are.

At the Arms Park on the last Saturday of March 1958, I played my final game for Wales. And at that time of year it was inevitably against France. I had already announced that

I was retiring, which caused a bit of fuss because I hadn't yet reached my twenty-eighth birthday. I had agreed to go back to South Africa with the Barbarians in the early summer, but that would be it; this was my farewell international. Unfortunately, we came nowhere near repeating the success of Colombes the year before: we lost 6–16. I must admit, I didn't play at all well that day. I don't know why. Maybe it was the occasion. I hope it wasn't because I didn't care. When you know it's your last game, you might feel you wanted to play your best to go out on a high note. Or you might think that if you didn't play well it didn't really matter; you wouldn't be selected next time anyway. On the whole I think it was that little things went the wrong way. But I didn't do enough to make up for that, I'm unhappy to say, and we lost the chance of winning the championship.

That may have accounted for some of the press stories on why I had retired – that I was worried I was losing my pace, or that I was jaded after playing too much rugby. This was simply not true. I had played pretty well for Cardiff and for Wales that season, and I was to have a good tour with the Barbarians. I was still enjoying the game and felt perfectly comfortable with it. The explanation was much simpler. I couldn't afford to go on playing big time rugby. If I had continued to play in 1958, I'd have been in the running for another, bigger tour at the end of the season: the Lions to New Zealand. I couldn't contemplate another six months off work. Nuala and I, after living in one room at my parents' house, had moved to a tiny flat in Cardiff. Our first baby, Catherine, had arrived. We had no money and I knew I had to get a serious job and settle down to work.

By great good fortune the offer of a new career came on the evening of the French game. I felt slightly ill after being kicked about on the field and, though I didn't know what was wrong with me, any more than I had six years before in Dublin, I had broken two ribs. They're still sticking out, and I feel them occasionally with my thumb, just to reassure myself that I did play for Wales. During the match dinner in the Royal Hotel I felt a bit faint and went out of the dining room to get some

air. At the top of the stairs I met Gordon Rowley, the senior
medical man with the W.R.U. in those days, who was standing
there chatting with Hywel Davies, the BBC boss. Gordon asked
me what was wrong and, when I told him, said he'd better take
me for an x-ray. But before we left Hywel said to me: 'If you do
go to South Africa, Cliff, when you get back will you call and
see me at the BBC? I've got some ideas.' And so, on my last day
as an international rugby player, a new career in broadcasting
opened up.

7

The continent of Ireland

As I said, I never went North. But in 1954 I did what some people found it even harder to understand: I went west. In the middle of my Welsh rugby career I left home for Ireland, and for the next year lived and worked in Wicklow Town, played my club rugby in Dublin for Bective Rangers. I exchanged the argumentative style of Welsh conversation, which worries a subject to death, for the 'crack' – the quick, witty, convivial chat which is inseparable from Irish social life. And before I left Dublin, which is something I couldn't have foreseen, I met my wife, Nuala.

I mentioned being in the middle of my 'rugby career' just then, but that's not really how we looked on it at the time. A career was how you made your living. Rugby was quite separate, the sport to which you devoted your free time. A passionate, consuming affair, maybe, but not meant to interfere with your work. Even so, there were many who thought I was mad to give up my place in the Cardiff team, which I might never regain, and disappear from the sight of the Welsh selectors. I shared a few of those doubts myself, yet almost at once I knew I had done the right thing. I not only loved that year in Ireland for its own sake, I felt it did me a lot of good to be free of the daily pressures of

Welsh rugby: to play in a country where sport was for everyone's enjoyment, even the loser's; where winning was certainly the aim, but wasn't the only satisfaction; and where rugby wasn't the first topic of conversation. It also gave me independence – not from the ties of affection for family, friends, chapel, choir, but from the daily routine of the bus ride from Trebanog to Cardiff and back. At twenty-four, it was high time I made the break. Ireland gave me the chance to do it painlessly.

My move came about entirely through work. I had been with the Electricity Board since I left college, in theory training to become a member of the management, but in practice filling in meter books and other absorbing tasks like that. I won't say I was unhappy there, but I knew it wasn't going to be my life's work. This must have been clear to others, too, for one day in 1951, I was approached by a businessman, Kenneth Davies, through one of his reps, Jack Hopkins, who was coming up to retirement. At one time Jack had been a winding engineer in our local Coedely pit. Davies was then on the board of British European Airways, had an interest in Terrels, the Bristol wire-makers, and was the owner of George Elliot's Wire Ropes in Cardiff, in which he saw a place for me. His main home, though, was in Co. Wicklow, in a magnificent house called Kilochter. Davies had plans for expanding Elliot's and the prospects there sounded more exciting than pushing a pen at the Electricity Board. I took the job and started at the bottom, working in the factory. There I learned to make wire ropes, and splice on the various attachments. And though it ripped my hands to pieces, I became a pretty good splicer of ropes. Then, having got to know the manufacturing side, I was sent around England and Wales to sell wire ropes to collieries and crane-builders and all the other people in industry who used them. I was very happy at Elliot's. It had a family atmosphere; you felt you weren't working for an anonymous company but for Kenneth Davies and his wife Stephanie, a very beautiful woman who, beside being a model, took an interest in the business.

We all got on extremely well, and in 1954, after I had done

the groundwork, Davies told me he had bought a garage right on the quayside at Wicklow which he had set up as a workshop. A few people there were making covers for cables and working a simple little wire-twisting machine. He wanted me to go across and develop this little enterprise into a proper factory since, as he put it, 'They've never before manufactured steel wire rope in the continent of Ireland.'

In May, 1954, at the end of my fifth season at Cardiff, I left Rhoose airport in a Dakota to take up my new job. Lots of the boys – Jackie Matthews, who was the captain of the club, Bleddyn Williams, Rex Willis and others – had come along to wish me well, as if it was the last time they were going to see me. My boss, Kenneth Davies, was there too; he was coming over to show me around. We were all hanging about talking by the steps of the plane, as you wouldn't be allowed to do nowadays, and so delayed the take-off. But this being an Irish plane, nobody seemed to be put out by that.

I felt awful leaving everybody behind, but also excited and apprehensive at the same time. In fact I was just being very Welsh. The Welsh like to feel a length of cloth before they buy it, and I didn't know what I was going into, or whether I was capable of building up a successful business in Wicklow. I had never seen the place or lived away from home before. On the plane my mind was racing with all these things. They brought around sandwiches and tea. It was always tea at home, so that's what I asked for, but I had to wait for it because they served the coffee first. I remember I was a bit in awe of the Aer Lingus stewardesses. They were far more important than waitresses; they were in charge and gave instructions. Probably I was still feeling impressed by them nearly a year later when I first met Nuala, herself an Aer Lingus stewardess.

Yet flights to Ireland from Cardiff, or from London, in those days were not in the least formal. They were full of race horse trainers, jockeys and owners who were all great talkers, not just among themselves but to everyone around. The planes were small and intimate. We didn't even have Viscounts; it

Bleddyn Williams, prince of centre-threequarters, ball as ever in two hands, makes a break in the Lions' tour of New Zealand in 1950, watched by team-mates Ken Jones (left) and Randall Macdonald (right).

'My better half' – Rex Willis makes one of his famous breaks on the blind side, under the eye of C.D. Williams (left) and Sid Judd (right).

The unequalled Ken Jones shows his Olympic turn of speed with, on this occasion, Cecil Pedlow outside him and A.D. Stalder of Wasps coming up on the attack.

Roy John jumping in the wedge with hooker Dai Davies in support left and his captain John Gwilliam right at Twickenham 1952.

Rollo and Waddell of Scotland fail to hold English captain Jeff Butterfield, and Arthur Smith, grounded by Thompson, can only look on.

Dickie Jeeps passing the ball out from the scrum against Wales at Twickenham. Picked as third-choice scrum-half for the 1955 South African tour, he ended up playing in all the Tests.

Scoring at the Arms Park in 1955, with seven Irishmen strewn in my wake.

Springbok Hannes Brewis, the Brown Fox, a marvellously balanced player, gets the ball away before Rees Stephens can intervene.

Earl Kirton of New Zealand was not one of the mercurial fly-halves, but he read the game so well he was always in the right place at the right time.

The first try of the 1955 Lions tour to South Africa which I scored in the second minute of the game at Potchefstroom. But Western Transvaal went on to win 6–9.

Basic Van Wyk is eluded for once as I score my try in the first Test at Ellis Park, Johannesburg. We won by a whisker, 22–23, but it was a great game.

A pass out to Ken Jones against France at Cardiff, 1956.

Below left and right, the unstoppable Tony O'Reilly, one of the most powerful wings in the business. After all these years his seventeen tries on tour make him still the Lions' record try scorer. His record off the field is equally impressive as President of Heinz.

Jack Kyle, arguably the greatest fly-half in the world, mesmerises England at Lansdowne Road.

David Watkins (left) and Phil Bennett (right) were, like me, both 'chapel' fly-halves. David Watkins, star of Rodney Parade, went on to shine as brightly in Rugby League.

Whatever Gareth Edwards touched turned to gold, whether as fisherman, sports quiz team leader or, here, in the glorious 1973 Barbarian v All Blacks game at Cardiff.

Barry John was the master of every situation, a Welsh Duke of Wellington.

was Dakotas and Rapides with twin engines, and those planes which opened up in the front to take on cars, Wayfarers. The flights were slower, too, which gave everyone longer to get acquainted; the Wayfarer's journey time from London was four hours. When you reached Dublin there was no fuss either. You taxied in, jumped off and walked across the tarmac. It really was just like landing in a field.

This day Kenneth Davies's car was waiting at the airport, and he gave me a lift down to Wicklow where I had been booked into the Grand Hotel, a wonderful place on the front, just a short stroll from the Irish Sea. As soon as I went in I felt at home, literally so, for it took in several semi-permanent guests like me who had come to work in the town. There for three pounds a week I was to have a bedroom and a living room of my own and all my washing done.

Mr and Mrs Clancy, the owners, were waiting to welcome me, and there was no question of my going up to my rooms until I had been in to say hello to all the people in the bar. They included fellow residents like Larkey O'Brien, manager of the chemical factory, Eileen Nolan, the village bookie, Dr Alec O'Driscoll, the local medical officer, and regulars like the parish priest as well as many others I remember but can no longer put a name to. Although I had never met Larkey, I'd had a letter from him before I left Cardiff. A former player with Bective Rangers, and now one of its most fanatical supporters, he had heard on the Grand Hotel grapevine that I was coming over to Ireland. And since Bective badly needed a fly-half, he'd written to ask if I would join them. I accepted at once, for apart from needing to find a club with a vacancy at stand-off, I had to find one with an open membership. Most of the senior sides in Leinster were strict Old Boys' clubs which wouldn't have allowed me in.

Larkey was to become my closest friend in Ireland, and we must have talked and drunk, with the whole company joining in, for a couple of hours before I followed my luggage upstairs. I soon learned that this was the agreeable preamble to anything you tried to do in Ireland.

Next morning it was around 9.30 when I went over to our converted garage to meet Kenneth Davies, but those were the last gentlemen's hours I kept. From there on I was at the place and working like a fool from six, coming back to the hotel for breakfast at quarter to nine, returning to work the rest of the day and often rounding it off by going up to Dublin for a meeting. My title was Manager of Wire Ropes Wicklow Ltd, but I had only three people working for me when I started: Bob, a Protestant, Mick, a Catholic, and a young lad. And as we took on more people, we grew like a family. We always made tea in the mornings, and sat around with our tea-cans talking, and it took me back to what my father had told me about working in the pits. I enjoyed those times.

I was working harder than I had ever done. First we had to dig up the ground and lay new foundations at the factory. This was going to be a centrifugal operation with ropes spinning round, or machinery spinning round, so we needed a very firm base. It was months before we were ready for an engineer to come over from Cardiff and supervise the installation of all this precision machinery. After which came the little matter of recruiting more staff to make our ropes and sell them. We went up to six people, then ten, and by the time I left, just under a year later, we had sixteen. We also made a profit on that year.

I had been taught the manufacturing side of the business by Griff Jones, the manager at Cardiff. From Griff I had learned how to load machines to make locked-coil wire rope, how to test the rope and measure its tensile strength by increasing the pressure on it until it snapped. I spent hours and hours working on this. Griff had also taught me how to splice on a hook and eye, and a ring, and all these skills I'd had to take to Ireland with me and pass on to people who knew nothing about the process. I had terrific help from the engineers in Cardiff, but in the end you're on your own when you're spinning the wire onto reels, and spinning those reels into a rope, and spinning that around a jute or sisal core. You're bound to worry whether the finished product would be all right. A new responsibility, too, was working out exactly how many hundredweight of wire you needed to make a particular rope. Get that wrong and you threw away your profit.

I was really too busy to be homesick while I was in Ireland; the feeling only came through to me when I went home. In the late summer I was meant to sing with my mother and father in the Porth choir at the National Eisteddfod in Ystradgynlais, but a two-hour delay in the flight meant I missed the coaches that took them there. The choir won, and when they came back there was the usual big crowd of people at Porth Square to cheer them in. Then they moved across to the entrance of the old Cymmer Colliery where there was room for them to spread out, and thanked their supporters by singing one of their test pieces and some hymns. So in the end instead of being a participant I was just one of the welcoming crowd. That's when it hit me. When I stood there listening to my mother and father singing, 'O Lord, keep Thy people', the tears were running down my face. It was pure nostalgia for what I had been missing, even though I hadn't missed it at the time.

Of course I went back frequently to Wales. As part of my contract I was allowed two free flights a year to Cardiff. But I also flew across to buy wire from the mills. That autumn I paid a brief visit to Ebbw Vale where my new club, Bective, had a fixture. I went over to play in two of Cardiff's games with Newport, and during the Christmas holiday, turned out for them against the Wasps. I played for Micky Steele-Bodger's XV at Cambridge shortly before the Varsity match. And after proving to the Big Five in the first Welsh trial at Llanelli that I hadn't gone soft or picked up bad habits in Ireland, I was back to play twice at the Arms Park, as well as at Murrayfield and Stade Colombes. It might have been fun if Ireland had been home to Wales at Lansdowne Road, but I had picked the wrong year.

That I felt so quickly at ease in Ireland was largely due to the Clancys, who had become like parents to me. That first summer I brought my mother and father over to stay with them. My mother had never ever flown before, and as it happened the

Dakota in which they crossed ran into an electric storm. I was told about this as I waited at the airport, and worried that my mother must have been scared stiff. Not at all. Her first words when she stepped off the plane were, 'Oh, it was lovely.' My parents got on tremendously well with the Clancys, who never charged me a penny for their stay. It was as though, in adopting me, they had adopted my family too.

What also made the Grand Hotel, Wicklow, a congenial place to live was this hard-core of residents from local business and the professions. They had the key to the back door and practically everything else, and they turned the place into a perpetual talking shop which you could join any time you were at a loose end. We played a lot of snooker, and shortly before Christmas there was a big tournament with a turkey as first prize. I got through to the final where I was due to meet the parish priest, and I fancied my chances. But just before we began playing – and this was another example of the ambivalent Irish attitude to competition – Mr Clancy took me aside and said, 'Make sure you don't win, because the priest always takes the turkey to the nuns at the convent.' I understood the message, for this was a nearby convent school where I used to go and teach a bit of rugby. So that the priest could keep up the tradition, I had to go in off the pink.

You never knew who else would turn up at the hotel from time to time. Once Mrs Clancy asked if I would mind giving up one of my rooms for the night. She had more guests arriving than she had beds for. It didn't bother me to sleep on the couch in my sitting room, and next morning when I came down I found that my lodger was the great Welsh landscape artist, Kyffin Williams. He was on his way to visit the boss's house, Kilochter, and the Wicklow mountains where he would paint those stark, slatey pictures he was famous for. We had breakfast together and then walked outside where he painted me a black-and-white wash picture that I treasure. Very simple, just a little boy and a dog in the road. Yet somehow you knew just by looking at it – perhaps it was from the shape of the houses and the attitude of this kid – that the road they were walking down was going to the sea. He wrote on it, 'To Cliff Morgan from Kyffin Williams, Wicklow, 1955.'

Among the occasional pleasures of living in Wicklow, too, were invitations to the weekend parties at Kilochter. I have to say it was a good deal bigger than 159 Top Trebanog Road, a typically grand Irish country house with a high flight of steps leading up to the front door and into the wide entrance hall. Off that were magnificent reception rooms. A home farm surrounded the house, with a large field running alongside the drive where Kenneth would land his private plane. He came most weekends, bringing guests and inviting people down from Dublin and turning Kilochter into a kind of cultural centre. When, for instance, Emlyn Williams was doing his one-man performance as Charles Dickens in Dublin, he came down on the Saturday night as soon as the show was over. Kay Kendall, the star of the film *Genevieve*, about the London–Brighton vintage car run, was a friend of Stephanie and used to stay there. There were always interesting guests, splendid dinners and great conversation. Also White Lady cocktails, which it was one of Kenneth's vanities to mix himself. The Davies children were an added attraction. David, a friendly ten-year-old, became a top businessman in Hong Kong, and Christine, some two years younger, grew up to be one of the most beautiful women I have known.

But building up the business was what I was there for, and even after we had dug the foundations and installed the machinery, it was still largely physical as well as mental work. I used to go up to the docks in a jeep-type van drawing a big trailer into which I had to throw hundredweight hanks of wire from the boat. Then I'd drive them back and unload them at the factory, all by hand again. I got like an ox. In fact, I think at that time I was stronger than I have ever been. Having never drunk very much before, I now drank Guinness. And since I was burning up my energy as I went along, if you believed what the posters used to say, that may also have helped my body-building. There wasn't a pick of meat on me, as they say in Dublin; it was all sinew and hardness.

It gave me that little edge in rugby not only when I started playing for Bective in the autumn, but right through to the next summer when I went to South Africa with the British Lions.

Rugby at Bective was a totally different experience. I played in the opening match of the season, away to Old Belvedere at their ground in Anglesea Road, Ballsbridge. When I went into our dressing room for the first time there was my jersey hanging there, and folded up on the bench just below it were my shorts and stockings and things. I picked these up and a piece of paper fluttered out. It was the bill for my kit. Naturally, you expected to buy your own boots, but having to pay for your club jersey, shorts and stockings was something new. I can't remember exactly what the bill was, but it seemed pretty substantial at a time when I was earning less than £300 a year and paying for my digs out of that. We also had to pay ten shillings a week into a kitty. Half of this went towards buying food for the visiting teams at our home matches, and covering our own expenses when we were away. The other five shillings was kept for a party at the end of the season. And some party that turned out to be since, for the first time in twenty years, Bective won the Leinster Cup. Anyway, that was the system. You paid to play. Simple as that. It summed up the whole spirit of Irish rugby where, compared with Wales, amateurism was still in its innocent infancy.

I wouldn't say the same for the game itself. There was a freedom about Irish rugby that excited me, but it was tough all right. That year Wanderers, the Cup-holders, had a back row of three brothers, Ronnie, Gene and Paddy Kavanagh, all arch-murderers. Ronnie was a fabulous forward, and when we played them later in the season, I remember him saying, loud enough for me to hear, 'Leave the little fellow to me, I'll sort him out.' That's what you had to expect, but being cheeky and arrogant, I had a go straight away on the blind side and for some reason got away.

Against Old Belvedere I was pretty quiet for the first half hour, and then saw the chance to make a clean break. Running up outside me was our wing, Maurice Mortell. I pulled in their full-back, slipped Maurice the ball, and left him with sixty-five yards to go for a try. Nobody in front of him, he only had to run and run. There wasn't anyone near him when he reached the line, but all the same he insisted on diving full-length across it. 'What are you doing?' I said, and then I realised. He'd thrown himself on the ground to be sick. He swore he'd never run that far in his life before, and there I was making him do it in the first game of the season.

Bective is a little club at Donnybrook, which is not far from Lansdowne Road, which is not far from the centre of Dublin – not far from anywhere, in fact, since the scale of the city is so small. In my day it had a little grandstand which was never full, except for one of the Cup rounds, and an equally small clubhouse, not posh at all, where you had to walk through the dressing rooms to get to the dance hall. Nobody minded, for they had a sense of fun about rugby, which I enjoyed so much that it probably means I wouldn't be any good playing serious rugby today. The atmosphere was totally different from that in Wales. Instead of the 12,000 capacity crowd at Rodney Parade or the average 49,000 at the Arms Park who'd be watching a game between Cardiff and Newport, at Bective there would be anything from seventy-five to 380. And whereas if you dropped a pass at Cardiff, the crowd would groan as if you'd done them a personal injury, in Dublin they'd just shout, 'Ah, you eejit,' and immediately forget about it. It took away all the tensions that had been building up in Wales.

I have to admit that the standard was a bit lower than in the first-class game at home. You were up against some terrific opponents in Ireland, and you took the Cup games seriously, but there wasn't that remorseless succession of matches against Aberavon, Pontypool, Llanelli, Bridgend, Swansea – with only the occasional treat of playing Blackheath for a day off. You didn't feel the weight of the world on your shoulders every time you ran on the field.

For all that, Bective were a pretty good side. We had some players with real class, like Maurice, who played on the wing for Ireland, Joey Molloy, one of the regular centres, and the Cuddy brothers, one a centre, the other a prop. But our great advantage was the sense of unity in the team. We were always together, having drinks after the game, meeting each other away from the club. There was a family spirit within the Irish game – and in Ireland generally – which I adored. After all these years I still believe that this was the funniest, the happiest time I ever had playing rugby. And I would say this was largely due to the fact that all the fellows in the team had real jobs they were involved in and could talk about many other subjects beside rugby.

Because my period in Ireland coincided with my feeling particularly fit and playing well, there was lots of nonsense in the Irish papers about Welsh Magicians and Morgan Rangers and so on. But whatever I did for Bective was matched by what playing with them did for me. Training sessions, as they were loosely called, occurred whichever day you could get up to the club. It was just the odd times, perhaps before a Saturday Cup match, that we made a point of all meeting on the Thursday. Their more relaxed attitude made me more relaxed. I know it can be highly infectious. Once, when Cardiff played Old Belvedere in Dublin, Stan Bowes and some of the boys brought Guinness onto the field at half-time. They've talked about it ever since, and why not? I can't help feeling sorry for players nowadays who have to perform all the time, and daren't misbehave if they want to be considered for international rugby.

The effect Ireland had on my game was not as extreme as that, but it made me more inclined to try new things, to let the ball go, bring in the centres, create gaps. I think it also gave me a bit more confidence in setting out to beat people. I was always darting backwards and twisting and turning, and experimenting in ways I couldn't have risked with Cardiff. And although I wasn't aware of it at the time, I'm now convinced that it was playing with Bective which took me to South Africa in such an unworried state of mind.

At one stage early in the season I was forced to drop out of rugby for a couple of weeks because my hands were in such a mess from splicing the wire ropes we made. It was a job I had to do since the others were even less experienced at it than I was. But, fortunately, when I went down to Arklow one day, I happened to see this man working with ropes on a fishing smack at the quayside. I immediately asked him to come and work for us, and he agreed, provided that we bought him a little house in Wicklow. That was easy, a cottage only cost about threepence halfpenny then, and after he joined us I was able to concentrate more on building up the business in Ireland. It took us nine months or so to win our first order – some galvanised hawser for a Spanish trawler that came into Bantry – but from that point we began to get some very good contracts.

I spent my time going the rounds of the Dublin port and docks, the Electricity Boards, the Peat Board, the big building contractors and factories, all the people who used wire ropes – and there are many more than you'd think. It was a way of life I'd never experienced, but which I soon latched onto and found very stimulating. You'd ring up, get an appointment and off you'd go. I'd never owned a car before. Well, I didn't own one now, but I had sole use of the company's Hillman Minx, and used it all the time to drive in and out of Dublin.

Selling was all to do with meeting people and talking to them, which suited me perfectly. It was serious stuff all right, but again, this being Ireland, you didn't have to pretend you weren't enjoying it. I used to do most of my business with big companies and powerful people in government positions, but you'd meet at Bewley's Coffee Shop, or you'd get the contract drawn up in the office and then go across to a bar to seal it.

Maybe it was due to the Catholic influence, but there seemed to be a family spirit running through the whole of Dublin in those days. It was all so casual. When you parked your car in the street you'd leave it open with brakes off so that the next person could push it backwards and forwards to fit their own car in. You could go into Bewley's for coffee in the morning, or wander around Brown Thomas, the big store in Grafton Street, and be sure to find someone you knew to chew the fat with.

Those same people would ring up and say, 'I've got a problem, can you help me?' Or you'd phone them and ask, 'Look, can you fix me up with this?' And it would be done without fuss. It was like living in a village.

Every day, too, brought something to amuse you when you least expected it. In Ireland there was drinking every other day of the year, but not on Good Friday, so with the day off and nothing better to do a few of us went to the Ballsbridge Dog Show. And I remember there was some fellow with a big dog on a lead walking through the crowd. And there was another man, with two bottles of Guinness in his overcoat pocket, walking directly across his path. He fell over the lead, broke the bottles, and said as he looked up from the floor, 'Such a place to bring a bloody dog!'

There was another marvellous example when Bective reached the final of the Leinster Cup at Lansdowne Road, and we were lined up before the match to be presented to the president Sean T. O'Kelly, a big figure in Irish politics but a tiny little man. As he walked out onto the field there was a respectful silence, but when he began shaking hands with us, out of the crowd came a shout, 'Somebody cut the grass and let's have a look at the president!'

It had been a good season for Bective, and winning the Cup in early April was something to celebrate for the rest of the season and well beyond. Again our opponents were Belvedere, whom we beat by a goal and a penalty to nil but, as so often with big tense occasions, it wasn't a great match. The urbane Paul MacWeeney, then rugby correspondent of the *Irish Times*, described it as 'not a memorable final', which gives me an excuse for not remembering much about it after forty years. I know I scored the only try right under the posts (and the only one I scored for Bective all season) and from then on, it's said, I ruthlessly kicked for touch. It could well be true. The fun came afterwards. Over the next couple of months everyone gave parties. I was the only one who didn't have a home in Ireland, so I gave my party at the Hibernian Hotel, which was slightly expensive. Afterwards I drove Larkey O'Brien back to his family home in Bray. We'd had a lot to drink, but I was in rather better shape so I put the key in the lock, and Larkey fell into this bungalow, knocking the hall-stand over. He was lying there, hats and overcoats everywhere, when his mother came out of the bedroom. She looked down at him: 'Well, Larkin?' And he looked up at her and said, 'Hello, Mum, did you hear Bective won the Cup?' And that was eight weeks later.

By then I was on the point of leaving Ireland to join the British Lions party, and, though I didn't know it at the time, leaving Bective and Ireland behind. I was sitting in the office when I got a call from Jack Siggins, the Lions manager, to tell me I had been picked (and so, I found out later, was a boy of eighteen and a half called Tony O'Reilly who had played in the centre against us in the final). Jack said he'd be confirming this by letter shortly, but I went at once to tell the boss, who did nothing to hinder or help me.

I could take the time off, but it would have to be as unpaid leave. It disappointed me, but I could also understand it – or so I thought. This was a small company in the process of being built up. It couldn't afford to pay hangers-on like me who would be away from the office for four months at a time. I decided to go anyway and manage as best I could. It was only when I was on tour that I decided I wouldn't go back to work for Wire Ropes in Wicklow. Although I could still see their argument, I felt that if they couldn't pay me when I was away then, in a sense, they didn't really value me.

Mind, it's sometimes hard to separate your own motives. I don't think I could have lived in Dublin for the rest of my life. I had begun wondering what I would do when I stopped playing rugby and settled down to a career. Even at twenty-eight, when I decided that the moment had come to retire, I was still unsure *exactly* what to do. But already at twenty-five I had an inkling that it would have something to do with broadcasting. What also prompted these thoughts about the future was that I was soon to be married. It was something I hadn't even contemplated until those last few weeks in Dublin.

It was indirectly through being picked for the Lions that I met Nuala. In order to go to South Africa I needed injections against smallpox and so on, which my local doctor in Wicklow, a woman called Dr Conway, gave me one Saturday morning. While I was there I must have mentioned that I was going into Dublin to play for Bective that afternoon, for she asked if I would mind taking in a parcel for her daughter who lived in a flat in Rathmines round the corner from Merrion Square. No trouble. I went into Dublin, played my match, and was driving home when I thought, God, I've forgotten to drop this parcel off.

I turned round, found this basement flat, knocked at the door after midnight, and told the girl who answered – and turned out to be called Nuala Martin – that I had a parcel for Sylvia Conway. The two of them had just come back from an Aer Lingus flight, and asked me in for a coffee. And that might have been the end of it if I hadn't driven in to the Welsh chapel in Dublin next morning, and on the way back to Wicklow seen Nuala standing in a bus queue. The rewards of virtue, I suppose. I parked and went across to ask where she was going, and gave her a lift to the airport. The next week she invited me to the Aer Lingus dance, the week afterwards we got engaged, and then I went to South Africa for something like four and half months. The next time I met her was when she flew in to Cardiff airport in the October, which was my first chance to take her home to see my mother and father. I said to my mother, 'What do you think, Mam?' And her first remark – because Nuala, with her red hair and green eyes, also had lovely hands with long red fingernails – was, 'Well, looking at her hands, she'll never bake a cake.' Her main worry was that her baby wouldn't get properly nourished.

In the few weeks I had left in Dublin, I went with Nuala to buy an engagement ring, the one she sold to pay Nicky's school fees after I had my stroke. And as far as I could in so short a time, I got to know more of Nuala and her extraordinary family. Her

Uncle Noel was a distinguished but eccentric Dublin barrister and senator who sometimes came to court wearing one slipper and one shoe. He appeared for the defence in two famous Irish murder trials, and was a big pal of Aneurin Bevan, who came over to Dublin after the war to work with him on the preparations for the National Health Service. But striking as Uncle Noel might be, he was no more formidable than the women of the family, who occupied a house in Dundrum no great distance from the flat shared by Nuala and her air hostess friends. It was next door to the home of Sean MacBride, and Nuala used to tell me that when she was about three she remembered looking through the high hedge that surrounded her own big garden and seeing an old lady in black in a rocking chair. It was Maud Gonne, MacBride's mother and the unrequited love of W.B. Yeats's life, the inspiration for much of his poetry.

This was where Nuala had grown up, and she often went back to spend the night there with her grandmother, mother and two sisters. The grandmother, called Mush by the children, was Italian, though the family was from Kenmare in County Kerry, and she lived on the first floor with her personal maid, Mary. She had been claiming for years that she wasn't well, but she ran the house not so much with a rod of iron as with an ebony walking stick which she banged for attention on the floor over the hall. Her convictions were that the girls shouldn't ever have to wash up dishes, or do any work at all if possible, that they should all be home by 11.30 pm, and that they should marry well. She regarded me as a rugby-playing pauper.

Nuala's mother, Sheila, was another interesting and independent woman. She had been jailed at seventeen with Mrs De Valera for carrying messages for the old IRA. Later she been awarded medals, and still received a pension of fifteen shillings and fourpence a week from the Fianna Fáil party for past services to the Republic. On that she had to survive. She had become a rather sad figure as her earlier wealth disappeared and her daughters prepared to leave home. 'There's a great loneliness on me,' she once told me.

Nuala was sent away to be educated at Le Bon Sauveur convent on Anglesey, but there was no question that she had to work as soon as she left school. Her first job was in the Blood Bank, where the donors were given a pint of Guinness in exchange for the pint she took from their arms. She was a great favourite of the Dublin lads, who'd say, 'Aye, you can take two pints of mine if I can have the redhead!' She stuck it for years until she found a job at Aer Lingus as one of their early air stewardesses. The salary wasn't that much of an improvement, but at least they had first refusal of the sandwiches, cakes and biscuits that the passengers had left. That may seem to be pitching the hard luck story a bit strong, but things were pretty tough in Ireland just after the last war.

My year there, when every day brought a new experience, nearly always funny and challenging, changed me a lot. I found my independence, even if now I was going to share it with Nuala. I worried less about rugby, enjoyed it more and, I think, played it better. I came to acknowledge to myself that I wasn't deeply religious, and that it was some relief not to attend chapel three times every Sunday. At the same time I realised that I had to go to services from time to time to join in the singing and refresh my spirits. I now knew what it was like to carry responsibility for a small manufacturing company, and had done it well enough to regain confidence after throwing away my university chances. And at least I had established one claim to fame by making the first wire rope ever spun in the 'continent of Ireland'.

While I never lived in Ireland again, I have always visited it several times each year. It has become a far more prosperous country now, a process which always seems to involve destroying the very places – squares, hotels, restaurants, pubs – that you were fondest of. At the same time the basic Irish belief that business should always make room for pleasure keeps asserting itself. Whenever I stayed in Dublin, whether with Cardiff, Wales or the BBC, it was always at the Hibernian. There was a taxi rank outside the hotel and I got to know the drivers well. Years later I took a cab from the rank to go to the airport and the driver said:

'How are you Mr Morgan, I haven't seen you for years.' Then as he drove away he asked, 'What time's the flight?' I told him and he said, 'Well in that case we've got time for one.' He pulled off the road, we had a pint of Guinness together, and chatted until he decided it was time to go. As we got to the airport, just for something to say, I remarked on the changes there – no left turns, no right turns, parking here, departures there, all these new signs and new buildings. Straight away he said, 'Ah, Mr Morgan, ever since that BEA is flying to Dublin the place is fooked.' He blamed British Airways for all those differences. If it had been left to the Irish it would have been all right. Typical! When I heard that I felt as if I'd never been away.

8

Lore of
the Lions

I never really thought twice about accepting Jack Siggins's invitation to join the British Lions tour of South Africa in 1955. I admit I was put out when my boss, Kenneth Davies, said he couldn't go on paying me when I was away. But the pain was to my pride not to my back pocket. I knew my parents would help with my few expenses, as they did; otherwise I would make out. At that period Lions tours were four or five years apart; you needed to hit the top at just the right time to be included once, and you had to have a long international career to be asked a second time. It was an offer you couldn't refuse, a chance and challenge to pay the best rugby in your life. I felt that once I had been a Lion I would have done everything I could in the game. I looked at the company I would be keeping. The other nine Welshmen in the team I knew well, of course, but the buzz I got was from the thought of playing with Jeff Butterfield as my centre and Tony O'Reilly on the wing.

I went briefly back home, after which the idea was for the team to spend six days at the Cavendish Hotel, Eastbourne, to get to know each other. As it happened there was a rail strike on the day the Welsh contingent was due to leave. So, instead of travelling by train, Danny Davies, the British Lions secretary, organised a coach to pick us up on the forecourt of Cardiff station. I sat at the back, I remember, with Russell Robins, the Pontypridd lock-forward, and Trevor Lloyd from Maesteg (one of three scrum-halves in the party, which was one too many it seemed to me). Trevor had come up holding the *Western Mail*, and asked, 'Have you seen what that bloody J.B.G. Thomas have said about us? "The Test half-backs will be J. Williams and D. Baker of England." Cliffy, you train with me and I'll play you in.' That was Trevor's great compliment. We did play together in the opening match, and a couple of other times, but, unfortunately, I couldn't return the compliment by playing Trevor into the Test team. The job went to Dickie Jeeps.

We stopped for a beer just outside Gloucester, and after a long, long bus drive arrived at Eastbourne in time for the first essential of any tour, the fitting for our blazers. At least it gave us a good laugh because all the sleeves were too long, the shoulders too wide, and everything had to be altered. That broke the ice, and that evening we came to the decision that we were going to be a singing team. I was appointed choirmaster, with first call on the hotel piano, and every day for a week we practised English, Scottish and Irish songs in English, Welsh songs in Welsh and, in four-part harmony, 'Sarie Marais' in Afrikaans, which we thought would go down well with the people over there. We learned this parrot-fashion, and the words of the Welsh songs I wrote on a blackboard. It paid off eventually because, although there are always some hurt feelings when players are competing for a place, we were an extremely happy side.

Apart from our singing lessons and bits of training, that was what our get-together before the tour amounted to. I suppose on reflection the worst thing about the set-up was that the team didn't have a coach, which would be unthinkable nowadays. We trained every day just because Jeff Butterfield, who had been to Loughborough and taught P.E., was asked to take over responsibility for getting us fit, and we didn't want to let him down. We got fairly fit, all right, but as with most international teams of that time, we didn't go in for any strategic planning for the games ahead. What a difference it might have made if we'd had a coach to direct us and teach us moves and techniques. We didn't even have a physiotherapist or doctor. If we needed a massage or medical treatment in South Africa, we had to go down to the local hospital. The whole thing was run like a casual trip for amateurs abroad.

The last Lions party to visit South Africa, in 1938, had travelled each way by sea. We were booked to come and go by air, though not all that quickly. We flew on a BOAC Argonaut, a rather ponderous aircraft, via Rome, Cairo, Nairobi and Livingstone, arriving at Johannesburg five and three-quarter hours late. Coming down the steps of the plane we were amazed at the crowds who had waited so long to greet us. I turned round and said, 'OK lads, look at the people.' So we all came to a stop and sang practically our full repertoire from 'Sospan Fach' to 'Sarie Marais', cheered on by the crowd. And that was the spirit of that trip, everybody together. Later that week the *Rand Daily Mail* carried a front page headline: 'This is the greatest team ever to visit South Africa'. And we hadn't played a match!

Mind, the South African Rugby Union weren't so easily swayed. Shrewdly, on the Wednesday before our opening match, they took us to see one of their own games and put us in seats on the touchline which were below ground level, just as they were around the running track at Stade Colombes. We were looking up at the players, who all seemed fifteen feet tall, and frightened us to death. We looked at each other and, in comparison, we were all little fellows: how could we compete? Yet on the field in the months to come, the Lions team proved that size and weight weren't all-important, particularly in winning a reasonable share of the ball against the odds. Our forwards were terrific, tough, hard men. In the basic Test pack we had a Welsh front row, one Welshman in the second row and another, Russell Robins, in the back row. In other words, Wales provided five of the eight forwards. But in the first Test I was the only Welshman in the backs. The team was a curious combination of nationalities, but you got to know each other wonderfully well on a tour like that.

We also got to know the press much better than the modern tourists do. There were only three from the UK – Vivian Jenkins of the *Sunday Times*, J.B.G. Thomas of the *Western Mail*, and arriving on the eve of the first Test at Johannesburg, Roy McKelvie of the *Daily Mail*. What was unique was that all the players liked them and treated them as part of the tour. Vivian, of course, had been a Lion himself in South Africa, 1939. And J.B.G. became a father figure, going to a lot of trouble to get calls home for the players. Our three pressmen and even the South African writers and photographers were welcome to ride on the official team bus except on match days when the players wanted privacy. Nowadays you might get a couple of dozen home reporters following the tour, which can cause suspicion among the players that the journalists are using them.

Our opening game was against Western Transvaal at Potchefstroom towards the end of June, and, such was the stately pace of rugby touring then, it was over seven weeks before we would meet South Africa in the first Test. To avoid the worst of the heat, we kicked off at four in the afternoon on a ground which had set like concrete. Although we were living on only five shillings pocket money a day, we decided to put ten shillings each into a kitty which would go to the player who scored our first try. The chance came to me in the second minute of the game. I took the ball behind a ten-yard scrum, went on the blind side, sold a dummy and dived over to score. So I took the kitty – or almost all of it. Cecil Pedlow, the Irish wing who was outside me, reckoned that I should have passed the ball and given him the honour, so he refused to pay up. Cecil did get a try of his own soon afterwards, and we were looking pretty good at that moment. But Western Transvaal got two dropped-goals and a penalty, and we lost 6–9. In some people's eyes it was a bad start, but it taught us to tighten up and not be quite so frantic in our approach. We lost only one of our next fifteen games, proving that the lads could play a bit of rugby.

After our 31–3 win over the Orange Free State early in July, there were South Africans who were even prepared to make us favourites for the first Test. Jeff Butterfield scored three tries in that match, and those natural, logical angles of running which swept him through the defence and across the line were beautiful things to watch. Ever since 1951, when the Springboks beat Scotland 44–0 in Edinburgh, South Africans have referred to a crushing victory as a 'Murrayfield'. The morning after the Orange Free State match, one headline ran: 'It's not Murrayfield, it's Butterfield'.

During the build-up to the first Test, I injured my ankle playing against South-Western Districts, the result of twisting my foot in a loose ruck. I missed the next match, a surprisingly emphatic defeat at the hands of Eastern Province, which set us back a bit. But I returned for a fairly easy game against North-Eastern Districts, letting the threequarters do the work in the first half but scoring two tries of my own in the second. I was rested for the Transvaal game, in which the Lions scored seven tries, three of them to O'Reilly and two to Butterfield, and won 36–13. Transvaal was famously a cradle of the Springboks, and such a hefty victory over them greatly shortened the odds on the Lions beating South Africa. But whether I'd be on the field or watching the Test from the stand was still in doubt. I had to prove my fitness in Rhodesia, and it was only after coming through both our games there with nothing worse than a sprained and swollen thumb that I was named for the team.

Some weeks before he died in 1995, Dr Danie Craven, mastermind of the South African game, and probably the most famous rugby man in the world, said that the greatest international match he ever saw was the first Test match at Ellis Park, Johannesburg, on 6 August 1955. Because it was us, I like to believe him. And also because I know we produced great moments of rugby in a temperature of 78 degrees in the shade and at an altitude of 5750 feet, which left us gasping for air. To me that game epitomised what rugby and the whole tour were about – adventure, style, passing the ball and, about the most important thing in rugby, taking chances. We gave away stupid tries, I'm sure, but we went on taking risks, because when you play safe the game is impoverished. And we gained far more than we lost by that approach. Apart from the enjoyment we got out of it, we proved that you must throw the ball about to win matches.

The first Test selection was fairly predictable.* There was some discussion over whether Gareth Griffiths, who had come out as a replacement, should be on the wing instead of Cecil Pedlow. But Cecil was the number two goal-kicker, and would be there if our first choice, full-back Angus Cameron, were injured. As it turned out, picking Cecil cost us nothing on the wing either, for he scored the opening try.

Playing in that match would have been an extraordinary experience whatever had happened on the field. It drew the biggest crowd ever to watch a rugby international – officially 96,000. But thousands more got in without paying, since tickets were pushed back over fences to people waiting outside to re-use them. There was a grandstand on only one side of Ellis Park at that time, so the rest were crammed into standing areas. Their impact was almost overpowering as you came down the flight of steps to the field. And another thing that staggered us was that on the touchline twenty yards out from the front of the grandstand, the Springbok selectors sat in a row of chairs on their own. Everybody knew who they were, and so they were there to be booed, cheered or heckled or whatever took the fancy of the crowd.

Happily, the rugby lived up to the occasion. When we scored the first try, not one Springbok touched the ball. There was a throw-in to our lineout where Rhys Williams from Llanelli – not massively big, but a giant in every other sense – caught the ball, turned in the air and dropped it down to Jeeps. From Jeeps to me, and I made a half-gap. Phil Davies took my pass and running, as

* Cameron; O'Reilly, Butterfield, Davies, Pedlow; Morgan, Jeeps; W. Williams, B. Meredith, C. Meredith, Higgins, R. Williams, Thompson (capt), Greenwood, Robins.

he always did, with a tremendous sense of power in his enormous shoulders and hips, swept through the gap and gave the ball to Butterfield. Now Phil wasn't the world's best passer of the ball, and it went somewhere behind Jeff's right ear. But Jeff put his arm back and, without checking his stride, took the ball, brought it in front of him, leaned in and drew the full-back, and finally gave Pedlow the perfect pass which took him across the line. It was all magical, a flawless, text-book movement. There was great excitement and then the crowd went silent. You knew they were thinking, what is this? Angus Cameron didn't convert, but he kept us in the game with his goal-kicking after that.

I remember that we scored five tries and were 23–11 ahead midway through the second half. But in the final twenty minutes, and after we had been reduced to fourteen men, the South Africans came back at us so strongly that with seconds to go our lead was down to one point. And Van Der Schyff, their full-back, had still to take a conversion from in front of our posts. But it's less the pattern of play than certain vivid, individual moments which stay in my mind.

There was one magnificent disallowed try of Tony O'Reilly's, for instance. The Irish used to say, that fellow can't tackle, as the Welsh sometimes said about me. But at eighteen and a half he kept going down and down the touchline until he crashed over carrying three Springboks across with him. The referee went round and awarded a try before he noticed that the touch-judge six yards back had his flag up. According to him Tony had put his foot in, and so the try didn't stand. I don't think Tony was in touch, and nowadays I suppose there would have been hell to pay about it, people arguing with the referee and the touch-judge. Tony just walked away, and so did we all. And maybe that was the difference between the rugby that became professional and the rugby we played on tour. We wanted to play hard, wanted to win, but our attitude was basically carefree. Maybe we had scored a try, I don't know, but it didn't matter, it wasn't worth an argument.

I also recall from that match the remorseless covering of

an English back-row forward, Reg Higgins, before he was injured just over half-way through the game. He was a hard, tough Liverpool boy whom I'd met when he played his first international at Cardiff Arms Park. The teams were walking round the pitch before the match when he put an arm on my shoulder and said, 'Are you Morgan?' I said I was. 'Well,' he went on, 'I don't want any bloody platitudes. Come blind today and I'll bloody kill thee.' I said to Rex, 'Let's go blind and see what he's talking about.' I ran blind, and Higgins and I clashed, bang into each other. As he got off the ground he picked me up by the scruff of my shirt and said, 'Thar'll do for me, lad.' He'd just wanted to prove that you can't get away with anything; to win you've got to be hard, and that's how he always played. At Johannesburg Reg was injured in the lineout, badly twisting his knee just after half-time, and was being carried behind the goal posts when he told his stretcher-bearers, 'Stop here, I want to see the Lions score.' And what happened in the next moments was that although we were down to seven forwards, Bryn Meredith took the ball in the scrum and Jeeps threw out the perfect flat, shortish pass which was moving away from me. I had to run and stretch to get it, and as I caught it and swung my body, my great adversary 'Basie' Van Wyk just missed my backside. Then I swept in and beat Jack Van Der Schyff to score a try under the posts. Reg said, 'All right, you can take me in now.' And they took him off the field and out of the tour, for his knee required a more complicated operation than we expected and he was kept in hospital for at least a month before he returned home.

The South Africans then turned the pressure on us, scoring four tries, two of them from their wing, Briers. For the first of these he left me flat on my backside as he beat me on the inside, but it was the second, a joint effort by backs and forwards in injury time, which threatened to destroy us. Whether we won or lost by a single point all depended on the conversion. We were standing behind the posts – clapped out and searching for air – as Jack Van Der Schyff took the ball. He was a crocodile-hunter by trade and an ace goal-kicker, and since the try had been scored

less than half-way to the Springboks' left, it was an easyish kick
for him. I was thinking, 'Oh God, this is it, we've lost the game,'
when Jack stepped back, took the kick and as I looked up I
saw the ball floating past the posts. Within seconds the whistle
went and we'd won 23–22. So ended a match which, because
it created so much interest, took enough at the gate to pay for
the whole twenty-seven-match tour. I won't say that the home
crowd enjoyed the result, but they got their money's worth in
entertainment. And what the match proved to me was that if
you had players with talent and let them go, at the end you'd
see the best rugby in the world. Afterwards as we stood around
on the field wondering what to do next, W. O. Williams, the
Swansea prop, stuck his arms around me and said, 'Cliff, I'm
glad we went to chapel last Sunday!'

The chapel we'd been to was St Colombus Presbyterian,
Johannesburg, where the minister, Rev. Emlyn Jones, was
from Pontrhydyfen, the mining village north of Port Talbot
where Richard Burton was born. In fact some of us knew him
from his chapel there, and Emlyn and his family became great
friends of the Lions on that trip. The day after the Test at least
a dozen of us from the party of thirty-one went back to the
church, Catholics as well as Protestants, for we kept very much
together on that tour.

In Wales we regularly hold gymanfa ganu, singing festivals,
and Emlyn asked me if I would conduct one of these in the vestry
on the Sunday evening after a short service in the church. This
vestry turned out to be bigger than any concert hall I'd seen at
that time. It had a proper stage, where we were introduced, with
a pipe organ, a piano – everything. And the place was packed
with people perched on shelves and window sills, sitting on the
floor between the seats. I hadn't expected anything like this. I
looked round and said, 'What are we going to sing?' There was
a woman waiting at the piano and a man on the organ, and
somebody shouted, 'Llef'. I said, right, and we began singing
'O Iesu Mawr . . .' and we went through all the famous hymn
tunes. It was a fabulous night. Then when we had finished, up on

the stage came a man who said, 'Emlyn, I can't let this occasion go
without talking to the boy.' That was me. I didn't recognise him,
but he was Francis Russell from Tonyrefail, whose sisters had
taught at the village school I attended. He had once worked for
my grandfather in the levels and later become a celebrated tenor
at Covent Garden and many of the world's opera houses. Now
he was living in South Africa and was going blind. He sang a
song that was almost unbearably poignant in the circumstances,
'The Blind Ploughman':

> Set my hand upon the plough, my feet upon the sod,
> Turn my face towards the east and praise be to God.
> Everywhere the sun will rise on both you and me,
> God, who took away my eyes, that my soul might see.

It was fantastically emotional; we all felt it. The day before we
had won a Test match by just one point. Now we had reality
brought back into our life by Francis Russell. Emlyn said, 'Thank
you, we must now let the boys go,' but people were shouting,
'No, sing one more!' and so we sang the hymn everyone knows,
'Cwm Rhondda'. Early next morning we flew off to Durban. It
could not have been a more memorable weekend.

Taking all the results together, it was a successful tour. We
won nineteen of our twenty-five matches, drew another, and
tied the Test series 2–2. All the same, we were accused of being
naive in our approach to the second Test at Cape Town, which
we lost 25–9. There was some truth in this. The game was played
on a fairly wet day, following a very wet week, and most of the
South African papers had already predicted that we wouldn't be
able to run the ball as we had in Johannesburg. This was right,
but it wasn't so much the conditions that stopped us as the fact
that we hadn't prepared for them. South Africa had worked
and worked at their preparations. Danie Craven ran special
training sessions to teach them how to stop people and create
gaps. Although it was in the scrums that the Springboks really
stuffed us, the weather didn't stop them running in seven tries
as well. Three of them were from Tommy Van Vollenhoven, a

class player who had been switched from centre to wing and
would later become a Rugby League star with St Helens. The
strange thing was that the Lions were exactly the same in defeat
as they had been in victory. After losing we came down singing
into the hotel dining room, where the Springboks were waiting,
and we went on singing all the way to the table. Even now I'm
still not quite certain whether or not that was to our credit. I
suppose it bears out the charge that we were naive.

The conditions in Pretoria for the third Test in early September
were totally different; the ground was as hard as it had been in
the Transvaal. Robin Thompson, the tour captain, had injured
a knee and I was made captain for the day. I'd captained the
Lions in Rhodesia and a few other games, but this was my first
Test. W. O. 'Billy' or 'Stoker' Williams led the pack. And Jeff
Butterfield, who had never dropped a goal in his life – who had
never even kicked a ball with his left foot before – dropped a
left-footed goal. He also scored a try, and Doug Baker kicked
a penalty, while Roy Dryburgh kicked two penalties for the
Springboks. It wasn't a spectacular game, but it was hard and
tight, and by winning it 9–6 we went one up in the series and
knew that at least we couldn't lose it.

In this Test, as in the first, we had a try disallowed. And the
circumstances of that were almost more interesting than the
rest of the game. As we were walking on the field I went back
up the line and said, 'O'Reilly and Griffiths, change wings.' I
knew that Tony had a thing about Van Vollenhoven, the wing
he'd have been marking, and I thought Gareth Griffiths would
cope with him better. They swapped, but I'm sure Tony didn't
like it. The first thing he did was to run up the left touchline
like a rhino, knocking people over, handing them off, almost
scoring a try in his determination to show us he wasn't afraid
of anyone. Then Gareth went round Van Vollenhoven, and a
beautiful move developed with O'Reilly going outside Briers and
inside the full-back to touch down under the posts. There was
tremendous cheering – until we noticed that J. E. Williams, who
was our touch judge (in those days you gave the job to whoever

wasn't playing), was standing about fifty yards back with his flag in the air. He said O'Reilly had put his foot into touch. The Springboks weren't even arguing about it, but Johnny had seen it. He needn't have bothered, but he kept his flag up. We called him a few names, but you wonder how many other British Lions would have had the honesty to do it.

It's funny, as captain you wanted the best out of everybody, and I knew that Tony would play better on the left wing. I had great admiration for him since, even at that age, he had all the classic virtues – body turned slightly away from the tackler, knees and legs high as he ran, tremendous courage. The Irish tend to say, ah, lucky fellow. Everything's lucky in Ireland. But there was nothing lucky about Tony's life. He was already twenty-five years older upstairs in his mind than anybody I'd known. He was handsome; everywhere he went in South Africa, girls used to say, 'I've touched Tony, touched his blazer.' And he was ambitious. I wanted him to do so well in the Test match, and my God he did.

After the third Test in Pretoria I had a room of my own, the captain's perk, where the boys would come and use the telephone. In South Africa there was no post-match dinner, just a short reception at which both captains made a quick speech. I'd got back early to the hotel for a bath, just to relax a bit more, when there was a knock at the bedroom door. I opened it with a towel around me, and there was a little red-faced Afrikaans farmer carrying a box. 'I wanted to give you this,' he said; it was a box of biltong, the sun-dried meat that kept the soldiers and settlers alive in the Boer War. Then he gave me an envelope full of red £10 notes – that was then the South African currency – to buy the boys a drink. When he left, not wanting to stay and explain himself, I found it came to £150. I passed the money on to Charlie Du Plooy, the baggage man, to spend on drinks for us when we left Pretoria at six next morning for the Kruger National Park. We were spending a short holiday there, away from rugby, before we played the last three provincial games and the final Test.

What Charlie did was hire a van with a canvas roof and fill it full of bottles of Castle lager and other booze, only partly bought with the farmer's money, and follow our bus for 280 miles to what's called a national park but is more of a district. There we lived in the open and slept at night in *rondavels*, little thatched huts, in a stockaded camp. In the evening we would sit around the fires and cooking stoves like boy scouts, singing and doing our party pieces. It was simple stuff, but the Lions party had such a strong family spirit that the friendship within it survived even the strain of arguable team selections and inevitably unfair shares of the limelight. What you realise now is that bonds are created and people stick together when they haven't got too much to spend. You wonder whether that kind of bond will ever be attained in the future when players earn good money and they've got another commitment in two days' time to play somewhere else for somebody else. In our case the bond held, too, as our reunions afterwards proved. When Craven was eighty in 1991, Tony O'Reilly rang me up to say, 'We're giving a dinner for Danie.' I said, 'Of course, where are we having it, in London?' 'No, in Cape Town.' And he got Rhys Williams, Jeff Butterfield and Bryn Meredith to turn up, with Tony paying all the air fares.

This was typical of O'Reilly in its generosity and its flamboyance. Like the time he returned to international rugby in 1970. Only the Irish would have brought him back at Twickenham when it was eight years since he had last been capped and was now established as managing director of HJ Heinz UK. And probably only O'Reilly would have agreed to do it. When the Irish team turned up in an oldish bus, O'Reilly arrived in a chauffeur-driven car. On the field that afternoon he did something that he, like me, didn't much like doing. He fell on the ball. The English pack came round and kicked lumps out of him. Afterwards he lay there dazed, and as he put it afterwards, 'You know that silence that falls over a group of people, well, suddenly I heard an obviously Irish voice shout, "And while you're at it, kick his bloody chauffeur as well."' For him, half the fun of the game was in the telling of it afterwards. He swore that playing for Ireland they used an excess of embrocation, 'because if you're not fit, for God's sake smell fit.' And if he wasn't telling a story he'd be embellishing yours. On television one night with O'Reilly I repeated the one about my father losing his false teeth at Lansdowne Road when Wales scored a try. 'Jaysus, Morgan,' he said. 'I know a feller in Cork who's still wearing them.' What could you say to that?

The last Test at Port Elizabeth on 24 September was a bit of an anticlimax. After our success at Pretoria we went into it thinking we could pull it off again and so become the first official British Isles team to win a Test series in South Africa. Instead, suffering from three months' accumulation of injuries, we lost 22–8 and only drew the series. I shouldn't really have been playing. Ten days before, I had injured my ankle in the match against the Junior Springboks at Bloemfontein. With a week to go I still couldn't walk properly. Dr Louis Babrow, Medical Officer to the South Africa Board – a former Springbok who had played for Guy's Hospital and the Barbarians while he was finishing his medical training in London – x-rayed my ankle and found five chips off the bone. It was a mess and had to be bound up all the time. At home there would have been no question of my playing. On tour there were other considerations. The fact was that we could only just manage to get fifteen players on the field. I would have cried off if Dougie Baker could have taken my place at stand-off. But Angus Cameron and Alun Thomas were both unavailable to play at full-back and Dougie was needed to fill that gap. I wasn't the only player who shouldn't really have been there. Our tour captain, Robin Thompson, came back into the second row after a leg injury had kept him out of the team for a month, and then not surprisingly broke down during the game, which undermined the effectiveness of the whole pack. O'Reilly, too, dislocated his shoulder while scoring a late try, and although the issue had probably been settled by then, the Springboks were able to score a final try while we were reduced to fourteen men. I still think that with a fit side we could have won that match and the series, for we were still leading at half-time. But if victory was important, it wasn't the most important thing. It was pride that mattered, and we hadn't lost that.

I find it sad to contemplate a rugby world with no more Lions tours, and none of the opportunity they provide to play alongside former and future opponents, sharing their lives and their views on life. That tour to South Africa did a great deal to teach me that you had to have confidence in your fellow man and faith that he wasn't going to let you down. Your life was enriched by a feeling that everybody wanted everybody else to do well, which is what made the whole experience for me.

I took a few months' sabbatical from rugby when I got home. I stayed for the time being with George Elliot's, working on the road as a rep, and Nuala was still flying around with Aer Lingus, but during the few times we met we planned our wedding. If we had married in Cardiff or Dublin it would have been the kind of all-ticket affair we didn't want and couldn't afford. Instead we settled on a quiet wedding in a little church at Woking on 17 December. The previous night I slept at home, leaving the car in what had been my grandfather's garage on the other side of the street. To make sure of an early start I got up in the dark, forgetting that the garage had an inspection pit, and drove one of the wheels over the edge of it. I then had to go back, wake my father and get him to help me lift the car out. Just what I needed.

I still got to the church on time, but something else didn't go to plan either. With Nuala's sister Pam and her husband Ronan as the only witnesses, we thought we had kept the wedding a close secret. But when we came out a camera crew from BBC TV's Saturday night sports programme was waiting. At least we had the consolation, after driving west to the Seabank Hotel in Porthcawl, of being able to watch ourselves on television emerging from the church. The next day we flew to Dublin, and the day after that I left Nuala with her other sister, Sheila, while I joined the England–Wales team which I was to captain against Scotland–Ireland at Lansdowne Road. So began my first years of marriage and my last three seasons as a senior rugby player.

Nuala had already given up her job with Aer Lingus, and when we came back from Ireland we went to live with my parents in Trebanog. It was a bit of a culture shock for her. I went off to work and Nuala was left to help with the ironing, and making the tea in the morning and taking it in to my aunty next door. It wasn't the easiest of starts. But after about six months we found a furnished flat in Cardiff where we had to put books under the two single beds to bring them to the same level. That was short-lived but then we moved to the lodge of a house owned by Jim Dooner, whose father had run fairgrounds and boxing booths. It wasn't luxurious. If you looked between the lavatory floorboards you could see the gardener working in the potting shed below. But Wilf Wooller's wife, Enid, made us curtains, someone passed on an old-fashioned washing machine, and we had great times in the lodge. Our first child, Catherine, was born when we were living there. Still, there must have been times when Nuala wondered what she was doing in Cardiff and remembered her grandmother's warning against marrying a pauper.

Through Hywel Davies, Nuala was asked to do two radio series for the BBC. One we introduced together, 'Holiday Highway', going around all the holiday camps in Wales and talking to the campers about how they spent their time. Then I was dropped and the second series was called 'Nuala in Jazzland', which took her to all the jazz clubs. Both were successful, and must have given Nuala a boost. And as our situation improved we were able to buy a house in Cardiff for a couple of thousand pounds. That was where Nicky was born.

My attachment to the Lions' style of life made it all the harder to pass up the chance (which is all it was, a chance not a firm offer of any kind) to go with them to New Zealand in 1959. That would have been the ultimate Test. Although I did return to South Africa with the Barbarians in 1958, by then I was on the point of retiring from rugby. 'You can't retire, you must take the Lions to New Zealand,' Sir Wavell Wakefield wrote to me; not that the job was within his gift. But at that point, as I explained earlier, I couldn't afford *not* to resist the temptation.

It worked out for the best, but I still regret terribly that I didn't play in the country which, for me, represents rugby at its very best. People criticise New Zealand rugby for its rucking, but when rucking was invented in Dunedin by Vic Kavanagh it was executed with brilliance. Opponents might get scratched on their way out of the ruck, but they never got kicked when the All Blacks were going in. New Zealand always went over the top of obstructive bodies and got them out of the way. I'd love to have beaten them on their own grounds. For one thing, they've got the perfect conditions for rugby touring – raining one day, hot the next. You have to prove that you are the class all-rounder. For another, I have the happiest memories of playing the All Blacks and of talking rugby with the likes of Bob Scott, one of the greatest full-backs who ever breathed. To me the finest radio commentator on rugby was Winston McCarthy, a New Zealander who brought the game alive and made you feel you wanted to be part of it. Everything about the country and its people made me want to go, and see and conquer with the Lions. I never did, and it's a sorry gap in my education.

Instead I had to be content with playing the All Blacks at the Arms Park, something which came my way three times in the 1953–54 season. The first match was for Cardiff. We went to see the tourists playing Llanelli on a Tuesday, and afterwards Bleddyn Williams said, 'We have got to throw a long ball at the lineouts to stop their back row getting at Rex Willis and Cliff.' So we agreed on a signal for this; it was that Rex would shrug his shoulders. Then our wing, as it was in those days, would throw a long ball. What we didn't realise was that Rex naturally shrugged his shoulders; it was a kind of nervous tic with him. And so every throw at our lineouts was long. But at least it meant that their back row had to jump for it, and were too preoccupied to run at Rex and me if Cardiff won it.

It was a staggering game, with a big build-up and a terrific front-row battle. In particular I remember Stan Bowes, our tough naval prop, playing opposite Snow White, an equally rugged New Zealander. They struggled and hit and fought in that front row all through that game, and yet until the day that Stan died in the early 'nineties, Snow White would come across to see Stan, or he'd pay for Stan to go and see him in New Zealand, and they kept that friendship going for thirty-seven years. There is a special relationship, a kind of intimacy between opposing front-row forwards which I have always admired. I noticed it when I first played with Cliff Davies, and later Billy Williams and Courtney Meredith and other great props.

The All Blacks' full-back was Bob Scott, one of the first to come into the threequarter line to make the extra man and create a gap through which tries could be scored. Bob was a phenomenon. He kicked equally well with both feet, and part of his normal training was to kick goals from the half-way line with his bare feet. He forced us to think up another signal. If he came into the line, somebody would shout, 'Scott's in!' and we'd have an extra man there to tackle him. But he also made us think more adventurously. I'll never forget Bleddyn saying, 'We've got to try things, and if we fail we fail, but we've got to be different.' So once when the ball came out from Rex, I tried a little chip over the top of the New Zealand pack, chased after it myself, and as they all came out of the scrum to nail me, I caught it, and passed it immediately to Bleddyn who shot it out to Gwyn Rowlands on the wing. He was boxed in on the touchline but kicked inside where our flanker, Sid Judd, who was majestic, won the race for the ball to score a try. At that point, only six minutes into the game, you knew that there was something on that day. And it's true, the game was decided already. Gwyn converted the try and kicked a penalty; Ronnie Jarden kicked a penalty for them; and we won 8–3.

That still left us with seventy-four minutes' defending to do. But the 45,000 spectators were unbelievable; I've never known them so solidly behind us, even playing for Wales. I felt that every yard you ran you'd been pushed forward by the crowd, and every time you kicked to touch, the ball went twenty yards further because the crowd were willing it to do so. People said in those days that Cardiff couldn't tackle, that we never had a tackler. Well, we did tackle, we did fall on the ball and keep possession. And then in the last moment of the game, Geoff Beckingham took the scrum against the All Blacks' put-in, Rex just lobbed the ball out to me and I whacked it up into the north stand, out of the way, because I knew it was the final whistle. We were the only club side, as Wales were the only home country, to beat New Zealand on that tour.

Every year since then, the Cardiff side who brought off this victory have held a reunion in Cardiff on the Friday evening before the date of that match. Sadly we are down to nine now, but all the survivors get there from wherever they are, paying their own way and buying their own meal. Once I remember flying in from Geneva to London Airport, catching the train at Reading and arriving for a seven o'clock dinner party at half-past nine. We have no speeches, just conversation, and only one toast – to absent friends. This is at nine o'clock, which is nine in the morning in New Zealand where our old opponents – and most of them are still alive – have a similar anniversary breakfast. After the toast we make a quick phone call: Bleddyn, our captain, speaking to theirs, Bob Stewart. It keeps the true spirit of the game alive, and that's the most remarkable thing as far as I'm concerned. We've always wanted to whack New Zealand, but also to be with them afterwards to share the bumps, the bruises and the memories.

The Wales game, which followed, will always be remembered for a try scored by Ken Jones from a cross kick by Clem Thomas. The ball was loose, Clem Thomas picked it up and, it seemed to me, didn't know quite what to do with it. I was on his left, and thought he was going to give it to me. But suddenly he turned and thumped it across the field. There are only two bounces, lucky and unlucky, and this one couldn't have been kindlier. Ken Jones, steaming up, plucked the ball out of the air, came inside Jarden, and scored under the posts to win the match for us. The conversion put us 13–8 up. What makes that story more extraordinary is that Ivor Jones, a great back-row forward for Wales in his day, who was working the touchline that afternoon, claimed to have had a hand in that try. I can see Ivor now: blazer, grey trousers tucked into his socks, flag in hand. And Ivor Jones always said afterwards, 'I told Clem to cross kick.' But I very much doubt whether any conversation at all passed between them.

We lost Gareth Griffiths with a shoulder injury towards the end of the game and had to play it out with fourteen men. I'll never forget the pressure they put us under. They had a constantly rolling machine up front which we had to fend off. I don't think we were a better team than New Zealand, but there was a certain spirit in the Welsh side which pulled us through. Again in those last ten minutes we defended, we fell, we tackled, we caught the ball, scooped it away to touch. All the little things that mattered.

The third match, the traditional Barbarian farewell to the tourists at the Arms Park, we lost 19–5. And they looked pretty comfortable playing our style of game. I had just one moment of glory on the right-hand touchline when I went blind, came in off the right foot, beat Bob Scott and scored a try. Or so I thought and felt pretty pleased about it. But the touch-judge was Laurie Haig, a veteran All Black stand-off who had been displaced on this occasion by a youngster, Guy Bowers. When I looked back, Laurie had his flag up on the 25. I knew I hadn't strayed into touch, and years later when I happened to meet him in Dunedin, I told him so. 'Ah,' he said, 'but I had the flag.' We left it at that.

Even if it hadn't been for rugby, I would still have had a soft spot for New Zealand because of Murray Halberg. I first saw him running for his country in the 1958 British Empire and Commonwealth Games in Cardiff where he won the 3 miles. Two years later he took the Olympic 5000 metres gold medal in Rome, and then set world records at 2 miles, 3 miles and the 4x1 mile relay. He was a runner of remarkable persistence who had triumphed as an athlete after his choice of sport had been restricted by a teenage rugby accident which paralysed his left arm. He went to the United States to run and coach and was given a leaving present which he didn't open until he got home. He found it was a parcel of money and, without thinking of spending it on himself, wondered what to do with it. Because of his injury he had the idea of opening a home for handicapped children, and started the Murray Halberg Trust. Now his homes are all over New Zealand, supported by golfers who, when they go out for a round at the weekend, always put a dollar in the kitty for the Trust. Every year there are Murray Halberg dinners and special charity nights. I've been out there to do two for him, and no-one in the world could refuse to do the same. He's quiet, he smiles and talks, and people make millions of dollars for the Trust just because he wants little or nothing for himself. At sixty-five, having brought up his family, he still works as a sales assistant in the same ironmonger's shop in Auckland.

We all need heroes, and Murray is a great hero of mine because he represents the good that sport can do. Having been a great athlete, he has spent the rest of his life in a very simple, ordinary way, not expecting any luxury, and every day lifting the gloom of the world for some unlucky kids.

9

'And a jolly good way, too'

Oddly enough I played my first and last games of senior representative rugby for the Barbarians. The first was in the Mobbs Memorial match at Goldington Road, Bedford, in February 1951, the month before I won my first Welsh cap. The other couldn't have been more different in climate or context. It was at Ellis Park, Johannesburg, on 24 May 1958, when we wound up our tour of South Africa with a match against Combined Transvaal. And in the years between, playing for the Barbarians, or against them for Cardiff over the Easter weekend, touring with them or appearing in their farewell matches for visiting tourists, they gave me many of the most rewarding hours I spent in rugby.

It must have been Bleddyn Williams who first told the Barbarians about me. They didn't go in for formal selection committees meeting round a table; they arranged it all by post and telephone. And when they introduced new players into their teams, they went on the recommendation of older members who knew the style of person they wanted. Bleddyn was certainly an established Barbarian, and the idea of picking me against the East Midlands at Bedford must have come from him. Another Cardiff player, the prop, Cliff Davies, was also picked for the

first time that day. I can remember practically every detail of
it. Cliff left Kenfig Hill on the N&C Express, and I left the
Rhondda on the double-decker bus, and we met in Cardiff
station at twenty to eight on the morning of the game. We
bought our third-class tickets, and took the eight o'clock train
together to London. With a bit more difficulty we found our
way across London to St Pancras station; taxis were unheard
of in those days, at least they were by us. At Bedford we asked
the way to the rugby ground, walked a mile or so to get there,
found the visitors' dressing room and introduced ourselves.

Nearly all the other players were complete strangers. In fact
the only one I'd ever talked to, and that was just in passing,
was the East Midlands captain, Don White; he had played
in the back row for Northampton at the Arms Park. It was
like moving up to a new school: the same unfamiliarity and
stiffness. Our captain, Philip Moore, who was a member of
the Blackheath back row and had just won his only England
cap, greeted me like a headmaster: 'Hello, young Morgan, how
are you?' And there was a lot of that sort of thing; we were on
very polite terms. Later of course that formality broke down,
and much later still, when I was Head of Outside Broadcasts
at BBC Television, I found myself working with Philip. He had
become the Queen's private secretary and so a key figure in any
arrangements to broadcast royal events.

Still, the game went pretty well. In the centre I had Noel
Henderson from Ireland, and my scrum-half was Gordon
Rimmer of Waterloo. We'd never met, but it didn't matter
because we were playing for the Barbarians, and if there was
any misunderstanding between us, it was all in the game. You
had to make the odd mistake to achieve anything at all; that was
the Barbarian philosophy. Don White, a terrific wing-forward,
knocked me around a bit that day, I seem to remember. He
was a hard nut, rough and tough – some would say too rough
occasionally – but he also thought more technically about the
game in the 'fifties than anybody I've ever met since. He scored
a try, but since Bill Mackay, our Irish back-row forward, scored

a couple, we won 9–5. Afterwards, Cliff and I had just about enough money to buy a badge and a tie each. The ties we put on immediately, the badges we slipped into our pockets to take home to put on our blazers one of these days.

After a meal, we walked back to the station, got to London about 9.20 at night, spent the half-hour up to ten o'clock closing time in a pub near Paddington, and caught the midnight train home. We shared the carriage with a Women's Institute outing on its way back to Wales, and chatted with them until we got to Cardiff at about 4.20 am. Nothing moved at that time of day, of course, so we sat waiting in the Cardiff bus station for the first buses to leave, and I got to Top Trebanog Road with the milk. It sounds hard going, but you didn't think anything of it. It was a trip. I was twenty, and I'd never dreamt I'd ever play for the Barbarians.

And there it was. I felt I had been recognised in British rugby, even if I hadn't yet been recognised in Wales. And I know many players who felt that being picked for the Barbarians was just as important as being capped by their country. For one or two it mattered even more. On Sunday mornings I take my young grandson, Jack – Catherine's son – to play rugby at London Welsh. He may go off the game later, which wouldn't trouble me at all. But he loves it now, and if he does go on improving it would give me more pleasure to think of him playing for the Barbarians than for any other team I can think of.

It isn't easy to explain exactly what it is that makes the Barbarians so special. It's a mixture of views and values. The club is over a century old, and to me part of its romance is that it was thought up spontaneously over a pint of porter and a plate of oysters at a time when there were trams in the street and the cotton mills were booming. There's more than a touch of the Pickwick Club and 'Three Men in a Boat' about it. Again, some of the world's most celebrated rugby players have felt honoured to turn out for it. And the great touring sides from the southern hemisphere have felt equally honoured to play against it. Yet for all that, it is only a casual, touring club with no fixed place

of abode and no official status beyond being affiliated to the
Rugby Football Union. Despite its humble beginnings, I found
it could be surprisingly autocratic in manner. Jack Haigh-Smith,
the then Hon. Sec., used to send you a rather curt note which
began, 'Dear Morgan, You have been asked if you could play
at Bedford . . .' or wherever, on a certain date. And in those
days you made pretty sure you would be available. The club
could take against those who didn't fit in with their plans, or
with their ideas of acceptable behaviour on the field and in the
hosts' clubhouse. That could be off-putting at times, but I came
to love the Barbarians for their other qualities, in particular for
their insistence on playing a recklessly attacking game, even if
it cost defeat – not that winning or losing meant a great deal to
them. It was the kind of rugby I enjoyed, and, as you discovered
when you got to know them, enjoyment and entertainment were
what they were promoting. I just hope that spirit can be kept
alive even in an otherwise professional game.

I looked forward to the Barbarians' Welsh tour at Easter more
than anything in the year. They played Penarth on Good Friday,
Cardiff on Saturday, and golf over the Penarth course on the
Sunday; that was for recreation after plenty to drink on Saturday
night. Then it was Swansea on Easter Monday, and Newport,
Tuesday. I would sometimes be a member of the touring party,
but even if I wasn't I'd be playing against them for Cardiff. This
was always a joyful event with crowds of anything up to 35,000
attracted by the chance to see the most skilful internationals of
the day playing in the open Barbarian style. Afterwards some of
us would join the drinking, singing and late-night conversation
at the Esplanade Hotel in Penarth, which was their centre for
the weekend. The following morning we would play golf with
them and stay on for the very good lunch they served at the
clubhouse. The annual Barbarian matches against the East
Midlands and Leicester were comparatively short in-and-out
affairs, but the Easter tour was treated as an end-of-season
holiday in which the rugby was keen but all the rest was for
fun. At the end of it you had got to know some of the other

players really well. I particularly think of two lock-forwards, 'Squire' Wilkins of England and Tom Reid of Ireland, whom I met on the Barbarians' Easter tour and who remained friends for life.

Although the Easter tour of Wales dates back to the turn of the century, the idea of the Barbarians providing a send-off for visiting tourists came up only in 1948. The Australians had been over – the Third Wallabies as they were known – and were keen to travel home by way of Canada so that they could play some exhibition matches in British Columbia. Unfortunately, they couldn't afford it. So to help raise the money the four Home Unions invited the Barbarians to play an additional game against the tourists at Cardiff, where they'd be sure of a full house. The Barbarians were a bit dubious about it. They wanted to remain themselves and not be mistaken for a semi-official British Isles team, but they finally accepted, and the game was played on the last day of January that year. I went to watch it as a seventeen-year-old schoolboy. The Barbarians won 9–6 with a flourish of three exciting tries, and the event was so popular, largely because the Barbarians hadn't compromised their principles, that a farewell match against them was written into the programme of all future major tours. Micky Steele-Bodger was in the back row on that first occasion, and ever since has carried the flag for Barbarian principles in rugby.

Haydn Tanner and Tommy Kemp, a classical, straight-running English stand-off, were the halves in 1948. Four years later, in the last match of the Fourth Springboks' tour, it was Rex Willis and myself. It brought a very different result. We got beaten 17–3 by what I still consider the best touring team that I have ever seen or played against. The spirit of the game was terrific – unbelievably hard and tough, because although we wanted to play traditional Barbarian rugby, we wanted just as badly to beat South Africa. And they were just as anxious to whack us. We did hold the lead at the start for W.I.D. Elliot, the Scottish back-row forward, sprang on a loose ball bobbling about on the Springboks' line to score the opening try. Doug was a sheep farmer, and a month later, when I played against him in an international for the first time, he picked me up in his arms as if he had a sheep there, squeezed until I was gasping for breath and then dropped me on the ground. 'Now you know what the game's about, son.' But we weren't the only side with rugged back-row players. The Springboks had Hennie Muller, Stephen Fry and Basie Van Wyk, and I was constantly aware of those last two bearing down on me. It was a hard introduction to the occasion, but I was lucky enough also to be picked by the Barbarians for the other two tourist matches which were played in my time, against New Zealand in February 1954 and the Fourth Wallabies four years later, our only victory.

The All Blacks game I talked about in Chapter 8. It was another hard game, and although it was a little disappointing to lose 19–5, one mustn't be greedy; I'd already played against them in two winning sides, Cardiff and Wales. When I'd watched the first of these Barbarian fixtures from the terraces, Nick Shehadie had been propping for Australia. In the third and last I played in, Nick, now thirty and the most-capped Wallaby, was invited to swap sides for the afternoon and play for the Barbarians. I was captain of the team that day, and I'll never forget him coming into the dressing room, sitting down beside me, taking out three pairs of rugby boots and putting them under the table. 'What have you got all those for, Nick?' I asked him. He said, 'They tell me they fill the bastards here, so I brought three pairs!' Exchanges like that in the dressing room conjure up the Barbarians for me far more vividly even than the movements on the field. I knew that this was the last time I'd run out at the Arms Park in one of these matches, wearing the Barbarians' distinctive black-and-white jersey and, by custom, one's own national or club stockings, which always made our legs look pretty exotic. But what made up for it was knowing that I had the Barbarians' tour of South Africa to look forward to at the end of the season.

This would be my second Barbarian tour abroad. In 1957 I had gone to Canada on the first they had ever organised. Although there were hundreds of ex-pats and college students playing rugby over there, the game was nothing like as well established as it is now. The enthusiasts were longing to watch and to play against genuine Home Countries internationals, and the Barbarian hierarchy saw us as spreading the rugby gospel, though I can't pretend that we always behaved as missionaries should.

We no sooner got to Toronto than we were whisked onto a television programme called 'Tabloid'. We were standing around on the set, idly watching carpenters hammer together a glassless shop window frame, when this little producer with bow tie and long cigar told us: 'OK, you guys, we want you outside the window, and when we give you the signal we'd like you to wave.' At that point a commentator with a microphone in his hand, looking a bit like Eamonn Andrews, addressed the cameras, 'Ladies and gentlemen, meet the Barbs. These are the Barbarian football team, who have come here to show us how to play the game of rugby football. Here we find them window shopping in the streets of Toronto.' At that we had to wave, and we saw that inside the window now there were these beautiful girls modelling dresses. And as he announced, 'These are the Barbarians . . .' Tom Reid of Limerick stuck his arm in where the glass should have been, patted one of the girls on the bottom, and said, 'Jaysus lads, what a great bird.' The commentator went on, '. . . Barbarians – they sure are barbarians!'

On a later visit to the studios they began interviewing players individually, one of them, Ron Jacobs of Northampton, a tremendous front row and a very solid, laconic character. 'And who are you?' the interviewer asked. 'Ron Jacobs.' 'And where are you from, Mr Jacobs?' 'Northampton.' And the interviewer, clutching desperately for any straw, said, 'Boy, that sure must be some local derby between you and Southampton.' Ron wasn't famous for his sense of humour, and his face didn't change. 'Southampton,' he said flatly, 'are a second-class club.' The interviewer didn't get much change out of some of the others either. He came across to one of our threequarters, Gareth Griffiths: 'And where are you from?' 'W-W-Wales.' 'So what do you think of our country?' And Gareth said, 'B-b-beautiful.' And that was it. Our relationship with the media was generally one of mutual incomprehension. I remember verbatim parts of one running commentary on radio which never even began to catch up with the action: 'We're now on the 25-yard stripe and the ball comes out to O'Reilly. He's red-haired, he's six foot two tall, and he's got long white legs, and . . . now the score is 15–nil.' No mention of how the try was scored. Then the commentator would start describing players again and break off to say, 'The score's now 22–nil.' The nearest he ever got to describing a try by Tony was, 'Boy, oh boy, this sure is a bang-up ball game.'

We were in Canada for about three weeks and played six games, winning them all and scoring just about ten points for every one that was scored against us. That makes it sound easier than it was. In fact, although losing any game would have been embarrassing, winning it wasn't our only aim. We were there to demonstrate, as far as we could, how skilful, thrilling and enjoyable rugby could be. All the same the strength of the opposition varied a great deal. We began in Ontario with wins of 47–3 and 52–0, enormous scores when you think that a try then was worth only three points. But when we moved west to British Columbia we had only one victory on that scale. The other two games we won by just fourteen and thirteen points. The difference, I think, was that in the east we mainly met recent immigrants who had played the game in Britain but not to a very high level, or they were rusty, or whatever. In the east you could afford to have a drink before a game, it didn't matter twopence. In fact after a mayor's party at lunchtime, one of our scrum-halves went to put the ball in the scrum and fell in after it. But on the west coast we were up against natives with little experience of rugby but hardened by a school and college background in Canadian football. It was in Vancouver that Ron Jacobs was tackled out of the tour.

We were lined up for the British Columbia kick-off, and the ball was in the air and coming straight into my hands when I was knocked out of the way and a Northampton voice said,

'My ball.' It was Ron. He caught the ball, brought his leg up in order to put it down to make a mark, when a fellow called Ron Hunt who played fly-half for the Canadian side – he's now teaching in the Princess of Wales grammar school in Vancouver – came in and tackled our Ron. I've never seen anything like it. In hitting his knee, he knocked Ron's hip out. And the Badger, as we called him, was lying on the floor squealing like a pig. It must have been agony. But the only attention we could give him was to bring duckboards from the side of the pitch and carry him off. So ended his visit to Canada.

Our manager on the tour was Brigadier H.L. Glyn Hughes of Blackheath and England. Hughie or Glyn – but only if you had known him long enough – had become the fourth president of the Barbarians two years before. He was a remarkable man, a much decorated army medical officer who was the first doctor into the Belsen concentration camp, a hospital administrator, an honorary physician to the Queen, an active and sometimes impatient leader, and a Barbarian to his finger-tips. He revelled in the freedom of the club's approach to rugby and the companionship of the tour, and was extremely loyal to his team. One night we'd all had a few drinks and become a bit raucous and somebody at the hotel had complained to the police. They arrived in force, in plain clothes and uniform, and started asking hard questions. Hughie took exception to that. He stood on the stairs and in that marvellous English way of his said, 'How dare you speak to my boys like that!' These detectives wanted to take him in and question him, and I had to step in and calm things down. It was really no more than noisy high spirits, but Hughie was so protective of us all and wanted the police to know that he was in charge. When we met in later years he often used to talk about the night I saved him from jail.

The players appreciated that and had a lot of respect for him. When we reached Victoria on Vancouver Island, we were billeted in a camp which had been used to house athletes at the 1954 Commonwealth Games. It had been empty for some time and was very spartan. We slept in bunk beds in dormitories, and had to go outside to the washrooms and lavatories as if we were back in school. Tom Reid had been horrified when he reached Canada to find that you couldn't go out to the pub for a drink; you had to buy what you wanted from a liquor store and take it back to your hotel. He didn't like this at all, and he didn't like the camp either, though not for personal reasons. 'Now I don't mind for meself,' he said, 'because I'm an ordinary Irish guy from Limerick. But I think it's disgusting that we're living in these conditions, especially for a man like Glyn Hughes, who is a great, distinguished man. It's not fair on him.' At the end of the tour the boys clubbed together and bought Glyn a small clock. After he died in 1973 his wife telephoned to tell me that Glyn had wanted me to be given that clock. I have it by my bedside still.

The Canadian hospitality was unbelievable. We were given everything, including cars to drive around in. But the social highspot of the tour was undoubtedly Tony O'Reilly's twenty-first birthday party held at the West Vancouver home of Edward Gibson, a wealthy businessman. Tony had been only eighteen when I first played against him in Ireland and then alongside him on the Lions' tour of South Africa that summer. Now he was only just coming of age, though mentally he seemed far more mature. He knew so much, was so well read; in conversations after the match he'd regale you with wonderful tales from Irish mythology. You somehow knew that he was going to be something remarkable. And so it proved: becoming chief executive of the Heinz Corporation (and the Americans don't employ bums) and buying newspapers on his own account, amassing academic honours as well as great wealth. It was all there at the time. He used to tell me that he always allowed the opposition to reveal itself to him before he revealed himself to them; that was his philosophy in business as in sport. In contrast to that sophistication, there was still something boyish about him. He was famous for losing his keys and leaving his camera at airports. Endlessly funny in conversation, a terrific piano-player, a singer, he seemed to enjoy every second of the tour. He was full of charm and wonderful company, and even if he hadn't been an international rugby player, I'm sure he'd have stood out just the same.

Of Tony's twenty-first I only remember that Andy Mulligan ended up in the swimming pool in his new velvet jacket, and that the evening closed appropriately with an improbable touch of Irish romance. We arrived back at the hotel, where three of us – Tony, Andy and myself – occupied the bedrooms of one massive suite, while Tom Reid, who had left the party before us, had a pull-down bed in our living room. The key wasn't at reception so we went up and hammered on the door which suddenly opened slightly. There was Tom and, as O'Reilly always said, 'All he had on were his glasses and a pair of parish priest's socks.' Tom said, 'I'm not coming back to England with you fellows, I'm in love.' And Tom never did come back, except on visits. He stayed in Canada, worked as a lumberjack to pay his way through college, got his degree, married and did well.

Tom represented for me what Cliff Davies did in Wales, something strongly individual, dependable, unspoilt. If he was standing in a room at the Lord Mayor's party or any big reception, you only had to say, 'Come on Tom, let's have a song.' You'd play three chords on the piano, and on the spot he'd sing 'September Song'. And because he had a beautiful voice, and could easily have had a stage career in musicals, the people there would stop and listen and think differently of the team. Singing is one of the great traditions of rugby – real singing, not just the bawling of so-called rugby songs – and under Glyn the Barbarians kept it alive. In the same way he insisted that we should represent ourselves and our country by playing with adventure, which was one of his great words. By that he didn't mean stupidity, but style and dash, giving it an almost inspirational quality. And that's what kept this amusing, unlikely collection of people together as they entertained the spectators and did an awful lot of good for rugby in Canada.

Another member of the party whom I greatly admired was Eric Evans, the first captain of England to take an assortment of shire farmers, Cornish miners, young men in the City, policemen and Oxbridge students – the kind of mix, in fact, that we were used to in Wales – and by force of character get them to talk and play together. Hookers are a bit different from the rest of us, anyway, but Eric was exceptional; he trained with Manchester United, for one thing, which, in the eyes of the rugby establishment, was better than training with St Helens, but only just. He thought he could sing; he always sang 'This Is The Garden Of Eden', and he was always out of tune. But he was a noisy, lovely, lovable Lancastrian, who inspired teams to play for him. I admired his spirit more than I can say, and the marvellous work he did later with handicapped children in the north, enabling them to go boating on the canals. When he died his ashes were scattered at Twickenham. There were just about half-a-dozen of us there, including his wife who was in a wheelchair, and his daughter. We went first to the half-way line, but just for something to say I remarked to the secretary of Lancashire, 'I don't think this is the place to do it, because Eric never was on the half-way line, he was always on the 25, waiting for kick-off.' He agreed, so we moved there but as he took a handful of these ashes, and began to cast them over the ground, the wind blew them back. The next thing, we were all covered in ash. There was an awkward sort of silence, and stupidly I said, 'Eric never liked playing against the wind did he?' There was laughter, thank heavens, for it was typically Eric. Those are memories that make me feel lucky to have played rugby.

My other Barbarians tour, in 1958, was to South Africa, where I had been with the Lions three years before. I had already played my last international for Wales and my last club match with Cardiff. Although some newspapers insisted that I would change my mind, I was even more convinced that I had left the stage for good. South Africa was to be simply a curtain call.

Where the Lions programme had been spread over four months, the Barbarians were playing just five matches, all against provincial sides in the Transvaal and Western Province, with an encore in East Africa. The first was on 10 May and the schedule was completed within the same month. There was another big difference. On the Lions tour we had training sessions under Jeff Butterfield and we were out there to win. It was important to us. The Barbarians would also have said we were there to win, but on the other hand it didn't matter all that much if we lost, as long as there were three tries or three movements which would last in people's memories. The pressures weren't there. We trained a little and we had a few plans in mind, but our moves didn't have that seriousness which can quite often lessen your impact as a team.

The Barbarian party was not far short of Lions standard. O'Reilly and Mulligan were there again, along with Malcolm Thomas and Arthur Smith in the backs; and we had a good pack, including Ron Jacobs, none the worse for his Canadian caper. Yet we won only one of our five matches in South Africa itself – against Northern Transvaal in Pretoria – and as luck had it, I didn't play that time. Gordon Waddell was at stand-off. All the same we had five close, exciting matches which made it all worthwhile. We lost one match by a single point, another by two points, and our only 'bad' defeat was by eight points. Our opening match against Transvaal at Ellis Park we drew 17–17, and that didn't do us justice. We had a brilliant move from our own 25 at the end of which O'Reilly crossed the line in the corner but fell over a photographer who had strayed into the in-goal area to get his picture. O'Reilly picked himself up and still had time to run round and put the ball down under the posts, but the referee awarded the try back at the corner where Tony had been baulked. The try levelled the scores, but the conversion failed; if it had been taken from in front of the goal the two points would have given us a win.

We played our last game in South Africa, which was also my last official game in senior rugby, against Combined Transvaal at Ellis Park on 24 May 1958. I was asked to captain the team. As far as I could see, the ground hadn't been altered since I had been there with the Lions. There was still just the one grandstand, with terraces for the rest of the spectators, and that long flight of steps which the teams had to trot down to reach the field under the eyes of everybody. As captain I led the team down carrying the ball, and as I got onto the pitch I looked round to see who to pass to. There was nobody there. The other players had waited at the top of the steps, and I found myself alone on the field while the loudspeakers announced that this was my last game. I didn't know what to do with myself, so I did something which, because of Ned Gribble's influence, I'd never done in all my games with Wales and Cardiff. Never done except in my dreams. I dropped a goal, whack and over. I can just imagine what would have happened if I had done that during the match – the frowns from the Barbarians in the grandstand: 'What do you think you're playing at, laddie?' But at least I'd got it out of my system, and once I had, the team came out.

For my last game, I couldn't have chosen better, I think, than to play with the Barbarians, a privilege in itself; to play at one of the world's great rugby grounds; and to play not in front of your own people, but in front of the South Africans. Touring showed me that, while it's all very well to be good in front of your own, you've really got to prove away from your own soil that you can play a bit. I had always loved playing with the sun on my back, and on the point of retirement I think I played some of my best rugby. There was something special about that trip . . . as there is about the Barbarian club itself. In a film to celebrate the centenary of the club – superbly produced by my close friend Bob Abrahams, who had already made 'The Runners' and recently completed a film on the Olympic triple jumper, Jonathan Edwards – these special qualities stood out like a beacon. The Abrahams touch, when he laid the music from 'The Magnificent Seven' over pictures of the seven Barbarians involved in that often re-played Gareth Edwards try scored against the New Zealanders at Cardiff in 1973, will forever represent for me everything that is good in the game.

I've said that the Ellis Park game was my farewell, and so it was. When the final whistle blew, I retired – in order to spend more time on making a living. I went on playing charity and benefit games, but I never felt tempted to take up serious rugby again. By chance, though, I did play one more game of senior rugby. I was going up to London to introduce the St David's Day Festival at the Albert Hall, and when I got on the train at Cardiff I found that the Llanelli rugby team were already aboard. They were on their way to play Wasps that afternoon but, unfortunately, Carwyn James had missed the train. Could I take his place? Impossible. I had to rehearse that afternoon. But of course I weakened. I went to ask the organisers' permission to be absent for a couple of hours and took a taxi out to Sudbury. After the game, which incidentally we lost, they gave me a scarlet Llanelli jersey and two pounds. It didn't cover the cost of the taxi, but technically, I suppose, it made me a professional long before it became the fashion. It also made me a Sospan, which is no light matter.

10

Spoken words

While I was in South Africa with the Barbarians, I suppose I thought mostly about the rugby and the incidental fun of the tour. But I was still excited by that chance meeting with Hywel Davies on the night of my last international, and his apparent offer of a job at the BBC. I knew, and everybody else knew, that I was on the point of retiring from the game, so it kept coming up in conversation and interviews. And although Hywel's offer was too vague to tell others about, it was never far from my mind. When I got back to Wales after two and a half months I found a letter from him in my mother's house asking me to come and see him at his office in two days' time. This was a Saturday, and when I turned up at half-past eleven in the morning his first question was, 'Do you want a coffee or a gin and tonic?' I said, 'I'll have a gin and tonic, if you like.' Then after another twenty minutes of questions and chat, Hywel said, 'Ten weeks next Monday night, we'll be doing the first sports programme on television from Wales. I want you to introduce it, and produce it. Can you do it?' And being totally ignorant of television, which I'd never really seen, I said, 'Yes.' Which is how I came to join the BBC in Cardiff. It wasn't so casual on Hywel's part. He'd obviously been planning for some time to bring me into the BBC to do something, but until recently I don't think he'd known exactly what.

I'd worked for the BBC an awful lot since I began playing international rugby, and my fascination with broadcasting went back much further than that. Back, in fact, to the excitement of the concerts which Tommy Tumble used to present at the Urdd Gobaith Cymru holiday camps in Llangranog, West Wales. I wanted to be like Tommy and command an audience. And I was enough of a performer at the time to take fairly easily to broadcasting a few years later. The first BBC interview I did was for Welsh radio on the Friday before my first cap in 1951. I had to leave the practice to go up to the studio because there were no portable recorders in those days. What they had were enormous. As far as I remember, I talked about looking forward to the game, and what a thrill it was to be picked, how I hadn't known about it until the Monday night, and since then hadn't had a chance to breathe. That was why I wasn't anxious about it. All the obvious things. A year later, when I told the story on air about my father losing his teeth at Lansdowne Road, I'd begun to pick up a few hints on broadcasting. I was so attracted to it that I used to pop into the Cardiff studio at times when I was pretty sure that certain people would be sitting in the canteen. I had got to know Alun Williams quite well and Hywel Davies a little, but I was welcome to listen to them talking about the programmes they had just finished or were about to do. 'That was good, that surprised people, that made them think,' Hywel would say. Once, I remember, he asked the question, 'What is Welshness?' And then he answered it himself: 'It's like a wine you can never chill, it's a welcome you can never outstay, it's about friendliness and gregariousness, and a sense of fun, and much much more.' And he ended, 'Whenever people gather together who tell tales, breathe fire, make intricate poetry, define the rights of man, sing the *Messiah* or score six tries for Wales, there'll be somebody in that company to remind them all of Merlin, the *Mabinogion*, the Act of Union, Thomas Jefferson and the Royal National Eisteddfod.' This studied eloquence was a characteristic of his. Later he asked another question: 'Isn't this man's face worth watching? Isn't his attitude worth considering? And isn't his heart worth sounding?' He went on talking along these lines, about programmes and attitudes and language, every time you saw him because he believed that Welshness was about fervour. It was heady stuff for a boy scarcely out of his teens, but it was part of my broadcasting education. I was lucky that this was such a fertile period for good conversation.

After Cardiff, then Wales, beat the All Blacks in 1953, the BBC asked the players into the studio for coffee, soft drinks and sandwiches, and then presented each of us with a record, an acetate disc, of the commentary on the matches. And during the presentation Hywel Davies introduced one of his pet themes, 'Everything should be worth while.' Worthwhileness wasn't a word he'd created, but he insisted that either something was worth doing, or it shouldn't be done at all. And I suppose that stayed with me when I was compiling my own programmes later.

I'm eternally grateful for that time when I played rugby, did a few interviews, and on the strength of that I could use the BBC canteen like a social club and listen to these extraordinary people. You never knew who you would meet there. Heber Jenkins, head of administration and a brilliant talker, would be sitting alone with only the *Sporting Life* spread out before him like a tablecloth. The novelist, Gwyn Thomas, was often around; he used to write and read these wonderful stories of Rhondda life. And Saunders Lewis, who wrote only in Welsh and went to prison for the cause of Welsh independence. You'd meet these people, listen to their programmes, talk with producers. And the strange thing was, because you had played rugby for Wales, they all seemed to want to talk with you as well. It was encouraging and made you feel you had something to offer in return.

It's staggering how when you say something different, like telling that story of my father's false teeth, it sticks in people's minds and they ask you back. Straight after the successful Lions tour in 1955 I spent a Saturday in the company of G.V.

Wynne-Jones, the Welsh rugby commentator whom everyone knew as Geevers. We left Cardiff for London on the early morning train to do a conversation piece on 'Sports Parade' at 12.30. Then Geevers took me to a restaurant in Soho called L'Escargot. I'd never eaten snails in my life, and I didn't know how to use the little tongs you hold them with. I didn't know how to do anything, I was like a little boy up from the country – you know, brown shoes and cloth cap. But I lapped up every new experience.

In the afternoon we went to do something for the World Service. Then in the evening it was 'Sports Report'. I remember walking into the little room and meeting J.L. Manning, an outstanding investigative journalist of the day. The Duke of Norfolk was there, and with him the Arsenal player, Bernard Joy. You were in good company. People like that had a great impact on me. On a later programme I listened to John Arlott making a two-minute contribution with just three words to jog his memory. These were written down on the back of his packet of Passing Cloud. He made his points brilliantly, and finished precisely on cue. 'Sports Report', which has influenced me in all my working life in broadcasting, was in effect the Sunday back pages produced on the Saturday night. By six o'clock everything was wrapped up, and yet very few stories were ever missed. It was a totally different experience for me. Playing rugby was one thing, but mixing with all these people you'd read or heard about or listened to on the wireless, that was thrilling in another way.

After that I was asked to be a panellist on a Welsh BBC programme called 'Sporting Call', again with G.V. Wynne-Jones. This particular night it was broadcast from Sully Hospital with a panel of famous names – that stylish England cricketer, Tom Graveney, whose off-drives were etched on your mind if you'd ever seen him play; John Snagge, the voice of the Boat Race, who sat on the platform in his Leander cap, which the audience loved; and as special guest, Jimmy Wilde, perhaps the greatest boxer we've produced in South Wales. To be on the same programme as those three! But there was something sad about Jimmy's contribution. He wore his Lonsdale belt under his coat that night, and seemed rather lost. Before the programme, he'd asked Geevers: 'What are you going to ask me, Mr Jones?' 'Oh, I'll just ask where you had your first fight, and how much you got for it,' said Geevers. 'Little things like that.' 'No problem,' Jimmy said. Then we got to the moment for Geevers's introduction: 'And now our guest of honour, the Ghost with a Hammer in his Hand, the greatest fighter pound for pound the world has ever seen, ladies and gentlemen, Jimmy Wilde!' On he came, but before Geevers could ask him a question, Jimmy put his mouth to the microphone and said, 'Porth, and three-and-sixpence.'

If I learned a lot from Geevers, I picked up even more from working with Alun Williams, a dapper, precise and highly knowledgeable man who always used to say, 'My name isn't Alan, it's Alun; it rhymes with gin and sin.' He could turn his mind to anything, like nearly all the commentators in that post-war period. For instance, Stewart Macpherson from Canada who could cover boxing, football and the Boat Race with equal understanding; or John Arlott, whose voice commentating from cricket grounds was as familiar as the sound of a lawnmower on a summer's day, but who was also an expert on poetry, politics, cut glass, book collecting and wine. Rex Alston and E.W. Swanton had similarly broad interests. Alun was exactly like them, equally at home doing a football or a rugby commentary or playing a piano to an audience. He was bilingual, with a beautiful command of the Welsh and English languages. He also confirmed for me what I had always wanted to believe, that my life ought to be about taking chances, having a go.

It was some years later that I became a presenter in my own right. That was in a quiz programme in which a team from South Wales competed against one from the north, with Alun Williams as questionmaster at one club, and me at the other. I was in North Wales on the first night, and I remember that Alun, at the other end of the line, decided to give me a lesson in

English. At one point I said something like, 'So that's fourteen, thirteen and twelve points. So let's have a check on this. We'll have the total score off Dewi Williams.' At which I heard Alun say from the other end, 'No, we'll have the score *from* Dewi. You take a cup *off* a table.' It wasn't a voice in my ear, it was over the air, and I thought, my God, don't they ever miss a chance to correct you? But Alun was a stickler. He hated people saying 'different to' – it was 'different from'. And now when I hear a television announcer say, 'No play today due to rain,' I can hear Alun Williams in my mind correcting them: 'It's not due, it's owing to rain, because only a train is due.' This may be pedantic but I agreed with him that it was important to try and get the grammar right.

Not that Alun was politically correct by modern standards. I remember that he had a regular routine for warming up the audience. He'd begin, 'We'll be on the air in a couple of minutes, so don't put the microphone down too hard on the table or you're liable to deafen millions.' Then he'd ask, 'Cliff, who's the announcer today on BBC Wales, is it that blonde girl?' I'd reply, 'I honestly don't know, Alun.' And he'd say, 'Oh, I hope it is, I like blondes, they get dirty quicker.' The audience used to laugh each week, and it seemed harmless to us, but if you said that today there'd be a walk-out at the BBC.

Those events all belong to the days before I settled down as a member of the BBC staff. I didn't make much money out of broadcasting, but that was something that didn't interest me. Unlike the players of today, we never had mortgages, couldn't even have spelt the word. Nor did we understand what you had to do to bring up a family. Perhaps one thing I regret is that I didn't know then that to protect yourself you have to know your own worth. I don't mean make a killing, just ensure that you're not being exploited. A big weakness of mine was that I wanted to be liked, which led me to do things for nothing. And for the most part people don't respect you for that. The best they'll say is, 'Well, he wasn't bad.' If you charged £1,000 for it, they'd think you were brilliant.

Mind, I had got a pretty good day job after returning from the Lions' South African tour in 1955. I stayed with George Elliot's for what was left of the year, and then, still as a salesman, I joined A. Gallenkamp & Company, who made laboratory equipment and machinery for schools, universities, research establishments and industries of all kinds. Its sales director was H.B. Toft, a former England hooker and science teacher, who combined his daily work with writing erudite articles and reports on rugby for the *Observer*. I had a lot of respect for him as a boss, and working for him paid around 2.5 per cent on sales and provided a large car. I had just about everything except contentment with my lot. At the back of my mind I felt that I wasn't meant to be a salesman. And I wondered whether I was doing anything creative that would be worthwhile in the end. So when in 1960 Hywel Davies offered me this television sports programme and a title he had plucked out of the air, BBC Sports Organiser in Wales, I accepted at once. I gave up Gallenkamp, took a drop in pay and sent back the company car.

At the BBC, with Hywel's encouragement, I tried to create a new style of Saturday-night sports programme on radio called 'Going Round the World'. Hywel said he wanted a series of complementary programmes to run for four weeks. So I organised a sports forum in which we visited people at home through a world-wide hook-up – Jack Dempsey in New York, Jack Peterson in Cardiff, Danie Craven in Stellenbosch. I wanted the programmes to be big and risky. In the same period I was also introducing the first Welsh TV sports programme to be shot in a studio, though one so small that it later became the paint shop. The first guests were Max Rawlings, a football commentator, and my old employer, H.B. Toft. And because there were two interviewees and room for only one camera (which funnily enough was pushed in and out by an Oxford student, David Parry-Jones, who was working through his holiday) we could fit in only two chairs. I found a cement bag, and so introduced my first programme sitting on that and was shot only from the waist up.

Straight after the programme came off the air, about 10.15 pm or whatever, I was told that there was a telephone call for me. I thought it must be my mother to say that my shirt had looked scruffy, but it was a man's voice which said, 'Dark, remorseless Welshman, I must have words with you.' I said, 'Who the hell is that?' He said, 'Gilbert here, Gilbert Harding. I'm down at the Angel.' He'd done a programme just before ours in which he had been grilled by the Lord's Day Observance Society. He went on, 'Come down to my suite, your dear friend Hywel Davies is here.' I rang home first to say I wouldn't be coming straight back. Then I went to the Angel where Gilbert was in his vest, and holding a large bottle of perfumed watery stuff to cool himself down on this hot night. He was telling a story to Hywel and some others who were there. 'I had them all in my flat, all the brains, Lady Vi, Kelly, all there in Brighton,' he was saying. 'I was in the middle of a very dramatic story, and I paused just for effect. And in the middle of that pause there was a Polish gentleman, who had frills on his cuffs and bracelets that jingled and jangled like a gypsy, and he had manufactured furniture before the war in Poland. And in the middle of my pause he had the audacity to ask, "I thay Gilbert, where is your lav?" And I turned upon him and I attacked him and said, "Be silent, you ignorant Polish cabinet maker, contain your urine, can't you recognise a dramatic pause when you hear one?" And the poor little devil said, "Oh yes, Gilbert, but I must pee in your pause!"'

It's not the sort of story you'd often have heard in Trebanog or the Cardiff rugby club, but on that note ended my first night on television. People say about Gilbert that he was hard and rude and malicious, but every year until he died he sent a birthday present to my daughter Catherine, who was two at this time, and he was always very decent to me.

You didn't get rich working for the BBC. While I was in Cardiff I was on what they called the B1 minus scale, which was about £520 a year – enough to live on but no more. But the beauty of working in that environment, which spread across radio and television, was that Wales was a very fertile BBC region where great drama and musical programmes were created. And any time that, say, 'Songs of Praise' came to Wales, I was lucky enough to have some role in it. I remember introducing one in the church at Briton Ferry, looking out towards the sea, and another from the Lido at Aberavon. I just felt good doing them, because I loved music, loved the hymns and knew them backwards.

I was fortunate, too, to be asked by Hywel to do various series, one of them being a four-parter, 'People who Sing'. This was when the 'Tonight' television programme from London went off the air for its summer break, and each of the five BBC regions was asked to fill in with one programme a week for four weeks. 'People who Sing' centred on four choirs: Treorchy, Morriston, Pendyrus and Rhosllanerchrugog. The last is a village between Wrexham and Ruabon where something happened that you don't easily forget. We'd been recording there for two days, and after working from very early in the morning in the pit, we were sitting in a churchyard eating a packed lunch – the camera crew, the producer and me – when a man walked through leading a little white Scottie. We were nibbling away and he would probably have passed on except that he looked at me and said, 'Cliff Morgan?' 'Yes, how are you?' I said, and we started talking.

Russell Walker, the cameraman, had the presence of mind to swing the camera round on this man, because he had the most beautiful voice. And without knowing whether what the man said would be of any use to us, he recorded a contribution to the programme which had a quality we could never have contrived. The man started off by talking about his life: 'I left Rhos on the day of the *Titanic* disaster. I was going abroad to seek my fortune in America, and I ended up in Canada.' He did well there and was invited to the opening of the new Toronto General Hospital. When he was young, he'd worked in the Ruabon brickyards, earning a penny a thousand for the bricks he made. 'And as I walked into the hospital, I looked down, and my feet was walking on Ruabon terracotta brick.' It brought back all his memories.

He talked about Lloyd George, and said they had all been weaned on his speeches, which were like powerful sermons which took you to heaven for a fortnight. And while he was on the ship going across to the other side of the world, he had read a collection of these speeches: 'My favourite was, "The world owes much to little nations and little men. Long legs have an advantage in retreat; the Kaiser chose his warriors from the six foot six nations. But the salvation of man came from a little nation, and if we had stood by when that wicked hand of barbarism struck Europe, our names would have been indelibly placed in the book of everlasting shame."' Then, having broadcast this during the next week, I had dozens and dozens of letters from people of all sorts, a lot of them running organisations, asking for a transcript. 'The world owes much to little nations and little men.' You suddenly realised how terribly important people's spoken words are, and these words were what the letter-writers wanted to pass on to their youngsters or their chapels or their societies.

Doing those series made me a bit more adventurous, I suppose, and more receptive when Hywel Davies sent for me one morning and said, 'I want you to go to London, there's a job going now I hear on "Grandstand". You must get that job, by any means you can, and work for Paul Fox for three years. Then you are to leave Sport and go and work for Grace Wyndham Goldie in Current Affairs for three years.' She was the woman who created the 'Tonight' programme and most of the little, hard jewels of factual BBC television in the 'fifties and 'sixties. But Hywel hadn't finished with me yet. 'Then, after sixish years in London, which will coincide with my being appointed Controller of BBC Wales, I want you to come back here as the Head of Programmes.'

Well, I went to London in 1963, though it didn't turn out quite as Hywel had anticipated. I didn't work *for* Paul Fox but *instead* of him as editor of 'Grandstand' and 'Sportsview', when he was promoted to the posh job on 'Panorama'. And afterwards I didn't go on to work in Current Affairs for Grace

Wyndham Goldie; I moved to ITV to produce the current affairs programme, 'This Week'. Meanwhile Hywel died in 1966 at the lamentably early age of forty-nine.

It was a terrible loss, not only to me, though I felt it keenly enough. Hywel was a genius in three different areas: as a performer, as a producer and highly original creator of programmes, and as an administrator, in which role he was one of the few who were capable of looking ten years ahead. He made you do the same, especially in terms of the developing technology of broadcasting.

Because Hywel died when he did, I never did go back to work on the staff in Wales. But I am not sure that I would have been right for the job. I think I would have enjoyed it for a few months, when it would have been like a Christmas party, but then I think I might have regretted it. It was by staying in London that eventually I landed – and I'm jumping ahead now to the mid-'seventies – the best job in the BBC open to anyone of my ability: Head of Television Outside Broadcasts. It was mine for eleven years. Having already travelled the world in rugby, I was able to do the same through the Olympic Games, the Commonwealth Games, the World Cup, racing, boxing, cricket. And the work wasn't just to do with sport, you had all manner of broadcasts which took place outside the BBC studios – the great royal occasions, opera, concerts, ballet, 'Mastermind'. It was a powerful job in the sense that a lot of money was spent to get things right, and it was more technically progressive because the development of television's huge potential came largely through outside broadcasts. It made big demands on the engineers' and technicians' capacity to solve problems, and so it led the advance.

But to return to 'Grandstand'. I had introduced the programme once for Paul Fox while I was still working in Wales. I was sent for one Friday evening and told I was needed next day because Alan Weeks had fallen ill. I said I had never seen it, which was true because I'd been working on my own programmes every Saturday afternoon. But Hywel said he thought I ought to go, so

I caught the sleeper to Paddington, a taxi to Lime Grove, and my first glimpse of the 'Grandstand' studio, which was unbelievably frightening. There were racing boards and results sequences and cameras and God knows what, but no autocues at that time. I was given this little script and from there on it was up to me to remember what I was supposed to be saying. In your ear, too, you got the alarming talk-back from Bryan Cowgill in the gallery. Cowgill must have been the greatest director we ever had in terms of studio work on a fast-moving, constantly changing programme. He was unbelievable. He made instant decisions which left you looking stupid and wishing you had thought of them first. He was always a great shouter, too. His 'Stand by', in a big Clitheroe accent, would frighten the life out of you. Still, I got through it, adding to my practical education.

Getting the job as editor of 'Grandstand' was alarming in a different way because at the start very few people were prepared to talk with me in London. Producers' doors on the corridor remained closed. Fortunately, I had inherited a marvellous secretary from Paul Fox, Avis Prior, who said to me, 'If I were you I'd go down and kick the doors, and say, "You're either with me or you're agin me. If you're with me, fine, if you're not, push off."' I think some of these people had been half-promised the job, and then I got it, this strange little Welshman who didn't know his way around London. I just wanted to be decent about it.

Another worry was that, because I'd had so little warning of the move, Nuala had to remain in Cardiff during my first year in London. I would go home late on the Saturday night, and get the first train back on Monday morning. Then we got a place in Godalming, which was near Nuala's sister, Pam. But Nuala still felt isolated, since I was working a six-day week, never getting home before ten and leaving at half-past six next morning. So we moved into London, finding a mansion flat in Barnes, practically on Hammersmith Bridge and looking right out onto the Thames. It became a focal point on Boat Race day, though I missed all the early parties because I was working on 'Grandstand'. We also had few family holidays, because with the Olympics, World Cup, Commonwealth Games and Wimbledon, the summers were even busier than the winters. It's one thing I regret for the sake of Nuala and the kids.

After a while there Peter Dimmock sent for me and said they wanted me to do 'Sportsview' on Wednesday evenings as well as 'Grandstand', for which they offered an extra £2000 a year – which I never got. I realised once more that I ought to be more shrewd in my handling of financial deals when they came up, but it's something I have never been good at, and I lost out. But where I didn't lose out was in the pleasure and profit I got from working with David Coleman, who was presenter of 'Grandstand' while I was its editor.

For me he was the best commentator who ever worked on television because he understood that his role was not to restate what the viewer could already see, but to add to the picture. He had this ability to put his finger on what was important. When the Olympics were held in Moscow while the terrible war in Afghanistan continued, and when the doves were released from their cages, Coleman's only comment was, 'I wonder will they turn south.' It was all that needed to be said. I also cherished his commentary on the 1500 metres from Rome, 1960, where the great Australian runner, Herb Elliott, was up against a hell of a lot of strong competitors. When they were on the far side of the last lap, Coleman's commentary went, 'If Elliott is going to go, he has to kick now.' Elliott kicked and the crowd went mad, carrying him round that top bend, and Coleman added only one line: 'There goes Elliott, the greatest runner in the world, running away from the greatest runners in the world.' I thought, oh boy. And then as Elliott went over the line to win, and he tripped on the kerb and the camera zoomed in, Coleman's sole comment was, 'This picture tells you the current price of gold.' There wasn't one obvious line in all of that. I thought it should have been put on tape and sent round to every sports commentator to say, this is the way.

All Black Andrew Mehrtens, for me the best of the present generation of fly-halves.

Joost Van Der Westhuizen, the player who won the World Cup for South Africa.

Two for the record books: Neil Jenkins, Wales's most prolific goal-scorer, under the eye of his record-breaking captain, Ieuan Evans.

What would England have done without Rob Andrew? Now he is all set for a brilliant professional career at Newcastle, while England hooker Brian Moore, behind, moves to Richmond as an amateur.

The sheer power of Jonah Lomu. The perfect hand-off of Alain Penaud of France (above) and it takes Pienaar, Van Der Westhuizen and Small (below) to tackle him in the World Cup final which, despite Lomu's size, strength and speed, New Zealand lost to South Africa.

François Pienaar receives the World Cup, Nelson Mandela receives the acclaim of the world.

The picture we never thought we'd see – Shaun Edwards of Wigan and Phil de Glanville of Bath leading the best in rugby league and union onto the pitch at Maine Road.

The cross-code challenge return match at Twickenham. For all his pace and fitness, the formidable Maori Va'aiga Tuigamala (above) is unable to break a typically rugby union tackle by Audley Lumsden at Twickenham. Below, England's new wing threequarter Jon Sleightholme runs away from Jason Robinson to score.

You get a much better picture on radio than on television!

Outside the Palace after receiving my CVO, with Catherine, Nuala and Nicky, 1987.

Two ex-sports reporters share a Christmas lunch at the Saints and Sinners Club.

The lighter side of Royal Liaison, cracking a joke with HRH the Prince of Wales during a rehearsal for his World Service reading of his book, *The Old Man of Lochnagar*.

A night to remember at the Royal Albert Hall. Two Welsh knights, Sir Anthony Hopkins (left) and Sir Geraint Evans (right), vice-presidents of the London Welsh Male Voice Choir, on a Night of a Thousand Male Voices from across the world, flank the musical director, Dr Haydn James, and the choir president.

A team of all the talents in London Welsh strip at Old Deer Park where I was surprised by Michael Aspel (front) with his big red book for 'This Is Your Life'. Back row, left to right: Sîan Phillips, Ian Robertson, Emlyn Hughes, Brian Johnson, Barry Davies, Dan Maskell, Owain Arwel Hughes; front row, left to right: Spike Milligan, Harry Secombe, John Howard Davies, Bill McLaren, Desmond Lynam, Nerys Hughes, Gloria Hunniford, Ruth Madoc.

Nicky, Nuala and a proud grandfather admiring Jack Alexander Morgan, aged three, but wondering if he is going to play for Wales or Ireland.

Coleman wasn't the only performer from whom I learned. I greatly admired the naturalness of Eddie Waring in rugby league and the restraint of Peter O'Sullevan in racing. Like Peter Bromley on radio, O'Sullevan had this gift of keeping the level just right. In a two-mile race they could gradually work up the tempo of their commentary to reach the climax at just the right time. They weren't screaming all the way through. During the Rugby World Cup in South Africa you heard commentators shouting at the top of their voices when the England pack pushed four yards forward. 'This is great scrummaging!' they'd scream. And the viewers could see perfectly well that it wasn't. They were about to lose the ball.

In broadcasting I've always respected the way people express themselves above almost anything else. And in Wales I had worked with a man, Wynford Vaughan-Thomas, who used words with consummate craft and fluency. I was asked to produce a series of radio programmes for him, 'Out of Doors' – about mountaineering, canoeing, underwater swimming, all that sort of stuff – and Wynford's reputation as a war correspondent had travelled before him. I could remember listening to his account of the bombing of Hamburg: 'Looking down from this aeroplane now I can see bombs explode. How can I describe it? It's as if you'd thrown a handful of jewels onto a piece of black velvet.' Now I had to work with him. I went to meet him with trepidation, and he was lovely, he was jolly, he was keen, he was fast – and he was climbing everything. We were in Snowdonia, at the bottom of what all the climbers know as Cloggie. And being new to it all, I didn't know how to set about the programme. 'How do I start, Wynford?' He said, 'Leave the tape recorder here, but switch it on. Now go up the road, then drive the car back down over the gravel. Stop, switch off, close the door, and walk towards me, saying nothing.' I did exactly what he told me. There was the sound of a car door slamming, then my footsteps coming close. And over those footsteps Wynford said, 'I've just got out of my car, and I'm arrived at the foothills of Cloggie, and the clouds are just touching the top of the hills.'

I thought, what am I trying to do? Wynford gave you that sense of excitement as simply as that.

Among all the marvellous things that Wynford did, I remember his contribution to the sixtieth anniversary of the Sports Department in London. Wynford was prevented by his doctors from coming to it, but he sent a poem and asked me to read it at the party. It was called 'The Commentator'. The sort of thing he might have written on the back of an envelope, and it's terrific:

> The commentator is, we know,
> The whitest man in radio,
> Handsome and sober, highly paid,
> Napoleons of the talking trade,
> Stern guardians of the spoken word,
> From him the voice of truth is heard,
> The honest truth? Well, let's admit,
> You've got to hot it up a bit.
> And then with cunning adjectival skill
> He gilds the lily and coats the pill.

It went on and on, and you suddenly found that the whole atmosphere of outside broadcasts was conveyed on that piece of paper. Wynford just encouraged you to think fast, and to pick on moments, and say natural things, 'Oh, isn't this a wonderful day.' And it was just as if he was talking to you in a pub or in the house having a cup of tea. And this, I think, is the most important thing. Whatever you're doing, the art of communication is very simple; it's one person expressing himself to another so that he can understand. It doesn't matter about syntax, which I suppose is the difference between the written and spoken word.

The other thing about that era of broadcasting was its extraordinary technical advances. It was a time of massive cameras and driving around the country in terrifically big vans. Now everything's lighter and more manageable in every way, and we were at the start of it all. The most remarkable thing about the 1964 Olympic Games in Tokyo was that we had a satellite called Syncon 3, which moved at the same speed as the earth and so provided constant pictures. But the sound travelled by a different route. It came not from the heavens but by cable from Tokyo to the United States and so on, until a boat sliced through the cable at Honolulu and left us without commentary for four or five days. We had to be pretty inventive then and try to find specialist commentators who, for some reason or another, hadn't gone to Tokyo. How lucky we were. We found Harry Walker for swimming, Norris McWhirter, a master of athletics and an all-round polymath, Dorian Williams on equestrian events, and a chap called Simon Smith on boxing. It was a better commentary team than we could reasonably have hoped for. They worked from the silent pictures on the box with help from a few little notes sent by telephone. And nobody guessed that the commentary wasn't coming live. That was a terrific achievement. It made you realise how important broadcasting is to the public, and how high their expectations have become. I recall when Peter Dimmock got a live picture from Hamburg, and people rushed home to catch it. That was the first Eurovision link. And then ten years later there were telephone calls complaining about the quality of the sound from the moon! How quickly people get used to things and refuse to accept second best.

I left 'Grandstand' in 1965, the year after the Tokyo Olympics. There were a few moves in television I didn't like, and Peter Dimmock, the Head of Outside Broadcasts, suggested that I should continue to edit 'Sportsview' in mid-week, but on Saturday, instead of continuing my studio job with 'Grandstand', I should do commentary for them on international matches. He also made it clear that if I agreed I would be free to report rugby for a Sunday newspaper. I went along with that, a bit reluctantly, but I did. The BBC was supposed to be negotiating a new salary scale, and meanwhile my agent talked to various newpapers. Within a week he came back with an offer from Frank Butler at the *News of the World*. We agreed terms, signed a contract and next Sunday the announcement appeared in the paper, 'Cliff Morgan joins the *News of the World*.' But the next time I went into the BBC I was told I would have to cancel the arrangement: 'It's not right and proper.' I refused; I had signed a contract with the paper, which was more than I had ever had the chance to do with the BBC, and I wasn't going to let Frank Butler down. After further argument and talks with my agent, the BBC said if I wouldn't cancel I would have to go. That afternoon I went in to collect my books and things from my office at the Television Centre. It was eight years before I worked there again, and then it was in Peter Dimmock's position as Head of Outside Broadcasts, the department which he created.

I had known Peter for some years, and have remained a pal of his ever since. We had a quarrel over a matter of principle: whether I could and should have pulled out of my contract with the *News of the World*. But we never became enemies over it, and as a result I was able to go back within weeks to contribute items for 'Grandstand' and rugby commentaries and whatever else was on offer. I also did lots of radio for Angus McKay. That's worth mentioning because Angus wasn't in the habit of treating those who went over to television and then wanted to return to radio as prodigal sons. He resented television. He looked on radio as a family medium – and in many ways it is more friendly and intimate – and he hated anyone leaving that family. Only two people who went to television ever came back to appear regularly in Angus's programmes; they were Harry Carpenter and myself. Together with reports and articles for the *News of the World*, which gave me a chance to see if I could write, that's what filled my next year or so until, out of the blue, came a call from Alasdair Milne at Associated Rediffusion which gave my career another twist.

Rediffusion at that time was the company which provided London with its independent television during the week-days (while Thames operated only at the weekend). Alasdair, who eventually went back to the BBC and became its Director-General, was there and he told me that they were looking for a new editor for 'This Week'. This was the big current affairs programme that Rediffusion produced for the whole ITV network. Was I interested? Well, yes, who wouldn't be? I next heard from Cyril Bennett, who was the boss of Rediffusion, and went in to see him. The result was I got the job. I was frightened of it, I willingly admit. But I decided that the only way I could do it was by using the people who were there and putting my future in their hands. I'd say, 'Look, I know nothing about this. Tell me how can we do it.' I did, and it worked because I was working with the most extraordinary bunch of reporters, a roll-call of the most talented there have ever been: Robert Kee, James Cameron, Ludovic Kennedy, George Fitch, Alastair Burnet from the *Economist*, Lew Gardiner. With their help I learned so much about producing programmes in that time.

For instance I remember we took Cameron to Brazil before the World Cup was staged in Britain. I thought it would be a good idea to do a programme about Brazilian football at a time when their currency, the cruzeiro, was about a thousand to the pound, and the most striking contrast between affluence and poverty in that country could be found at Copacabana beach. Here the best view of the sea belonged to the nearby slums. Two worlds met there. Millionaires lying in the sun being basted with sun oil by beautiful girls. And tiny kids from those slums playing brilliant football where Pele had once played it, between the twelve goalposts planted on the beach. At first Jimmy didn't want to go. He didn't know anything about football. But after I told him about all these details he agreed to do it. The BBC had also flown into Rio de Janeiro, and of course we got much the same pictures – the statue of Christ in Majesty, the slums, the beach. But we had Cameron. He was fascinated by these soccer-playing kids whose ball-control at ten or eleven was astonishing. They could bring the ball up with their toes and round the back of their neck and down the other side without letting it touch the ground. While the BBC commentators were using up all the superlatives to describe their skill, Jimmy just said: 'How can I describe it; it's a sort of rosary for the feet.'

At 'This Week' we did programmes about the fostering of coloured kids and doctors' pay and all the usual, indispensible items, but also it was the period when the Vietnam War was at its height. Sadly, too, it was when the Aberfan disaster occurred. I had already talked with Cyril Bennett about a programme I wanted to do about Wales, its music and poetry and prose – very Welsh. And then this world was shattered. Everybody felt that it was the most cruel act of spleen, or whatever it was from somewhere, that had caused these poor kids to lose their lives. And 'This Week' would be coming out on the Thursday, the day they were burying the children in a communal grave. Cyril said, 'Well, how are you going to treat it?' I told him I had no idea. This was the honest truth. I knew that as ITV's main current affairs programme we had to reflect this awful event. But I couldn't see how we could deal with it in an appropriate way. Cyril said, 'Do the programme you wanted to do about Wales.'

The phone went down, and within six hours I'd got Stanley Baker, Sian Phillips, Huw Griffith, Donald Houston, Anita Williams, a beautiful folk singer, and the Pendyrus Male-Voice Choir to agree to take part. We went out and bought the books of Dylan Thomas and other modern Welsh poets. We took Stanley Baker down to the Pendyrus choir practice on the Wednesday night with James Butler, son of Rab, who would be directing in the gallery on the night. There we went through with them the Idris Davies poem,

> Send out your homing pigeons, Dai,
> Your blue-grey pigeons, hard as nails.

And that was practically the only rehearsal we had before the programme went out. When the buses came up from Wales with the choir, and parked in the compound near Wembley stadium, we were almost ready to go on air.

All we said at the beginning was, 'Good evening. This is a programme about Wales, its music, its prose, its poetry. Here's Huw Griffith.' And I can see him now, standing in front of a lectern, with his half-glasses and his big eyes. He looked into the camera and he spoke the Dylan Thomas poem,

> I have longed to move away
> From the hissing of the spent lie
> And the old terrors' continual cry
> Growing more terrible as the day
> Goes over the hill into the deep sea . . .

And under Griffith's voice as he finished the poem came the choir singing, 'I feel thy presence every passing night'. This was terrific stuff.

The other thing I wanted in the programme, because it was about my youth and about kids, was Gwyn Thomas's 'Trip to the Sea', which Stanley Baker read beautifully: 'Even now, the rattle of a train means just one thing to me. It is the bizarrely entranced day each summer when we valley children poured in our thousands down the sloping streets to the station, and into the train to edge out of the close encircling hills through the lush fields of the Vale of Glamorgan.' We'd selected our extracts very carefully and, we hoped, not too predictably. And a compilation of extracts was made by Bryn Griffiths, who had been a longshoreman in the United States and who, because the University of Wales and the literary establishment wouldn't accept him as a poet, later went to live in Western Australia. One of his choices, 'Soliloquy for Compatriots' by John Tripp, was read by Sian Phillips:

> We even have our own word for God,
> In a language nourished on hymn and psalm,
> As we clinched to our customs and habitats
> All those decades in the chapels of the scarred zone,
> Clogged with feeling, ranting preachers on a rebellious frond.

It was the most memorable night. We went through it without once mentioning Aberfan or the word disaster, and yet I'd like to think we said everything important about it that was to be said.

Next day Nancy Banks-Smith wrote in the *Guardian*, 'Wow. What a programme.'

For ideas on the programme content I will forever be indebted to Mattie and Caradog Prichard – two pillars of London Welsh life and mine too. Caradog was an award winning poet and writer who in his time won several Crowns and Chairs at the National Eisteddfod of Wales. As a senior sub-editor on the *Telegraph*, he was impartial, generous and meticulous. Those who worked with him loved him. Mattie knew everything and everybody. If you needed a doctor or pianist, a solicitor or a Welsh translation, you simply telephoned Mattie. She was a Welsh Hedda Hopper! Their home in Carlton Hill was a constant buzz of music and poetry and everyone who came to London to further their future called there.

Emlyn Williams asked Caradog to translate 'Peter and the Wolf'; Richard Burton and Donald Houston sought words and inspiration; singer Ivor Emmanuel and opera star Sir Geraint Evans were visitors. Exiles from Wales found a real cultural home. The actress Katharine Hepburn used Mattie to learn about Welshness and accent before making the film, 'The Corn is Green'.

In the *Welsh Triads* there are three things which a man should have at home. A virtuous wife, a cushion on his chair and a harp in tune. The Prichards had all three.

I stayed with 'This Week' for two and a half years, and so, in my own way, I carried out Hywel's plan that I should spend three years in Current Affairs. I'd felt it was time for a change, and I never regretted it. Producing needs the same basic intellectual approach whether you're dealing with news or music or sport; the one thing I couldn't have done is drama. I wasn't a genius of a producer, but I was lucky to hit a time when the place was buzzing, and the whole television service was breathless trying to catch up with the next bit of technical advancement.

When I quit I picked up where I had left off as a television and radio freelance, which had its pleasures as well as its pains. One of the pleasures was to rub shoulders once again with Bill McLaren, the authentic Border burr of rugby, who would have played for Scotland if, after a successful final trial, he hadn't contracted tuberculosis. My working hours were often ridiculously long, but at least I wasn't tied to an office routine, and any interval between one job and the next I could spend as I liked. My work also took me frequently back to Wales, which allowed for me to keep in touch with my parents who were still living in Trebanog. I was also fortunate to be, in a sense, close to them at their deaths. My mother died in November 1969. I was in Wales to do a commentary on a Wednesday match between Newport and the Springboks, and I had phoned what was now a commercial garage opposite our house, to ask them to tell my parents I would be down around coffee time a day or so before. When I arrived my father was at the front door. I got out of the car, the lads from the garage came over to have a look at it, and my father shouted in to my mother to put the kettle on. I never got to speak to her. As she was carrying the kettle over to the hob she collapsed and died. It was a terrible shock, yet it was almost poetically apt that she should have died making tea for 'her baby'. Serving others was how she had lived.

Because my parents had been so close my father would say, 'There's no point in my being around now, is there really.' But he went on living alone in the house. He'd got a television now, and used to invite his friends round to watch 'Songs of Praise', football, rugby. He also swore he looked at 'Panorama' and all the posh things. But it was really there for the sport. He was watching Wales play New Zealand in December 1972; I was commentating. An All Black called Keith Murdoch, who was later sent home for misbehaviour, scored in the far right-hand corner and Wales went on to lose 19–16. It was then that my father had his fatal heart-attack, and the last thing he consciously heard was the sound of my voice doing the commentary.

I'd seen my father the day before but stayed in Cardiff that night to get ready for the programme. After which I was due to do an interview with Rolf Harris, the Australian entertainer. Dewi Griffiths, my producer, didn't tell me he'd had a message about my father's heart attack until I had finished the interview. Then he put his arm around me and said, 'Your father . . .' and drove me up to the Rhondda. He'd known it was pretty well over. In fact my father died in Llwynypia Hospital two days later.

After the funeral at Pontypridd Crematorium I was standing outside thanking people for coming to the service when one of his close friends said: 'Sad I am you've lost your father. But sadder still for me that I've lost my best pal.' He walked away miserably, then with almost an actor's swivel he turned back and added: 'But who could blame your father for having a heart attack in a second half like that.'

At that time it was nearly five years since I had left Rediffusion, and nine months since I had suffered my stroke. Some people I know can take freelancing in their stride and still lead a 'normal' life. I have always taken on too much work, whether I was paid for it or not. During the first four years I travelled the world. I went out to South Africa with the British Lions in 1968, a fairly disastrous tour which ended for Barry John when he broke his shoulder in the first Test at Pretoria. It was a hard slog; on my tod I did newspaper work, radio and television, and also made films. It was the same thing on the 1971 tour of New Zealand. I was producing a half-hour programme on a Saturday which included interviews after games, bits of commentary leading up to them and discussion looking forward to the next game. I put them together over there, cut the programme to half an hour, and sent it over to London. I was also covering for the 'Today' programme and Radio Wales, as well as doing newspaper work, so that I was always running from one place to the next with a tape recorder on my back, my notebook in one hand and typewriter in the other. Then when I'd get back to the hotel at half-past ten or eleven at night, I'd find a message on my bedroom door saying, 'We're at the so-and-so, come along, John Dawes.' Or there'd be a note from the Ponsonby Rugby Club or whoever asking me to spend an evening with them. I simply did too much work on that tour, and I think, as several others do, that this was the breaking point. I came back home, where I continued to work at the same pressure, and six months or so later I had my stroke.

During my final days at Farnham Park I spent many sleepless nights nagging away at my past errors. It caused me a good deal of pain. In practical terms it was obvious where I had gone wrong. At the back of my mind I had this idea of what a good life was – competitive, perhaps, but at the same time considerate of other people's needs and feelings. Now, as I looked back on it, I saw my own life as merely self-absorbed. The eight years of playing international rugby, and touring abroad looking for fame, to be followed by more rushing around as a rugby commentator, and television editor. And when I wasn't working I was speaking at dinners and receptions, playing charity rugby. I now saw the whole thing as showing off, being big-time, the centre of attraction. One of my great failings had been (and I haven't cured it yet) that I didn't like to say no to anybody. At the same time I hadn't done enough to secure the education of Catherine and Nicholas or the future of Nuala. We had no savings, and in cash terms we were, in effect, destitute. I'd not lived the life that I thought I should have done.

I left Farnham Park in September 1972, returning to London to continue my physiotherapy and speech therapy from home, and felt very nervous about my prospects of returning to work. The first night home, Nuala and I sat on the bed and decided to tip every penny we had on the counterpane. There was hardly enough to buy a packet of cigarettes. Nuala had already taken Catherine out of Francis Holland School because we couldn't afford the fees. Instead she had been sent to Le Bon Sauveur convent on Anglesey, which Nuala had attended with her two sisters from the age of six. We could just about manage that. Nicholas was at St Paul's School, and we decided that come hell or high water we would find the fees for that. Our car, a gorgeous bronze Ford Executive with real leather seats, power steering and automatic drive, would have to go. Worth a couple of thousand, we thought, but all we got for it from a second-hand dealer was £900. We had no car for the next three years. Then, for Nuala, the ultimate sacrifice: she sold her engagement ring, the only thing of real value we possessed. The comfort was that we now had no bills outstanding, and Nicholas was safe at St Paul's for at least a couple of years.

The first work I did was on a children's weekly, the *Tuesday Paper*, which Geoff and Mavis Nicholson, David Jefferis, a designer, and I launched in mid-September. We had been planning it long before I had my stroke. It survived for only twelve weeks and made us no money, but we enjoyed putting it together and it helped keep my mind off my problems. Then Angus McKay came up with something that did pay. He suggested that if I wasn't yet ready to face the microphone I could at least write a weekly review of the sports pages for someone else to read. And by mid-November my speech was sufficiently restored to let me comment on rugby matches on radio and television. This brought me back into the world of Alan Mouncer, the greatest outside broadcast producer I ever worked with, and Dewi Griffiths, the master director of live rugby programmes. Dewi was born in Pentre, so we were both from the one valley and felt exactly the same about the game and how to put it on the screen.

All the while a cheque for £2000 was burning a hole in my pocket. Jack Solomons, the boxing promoter, had sent it to me when I was at Farnham Park with a note which read: 'You may need this during the time you will be out of work. It comes with my love.' We never cashed it, and on the day I returned to regular television commentary – 20 January 1973, when Ireland played the All Blacks at Lansdowne Road – I sent the cheque back to Jack with the warmest thanks for his friendship and kindness.

The period of recovery had seemed never-ending. As is clear to any of the 120,000 people in the UK who each year suffer a first stroke, the hardest thing to accept is the inability to do the ordinary things you used to take for granted. Carers, too, have to fortify themselves against the impatience that comes from dealing with someone who is constantly impatient with himself. I was more fortunate than many, for I did make a fairly full recovery. And because of the kind of work I had done, I was buoyed up by the good wishes of hundreds of people I had never even met. Among them were listeners who wrote to say they missed me on 'These You Have Loved', and children who sent home-made Get Well cards decorated with Welsh dragons, leeks and rugby balls. They had been fans of another regular programme I did called 'Singing Together'. And if these were not enough to drive out self-pity, there were the half-crowns wrapped in silver paper which OAPs told me to spend on chocolates or fruit.

Another man who influenced me during my convalescence was George Thomas, then a Cardiff MP, and later to become Speaker of the House of Commons and Viscount Tonypandy. I had known him since his Methodist crusading days in the Rhondda, and it was understandable to me that he should say I must have faith. A faith which years later helped him to overcome cancer of the stomach and throat. He, too, wouldn't let me feel sorry for myself but made me direct my energies into helping others. It was George who brought me into the National Children's Home and other charities close to his heart in Wales.

The main result of having a stroke is to make you sit down and think what you're doing. And that's what started my involvement with the Disabled Olympics. I felt that because I had been helped through the harsh experience of suffering a stroke, I had something to offer in return. Then, as a result of running around doing what I could, I found myself getting caught up in other charities, mostly for those who had been handicapped by whatever cause. It's stupid, but having sworn I would cut down on my activities, I found myself doing more than I had before. But at least it was a more exhilarating activity. Doing something for young people who are physically and mentally disabled exposes you to a lot of sadness. But at the same time it gives you a boost because you know you are part of the same family.

For years we tried to get the Disabled Olympics on television, but the BBC weren't interested until 1980 when I covered the Arnhem Games with Geoff Goddard. They should have been held in Moscow but, if you remember, the Russians claimed they didn't have any blind or disabled citizens. Nowadays, of course, the Russians take part in the Disabled Games. At Arnhem we saw the most incredible things. We were able, for instance, to watch, from within a foot of her, a blind English woman playing bowls. She was called Bonnie and after she'd delivered her first bowl, her helper (this was allowed) told her: 'Two o'clock, and slightly lighter than last time, but stick to two o'clock.' And Bonnie's next bowl dropped within half an inch of the jack. You could hardly credit it.

Yet the outstanding moment of those Games was when the Canadian, Arnie Boult, who had one leg, cleared seven feet in the high jump. That's high. If you look at the front door of your house, he jumped over the top of that. He did all his training back in Canada with able-bodied sportsmen. At Arnhem, too, I first saw wheelchair basketball, which must be among the roughest, toughest, most exciting sporting events anywhere in the world. The players were aiming at the same height of basket, and in the manoeuvring below it not only were the bumps and knocks incredible, but anyone falling out of his chair had to get back in unaided.

Then at Seoul, on the same track where Ben Johnson had cheated his way to a gold medal, I saw a fellow called Dennis Oehler run the 100 metres. A former rugby and American football player, from the knee down he had pieces of steel with an artificial foot at the bottom. And yet he covered the distance only 1.9 seconds slower than Johnson had done.

These people who turn disability into ability stagger me, and they are marvellously heartening company. What they do is often extremely painful. A year or so ago I met a man called Ian Hayman (he had won the discus and shot put at Seoul) who propelled a wheelchair with his arms 1040 miles from John o'Groats to Land's End. He did it to raise money to send athletes to the 1996 Paralympic Games in Atlanta. I asked him how he had managed to face the steep Scottish hills, and he said his son had insisted on coming all the way on his bicycle to look after him. How old was his son? Twelve, Ian said. And it was the boy who had encouraged him: 'Come on, Dad, you can get to the top of this hill.' I don't know how you could hear that without feeling humbled, and wondering what you can do to help.

I would probably have missed all this if I hadn't had a stroke. I could certainly not have felt quite the same kinship with such people. At the time I was shattered but, after nearly twenty-five years and a pretty good recovery, I often think I should give thanks that it happened. The stroke changed my life. It stopped me being so self-centred and arrogant. I hope it made me a better person, but I'm not the one in the position to say.

11

The play-makers

It's one of the hobbies of rugby fans to make mental lists of their favourite players in any particular position. Especially the backs, since they are always out in the open for everyone to see. And extra-specially the fly-halves because even more is expected of them. They bear the brunt of making or breaking the play. My father, a soccer man but a fervent rugby follower, had compiled these rolls of honour for as long as I can remember. And even after I had been in the Welsh team for some seasons, he listed me down around number five as a stand-off, which put me in my place. The best he had ever seen, he said (and this was typically perverse and Welsh; anything for an argument), was Emlyn Jenkins from the Rhondda Valley. This was a man who had never played for Wales; he was spotted by the Rugby League early on and went North to play for Salford. He was a small man: funnily enough, I grew to be the same size as him. But my father told me he was the absolutely perfect outside-half. He could sidestep to the left and right, and catch any ball that went his way. And he could do that because his feet were in the right position. I never saw Emlyn Jenkins play, but I'm sure my father was right. Your hands don't matter; you should catch the ball one-handed, anyway. It's the footwork that counts. Watching a game I always look to see where the players' feet are.

Anyway, my father placed Emlyn as the best he had ever seen, even though we're talking now of the 'thirties, when our near-neighbour, Cliff Jones, was playing for Wales, and was brilliantly succeeded by Willie Davies. While still Gowerton schoolboys, Davies and his cousin, Haydn Tanner, who played as his scrum-half, had helped Swansea beat the 1935 All Blacks. So Jones and Davies, or sometimes Davies and Jones, occupied the next two places on the list; all Welshmen so far, you notice. And then, before I brought up the rear, the Ulsterman, Jack Kyle, claimed fourth place.

I have talked about my father taking me, as a schoolboy, to see Kyle play for the Barbarians in a Good Friday match at Penarth. 'That's who you want to look at and study and *emulate*,' said my father; it was one of his favourite words. Of course I never saw the other three in action, but I don't think I ever played against anyone quite like Kyle. He was a beautiful kicker of the ball with either foot. Kyle wasn't the fastest player in the world, but just when you thought you'd got the measure of him, and decided he wasn't all that special, he'd make you think he had let the ball go, suddenly take it back in mid-pass, and before you could recover, he'd scored under the posts. As he did in my first international. I later read all about a try he scored against France at Ravenhill in 1953; I also saw it on Pathé Gazette in the Central cinema at Porth. Everything about that try was perfect – Kyle's taking of the ball, his body action, the way he sold a dummy, went inside and side-stepped and so on. It had all the things I wanted to be able to do, and in particular his general command of the situation.

We weren't dissimilar in stature; at that time it was generally thought an advantage in our position to be fairly short and, perhaps not stocky exactly, but compact. At school Ned Gribble would look at you and measure you from your crotch to your ankles, and if you were too tall, you wouldn't make a stand-off. They're all six-footers now, so that theory has been blown out of the window, I suppose, but his argument was that you had to be the right shape to get away from trouble. He believed, too, that while the first five yards of a break counted for a lot, the second five yards were even more important. The first five set you up in an attacking situation, but it was the second that could get you away from the defence and allowed you either to run clear yourself or to make a gap for someone else. And this is what Kyle's play, with its marvellous sense of timing, represented. He was majestic.

He was also a terrific fellow to be with. He could talk about anything. Unlike those people who get keyed up before big games, on the morning of an international Kyle would be in bed reading poetry or studying his medical text-books. He was a good Christian soul, and a romantic in the sense that the library of books he carried around with him were probably more important to him at that moment than the game he was about to play. Yet his influence was on every aspect of the play. The one thing that marks a great fly-half is that the opposition must always be worried about him. And whenever you played Kyle, you worried what he would do next. That's why I place him on a pinnacle.

The first English stand-off who made a big impression on me was Ivor Preece of Coventry and that Warwickshire side which repeatedly won the County Championship. His international days came to an end in 1951, the same season as mine began, but we played against each other often in club games. Unlike the typical Welsh outside-half, he was slightly built, but he had a beautiful sense of movement, and everything he did, the line he took and the balance of his running, looked right. He reminds me of Nim Hall, against whom I played my first game at Twickenham. Nim had a similar slim build, and was another fine kicker of the ball and a beautiful controller of the game. Ivor also knew the game so well and probably thought about it more than most other outside-halves I've played against and watched. If anything I think he might have been a greater player if he hadn't thought about it so much.

Looking back it seems to me that England had a glut of

outside-halves at one period in the 'fifties and early 'sixties, when the selectors kept playing them and dropping them. (It was the same at scrum-half, where Gordon Rimmer of Waterloo would nearly always be picked for the opening international against Wales, but although he won a dozen caps never once finished the season for England.) You had Martin Regan, Bev Risman, probably the best England ever had, and later Tom Brophy. They were dip, dap, do. They could side-step and carve out an opening; they were bags of tricks. In fact they were typically Welsh. They looked like the people I played against each weekend at home. Unfortunately for Risman he coincided with Richard Sharp, who will remain famous for his great try against Scotland at Twickenham in 1963 when he sold three dummies to ease through a gap in the Scottish defence. Funnily enough, if Sharp had been a Welshman, he'd almost certainly have played in the centre because he was so unlike our idea of an outside-half. It would have given him extra time to think and turn into a truly great player.

Of the Scots, John Rutherford was also in a different class. He was taller than the accepted stand-off of the 'fifties, and in his thirty-five internationals with scrum-half Roy Laidlaw he produced memorable moments of drama. He had this ability to make powerful breaks and I saw him play some terrific games for his country. In the same class was Ollie Campbell of Ireland. As for the French, every back was an outside-half – not to mention one or two of their forwards. Jo Maso, for instance, who could switch effortlessly from centre to fly-half, did miraculously intricate things in the middle of the field. I've always said that on a hot day in Paris, the French are the best players in the world, because they pass the ball behind their backs, they split the field, they're not afraid to try anything. Just think of the exploits of Pierre Albaladejo, 'Monsieur le Drop', and the French stand-off during the period of 'Champagne rugby' in the early 'sixties.

The South Africa fly-half who made the most lasting impression on me in my early twenties was Hannes Brewis. He was called the Brown Fox, and you knew what people meant; he was a wily, independent character. On the Springboks' 1951–52 tour, it was he who made the two beautiful punts which caused trouble for Cardiff and later for Wales and led to tries by the wing-threequarter, 'Chum' Ochse. Mind, I'd swear to my dying day that Ochse was off-side in the Wales match, because when I ran up to Hansie I could see that Ochse was in front of him as he kicked the ball. All the same, Hansie was a precision player, slimly built but with a considerable presence. He had an enormous effect on the rest of the South African players, his punting to touch was good and his defence was terrific. Another stand-off I liked the look of on that tour was Dennis Fry, brother of Stephen, the flank-forward who would captain South Africa in all four Tests when the Lions toured there in 1955. Because of Hansie's presence, Dennis didn't get many games, but he was a beautiful player in the style of Ricky Bartlett – a stylish receiver and passer of the ball and highly polished in the way he brought others into the movement.

From New Zealand I think of a Maori, 'Mac' Herewini, very much my vision of the ideal outside-half. He was quick on his feet, a nimble side-stepper, always ready to have a go and to do cheeky things in defence, like starting a movement from behind his own goal-line. Then there was Earl Kirton, the stand-off in Brian Lochore's great side in 1967. The remarkable thing about Kirton was that, although he rarely looked as if he was going to make a score, whenever the All Blacks were in a tight situation he was always in the right position at the right time. In the Barbarian game at Twickenham which ended the tour, when Lochore fielded a mis-kick to touch, it was Kirton who was on hand to open up in his own half and send the wing, 'Stainless' Steel, through for the winning try in injury time.

Turning to Wales, the first real outside-half I came up against was Glyn Davies at Pontypridd Grammar School, an elegant, glamorous player with great judgement. He went on to play for the Pontypridd club and for Wales until he paid the price for defeat at Murrayfield. Also in the school side was the writer

Alun Richards who used to maintain that there were two kinds of Welsh stand-offs, Church and Chapel. Glyn was undoubtedly Church; so, to an even higher degree, was Barry John. Like all great ball players, like Pele and Best, Compton and Sobers, Barry always looked as if he had plenty of time to do things; it seemed so easy for him. On the other hand Phil Bennett and I were Chapel. We looked busy all the while, we were forever trying things, following the ball. It's very difficult to choose between Barry and Phil because they were both unsurpassed in their particular styles and eras.

In addition to everything else, Barry was a marvellous goal-kicker. On the Lions tour of New Zealand in 1971 I remember him turning up at Wellington to play the Universities with two left boots. He didn't make a fuss, he just went on the field in them needing just six points to equal the 100 points tourist record set by the South African, Gerry Brand, in 1937. By the end of the game, with three penalties, three conversions, a dropped goal and a try underneath the posts, he had brought his total to 115 in only eight matches. He would treat the opposition almost with disdain. 'Oh, he's not much good, a fish and chip merchant,' he'd say. But then you had to have a certain temperament to be like Barry, standing apart and remaining in total control with all the fuss and nonsense going on around him. Phil Bennett couldn't have achieved that sort of detachment. But though for Wales he might have been more constrained, for Llanelli, the Barbarians and the British Lions he invariably let rip with a great sense of adventure and experiment. He was the right size, as my games master would have said, since his legs weren't too long. And if he was shorter than most of the wing-forwards, that didn't matter too much in those days. He was dark and intense, a bundle of ideas, and he made the game so exciting that you'd have paid an extra £10 on the gate if you'd known he was going to be playing that day. I loved to watch him.

The best game I think I've ever seen a fly-half play for his country was against Scotland on a filthy ground at Cardiff in 1966. The player was David Watkins. While everybody else was bogged down, he was skimming over the surface, knowing exactly what he was trying to do all the time, and in effect beating Scotland on his own. Later he moved to Rugby League, and at Salford proved that he could play either game, just as Lewis Jones had done fifteen years before, and Jonathan Davies was to do twenty years later. Jonathan was very well looked after when he moved to Widnes, who gave him time to adapt. He wasn't allowed to play at first; he was taught the game. Then they would play him for twenty minutes and take him off. It was almost twelve months before he played right through. And the result of that care was that he developed into a thoroughly accomplished Rugby League international.

Jonathan became a star because he didn't have to think too much about what he was going to do next. It was instinctive. Any great fly-half, I believe, has to have that moment of inspiration when, whatever the book says he should be doing, he does something of his own. As I mentioned before, when I was playing in Cardiff from the late 'forties, there were six outside-halves who might have played equally well for Wales. There was so little to choose between us. I enjoyed watching and playing against all of them because they had that delicious difference, they were instinctive players. They knew without thinking when to break, when to pass, and when to kick and get out of trouble. Another characteristic they had was that they were self-assured and cheeky; they liked to show off a bit and entertain the crowd.

Once when writing about Jonathan Davies in Ireland, I quoted from a poem of Wilfred Owen that he had both mastery and mystery. There's that one thing as an outside-half, you've got to be a master of any situation. If he's getting things wrong, then whatever strength there is outside him doesn't matter. It's gone. And it'll always be like that I think. Now the fashion is for power and size, but I believe that little and quality is just as important. The player has to have this mysterious thing about him which leaves opponents wondering, what's he going to do now? And why? Of another person you can say, this is what he'll do. And even if he does it brilliantly, you can cope with that. When there's mystery, you can't.

Apart from his natural ability, his pace, his confidence, and that almost indefinable quality that is down to timing, Jonathan's play was marked by that ability to do things that no-one expected him to do. At Twickenham against England I saw him grub-kicking through a gap, chasing and catching, scoring a try – outwitting a whole side on his own. And while you didn't really associate Jonathan with hard tackling – after all it was his job to stay on his feet and start the counter-attack – when there was a need he would go for his opponents' legs like a terrier.

Against the All Blacks at Auckland in 1988, when Wales lost 54–7, his tackling on the film I saw was incredible. I first watched him at stand-off for Neath and, really, you only had to see him take a pass and let it go to know that he could play. He had opponents worried all the time. There was great excitement in Wales when he came back from Rugby League to join Cardiff in the autumn of 1995. But in that opening game I felt that the other Cardiff players weren't playing to him. He was coming into the line from full-back, but the ball was being passed inside. He's too great a player to ignore, and I wondered then whether the players and officials who had stayed with Rugby Union would give him an easy passage back into the game.

So what about Neil Jenkins, the record cap-winner and record points-scorer for Wales? I remember his first game. He looked a player, all right. Yet I still have a strange feeling that he would be a better full-back than fly-half. He's instinctively a terrific tackler; he kicks brilliantly; yet at fly-half there's something lacking. It's not that he's failing to pass to his centres, but it's at the wrong angle. There isn't that necessary sharpness about him, and his running is slightly unbalanced. You can't deny that he did a job for Wales that needed doing at a difficult period, but now it's at full-back that he could break all the records.

A stand-off unlike many I have mentioned, but a phenomenon in his own right, is Rob Andrew. When Ian Robertson was coaching Cambridge University he rang me up one day and asked if I would go up to Grange Road and take a look at a new fly-half he'd got. 'He's going to be good,' he said. It was Rob's first year up at Cambridge. I sat in the stand – there weren't many people there – and then after ten minutes walked over to the clubhouse. Robertson asked where I was going, and I told him I'd seen enough. Andrew was a great player. He was cutting through, side-stepping, doing all the things instinctively that an outside-half ought to do. And I still think that apart from winning internationals with his place-kicking and tactical kicking, Rob has never played as well for England as he played for Cambridge early on in his life. I believe that systems of play overcame the flair. For year after year you didn't see players showing any natural fluency because the stress was on power play – the need for possession and second-phasing and so on.

Rob played some fabulous games for England – he was a terrific operator – but I think he would have been all the greater if he'd been allowed the freedom to play with the initiative he showed at Cambridge. Because I like him, I've always wanted him to score or make a beautiful try. And he has made a few. But you won't hear people talking too much about the way he opened up the game. I'm sure he did at times, but it will have gone unnoticed because of the concentration on dropped goals and place-kicking.

That saddens me, because Rob was a far greater player than that. But then place-kicking has become the vogue with outside-halves. The Cardiff team, when I was playing, had goal-kickers everywhere, but with Bill Tamplin there the rest of us didn't get a look-in. And since it could be safely left to others, place-kicking didn't seem an essential part of the stand-off's skills.

It hardly needs saying that the stand-off is either liberated or confined by the type of service he gets from his scrum-half. I have already said how much I owed to Rex Willis who, for me, was the ideal partner – brave, resourceful, totally unselfish. But if we're talking about the greatest scrum-half, in fact the greatest rugby player, I have ever watched or played against, it must be Gareth Edwards. He was unbelievable. He was a fitness freak, his shape was right, and he was built like a bank vault – for, as you know, we've got small banks in Wales. He also had this wonderful quick-witted way of doing things. One Friday night on the eve of an international, he was talking to a few of us in the foyer of a hotel in Cardiff when Cliff Jones, then chairman of selectors, came in. 'Gareth, fitness test half-past eight tomorrow morning, across the road there,' said Cliff. Gareth had had a hamstring or something. 'Anyway, how are you feeling?' In reply, Gareth, without even taking off his blazer, did twenty back-somersaults on the hotel carpet. The fitness test was cancelled.

While Rex was injured in 1953 I played once with Billy Williams, a good, sound scrum-half closely identified with Roy Burnett, his Newport partner, and then twice with Trevor Lloyd who led the Maesteg club in their invincible season of 1949–50, scoring four tries, dropping five goals and taking place-kicks as well to tot up 112 points. He was a scrum-half in the mould of Clive Rowlands, keeping a terrific grip of the game when he was playing it. He came to South Africa with the Lions in 1955, and the tour wouldn't have been the same without him; we had some great fun in his company. But he played only a couple of games throughout because Johnny Williams and Dickie Jeeps were also in the side. In the past tours had often broken down because of injury to the scrum-halves, but this time the Lions over-compensated by taking three. It was sad that such a dominant player, and such a good-humoured tourist, should have drawn the short straw, but perhaps the style of the Lions didn't quite suit him. It was Dickie Jeeps from Northampton who emerged as the strongest scrum-half, and appeared in all four Tests, although he had not yet played for England. He served you like a dog, he was tough and he knew the game; I'm convinced that if his fellow Northampton player, Don White, had been in the party and working closely with him in the back row of the scrum, we'd have won the Test series.

After Rex retired from international rugby my new Wales

scrum-half was Onllwyn Brace of Llanelli, who had first made his name in partnership with Mike Smith at Oxford University. They had a marvellous understanding, and could have worked scissors movements blindfold. I think of him as an old-fashioned half-back – and this is no disrespect – like the James brothers, Dai and Evan, who played at half-back for Swansea and Wales in the 1890s, and were equally at home inside or outside. No-one knew which of them would put the ball into the scrum. In fact Onllwyn would probably have been better at stand-off. He was a natural ball player and breakaway runner, taking attention away from the back row, which were qualities that made him majestic in seven-a-side rugby. The only trouble playing with Onllwyn was that you didn't know when the ball was going to come to you. And although he was old-fashioned in one sense, in another he foreshadowed the modern game in which the scrum-half is often the more dominant partner.

Much as I admired Onllwyn, I never felt quite comfortable playing outside him, and he probably felt much the same about me. But often the partnership came off in spite of that. In 1956, when I was the Welsh captain, our second game was played against Scotland on a bitter day and a frozen pitch at Cardiff. Suddenly Onllwyn ran right across me and threw a reverse pass which I took out of sheer surprise. Then, because there were four people in front of me, I had to dive through them to score what proved the winning try. It was Onllwyn, I have to say, who made that try. But there was always an uncertainty about what he was going to do next. In the next match, in Dublin, we didn't play at all well together. We just didn't have that essential, instinctive rapport which you get with a club pairing. Life was less exciting, but more comfortable, when Onllwyn was succeeded by my regular Cardiff partner, Lloyd Williams. He fitted the new blueprint for scrum-halves. He was tall, well-built and durable, like Stan Coughtrie of Scotland and Dewi Morris of England. On tour with the Barbarians in Canada and South Africa I found I hit it off perfectly with Andy Mulligan of Ireland who was capable of making breaks on his own, so diverting attention from you, and was a beautiful passer of the ball. In that class too comes Van Der Westhuizen who, in my opinion, won the World Cup for South Africa in 1995.

When I grew up – and it's scarcely less true today – every Welsh boy wanted to play outside-half for Wales. Just as in New Zealand every boy wants to be flank-forward for the All Blacks. The ambition was fed by a succession of great outside-halves, running from the James brothers to Dick Jones, Percy Bush, Cliff Jones, W.B. Cleaver and so on – a long line of tradition which you had to respect. And you knew all their famous moves, which were passed down from one generation to the next. Rugby is peculiar in that there are players in the same side who are playing a different game from nearly all the others – hookers, wings, locks, scrum-halves. Unlike soccer, for instance, where everyone goes through roughly the same motions, and only the goal-keeper plays to his own set of rules.

The role of the stand-off has evolved over the years. I think that now he's expected to tackle more – or if not to tackle, to bang into people and get knocked down, so setting up the next phase of the game. But I was a great believer in the theory that if you made all these tackles – which was the job of the back-row forward anyway – then every bump cost you breath and energy. The result was that you weren't in tip-top condition to make the final break and snatch, perhaps, the one and only chance in a tight international to make the decisive try. I suppose we were spoilt by our back rows, who did all the donkey work and left us to show off a bit in the middle of the field. But they didn't seem to mind, it was the accepted practice.

It's what you look for in fly-halves. They do create surprising moves with the result that a try is scored. There are certain things I believe about them from my own experience. First, there's an emphasis now on angles of running; but they come naturally to you without having to be explained on paper or blackboards. If they don't you probably shouldn't be playing at stand-off. Again, everyone knows when to do things, but only the clever fly-half knows when not to do them. This separates the men from the boys. It's the people who know when not to break who eventually produce the jewels of the game and make you feel good walking out of the ground afterwards. Fly-halves have got to be cocky, and be allowed to preen themselves and be given the freedom to express their ideas.

What gives me the biggest buzz is to watch people who take your breath away with a beautiful run or a spontaneous move. I suppose to win World Cups you've got to play fairly dour, planned rugby. But nothing will ever take away for me the sight of a brilliant half-back creating a gap, racing through it, hair in the wind, making it look as if it's just occurred to him. Then somebody coming up outside, the ball pinging, and after seventy yards there comes a try. That may be romantic, but for me it's the ultimate in rugby.

12

Back to
the Beeb

Early in 1973, only three or four months after I left Farnham Park rehabilitation centre, I had a phone call asking me to go in and see Angus McKay at Broadcasting House. Angus had been the shaping influence on radio sport from the time I had done my first broadcasts as a rugby player. I admired him greatly, and had an extra reason to feel grateful to him since my stroke. He kept encouraging me to stay in touch by writing pieces for his programmes, even if problems with my speech meant I wasn't yet ready to read them on air. What he now proposed was a staff job: Editor of Sport on radio, with Bob Burrows, who later ran Sport on ITV, as my assistant editor. I understood Angus well enough to know what was in his mind. He was nearing retirement and wanted to make sure that a 'radio man' succeeded him. And in spite of my earlier defection to television, Angus must have decided that my heart was in the right place. Having so recently wondered whether I'd ever work again, I jumped at the offer.

It brought me some of the happiest times of my life in broadcasting since we set about re-shaping what was then 'Sport on Two'. Where previously it had been confined to the studio, we began to originate it from Wembley on Cup Final day, from Wimbledon during the championship fortnight or live from the Olympic Games with Terry Wogan in the chair. Angus had already been harbouring ideas like these. He knew that great numbers of men tuned in to his five o'clock show just in order to check their pools coupons with the League results. So it became compulsory listening for the rest of the family, who were probably not avid football fans, but would be sitting round the tea-table at that time on a Saturday afternoon. Angus saw the need to add newsy background features that would interest them too. I agreed and wanted to extend that principle to the whole of the afternoon's sport. Along with Bob Burrows, who was a brilliant editor on air, I tried to create a more varied type of programme which drew the listener in and was something new in radio.

That task became easier when, within twelve months, I was also made head of radio Outside Broadcasts. We had always had terrific commentaries on football, rugby, racing, but never co-operation between OBs, who covered those events, and Sports News. Funnily enough News, Sports News and OBs lived on opposite sides of the same corridor, but hadn't talked for ten years. So my first task was practically to introduce the members of these different departments to each other. I took them out to a series of lunches at the Rugby Club near the BBC, one or two from each side, and gradually they came out of their shells. It was only six months later, when my expenses were sent back, that I found that you weren't allowed to claim for entertaining other members of the staff. This made it a rather costly exercise, but it succeeded. The barriers came down.

In those days style was everything in broadcasting. And nobody epitomised this more for me than Peter Jones. Incidentally Peter died on the deck of a small launch at the Oxford and Cambridge Boat Race. In the middle of his commentary he just stopped talking and died. I don't think you can presume to say of anyone that he would have wanted to go this way – suddenly, and while doing what he did best. Yet there was a certain aptness in Peter's case, for he was the consummate professional, an argument in himself for not making false distinctions between sport and general reporting on radio. OBs may cover a church service in Tooting Bec, a general election, quizzes, the performing arts. And when you add to them the immediacy and the down-to-earth precision which are the special features of good sports reporting, you get broadcasting of a much rounder character. Peter, who was above all a football commentator, was equally convincing covering a memorial service from Liverpool Cathedral or the Heysel stadium or any other public event. This is because he had a command of language. A scholar in Spanish as well as English, he had this ability to communicate. He was never lost for words or caught with his head down consulting his notes. The facts he needed he kept in his mind, and that left him free to concentrate on what he was watching. It was qualities like these that I found exciting, and I wanted to exploit them fully.

Desmond Lynam was also there at the time. As soon as you heard him speak you knew his voice was right for radio. What bothers me is that today you often hear people in authority at the BBC argue that sound doesn't matter. The only thing that counts is what people say. Well, of course that is the essential thing, but it doesn't get you very far without a voice which makes your audience want to listen. That's what Raymond Glendenning had, and G.V. Wynne-Jones, and, to me, the best of all rugby commentators, Winston McCarthy of New Zealand. McCarthy had a sound which made you say, quiet a minute, let's listen to this. And that was the kind of impression I wanted our programmes to make. I was sorry to leave radio eventually because it was my first love, and because there are often more vivid pictures on radio, painted by the commentators' words, than there are on television.

My departure came in a curious way. One morning Ian Trethowan, the managing director of radio, asked to see me. I found him in his office reading the *Sporting Life*; he was mad keen on racing and later became chairman of the Betting Levy Board. He came straight to the point: 'Do you want to become the Controller of Radio One and Two, or do you want to go back to television? Tony Preston is leaving his job as head of the Outside Broadcasts Group.' I don't know what I had been expecting, but it wasn't that. I said I would have to think about it. The two radio networks were then under the same Controller, who was supposed to give them equal attention. Radio Two I was keen on, but as for One, I knew I would let them do what they liked. I didn't want to leave radio, but so as not to turn my back on promotion I chose television. I suppose I also took some ironic satisfaction from the offer. When I'd left television in 1965 it was after a dispute, over my *News of the World* contract, with the then head of OBs, Peter Dimmock.

My second arrival at the Television Centre in 1976 was almost a re-run of my first in 1962. Again I was cold-shouldered by people who felt they should have been sitting in my chair, but it didn't trouble me as much this time. In the first instance I had been this practically unknown Shoni Welshman arriving from Cardiff to take over 'Grandstand'. Now I was better known, but as a radio man who had been promoted to one of the most desirable positions in television. I could understand the resentment. I hadn't done a 'board', the interrogation before a panel by which people normally rise through the grades at the BBC. I hadn't even had many individual interviews. But I decided at the time that I was going to stick at it and work hard at it. Eventually, I got together with Sam Leitch, who was then the head of Sports Programmes, and we talked it out – pretty vehemently at first. Sam said to me, 'If you think I'm going to be going all over Europe carrying your bags you've another think coming to you. That's not going to be me.' And I said, 'Sam, I'm quite capable of carrying my own bags round Europe.' It was a bit childish, these disputes often are, but we became sort of pals. I knew I could count on old friends like David Coleman, Peter O'Sullevan, Bill McLaren and so on, and gradually the young staff and I got to quite like each other. From that point I began to enjoy myself there. The head of ITV Sport at the time was the enigmatic John Bromley. We were both very much alike in our attitudes and despite the fierce competition we became, and still are, great friends.

There had been great developments in technology my first time round, with the first videotape recording of any big event pioneered at the Olympic Games in Rome, 1960. But now techniques were changing even more rapidly. At the Games in Montreal in 1976 and Moscow four years later we were going in and out live instead of showing highlights. But I soon had interests outside sport. Peter Dimmock was still looking after the Royal Family and all state and royal occasions during the 'seventies. But it was a tradition that Royal liaison should be one of the responsibilities of the head of Outside Broadcasts, and I was asked to take it over. It involved making all the arrangements for such great national occasions as the state opening of parliament, Lord Mountbatten's funeral, the Queen Mum's eightieth birthday, the celebrations marking the twenty-fifth year of the Queen's reign, and the Prince of Wales's wedding to Lady Diana.

I had one great advantage in doing the work: I knew the Queen's private secretary. He was the Philip Moore who had captained the Barbarians side when I first played for them at the East Midlands in 1951. He was later to become Sir Philip and finally Lord Moore. Because of this connection I could phone him up for inside information on what to do, when to do it, what to wear, and so our friendship continued. One evening at a reception in Buckingham Palace I was standing with Philip and his wife and a few other people when the Queen came up to our group. Philip took something out of his pocket which turned out to be a 1951 match programme. He said, 'We played together, Your Majesty, for the Barbarians.' The Queen looked at it, then looked at the two of us, Philip with his silvery grey hair, and said, 'I don't know which of you has grown old more gracefully.' It was lovely.

I'm a great one for asking questions if I don't know something. You can't buy experience; it's only with time that you get to know the little nuances. So I was able to ask Philip whether we could have access to the Royal Family's philatelic collection, or use the forecourt of Hampton Court Palace for a play. Requests for facilities like these were coming through my office all the time from radio, television, the World Service. And one thing about dealing with the office staff at Buckingham Palace was that if you asked them a string of questions they would say, immediately, yes-yes-no-no-no-no-yes-no. You always knew exactly where you stood. There was never any messing about and saying well, yes, I'll fix that, but never doing it.

Another person I heavily relied on was Jane Astell, who ran my office and had been with Peter Dimmock. Then there was Ronnie Allison, the Queen's press secretary, who had previously been with the BBC and was always helpful with advice. Finally, there was available a great pool of expertise in covering, say, a royal wedding with forty-four cameras or whatever, which had been built up by Outside Broadcast engineers, technicians and producers. I spent so many hours asking perhaps naive questions, because it's better to admit your ignorance and find the right answers than to try and bluff it out. My job was to plan the operation, make it work, try and help if I could, but keep my distance if I had to. In the end this technique made a complicated task quite simple. It was a happy time for me, because I saw so much and learned so much. And looking back I realise what a privileged life I've had from my early days in rugby and right through broadcasting.

Royal weddings and royal funerals present much the same technical problems to broadcasters, but there's one essential difference. In the case of a wedding, you have six months from the date of the engagement to go through the millions of details involved, from laying cables through the gutters to dealing with the Army over the positions taken up by their street-liners stationed along the route. All through this six-month period you have regular meetings with the Army, the Department of the Environment, and so on, worrying out the agenda. To cover a funeral you may have no more than ten days in which to make much the same preparations.

The wedding of Prince Charles and Lady Diana took place at St Paul's Cathedral, the funeral of Lord Louis Mountbatten at Westminster Abbey; and what I found shattering was the toughness of our negotiations with these two places of worship. You think of churches and chapels as unworldly, but dealing with them was just like dealing with a boxing promoter or the Football League. Take the wedding. What we had to reach an agreement on was the facilities we would need for ourselves, for ITV, for the visiting radio and television commentators, and for the press and magazine photographers who were also our responsibility. We had to decide for how long before the wedding we would need the cathedral closed to the public so that we could move in the cameras, rig up the lighting and the microphones, and build the scaffolding for the photographers. Their negotiations were in the hands of a company employed by the cathedral. You could appreciate that if we wanted the public excluded for two days, then it was only right that we should compensate them for their lost revenue from visitors. But the sums which we and ITV were asked to pay seemed to be based on the supposition that they got five million visitors a day. We also had to pay the choir, the organist and practically everyone else involved. We came to some arrangement at the end, but it was still an astronomical operation. The same applied in the arrangements for the funeral, except that here we dealt directly with the Abbey. Both, by the way, were royal events; that is, they were paid for by the Queen. It is only on state occasions – the funeral of Sir Winston Churchill, for instance – that the tax-payer foots the bill.

Mountbatten was given a royal funeral because of his kinship with the Duke of Edinburgh, and it took place nine days after he was assassinated in Ireland. What helped in this case was that he had already specified precisely how the ceremony and the service should be conducted. We had it all written down in front of us, what was happening, and exactly where and when. Where the lying in state was to be, where the cortege should pick him up and take him to the Abbey. He had picked the hymns, decided which of the services should provide the street-liners and march in the procession. His horse must carry one riding boot turned backward. It's strange to remember that in the early hours of the Sunday morning before the funeral, we walked the route of the procession with Johnny Johnson, who was then the Comptroller at the Palace. He had a pedometer, a wheel which measured the number of paces so that the timing would be immaculate. The cortege was due to arrive outside Westminster Abbey bang on the hour, and so it did. When the horses got there and pulled up, starting to shudder as they do, so, boom, the first stroke of Big Ben rang out, absolutely perfect. This used to amaze me.

Despite these painstaking instructions, there was still a lot of planning to get through. There were regular meetings in the Jerusalem Chamber at the Abbey with representatives of the Abbey and the Church of England, the undertakers, the Brigade of Guards, the police and everyone else who was involved. I used to sit in on them for the BBC, since everything they decided would affect our programme.

The main speaking part went to Tom Fleming, the royal commentator, a Scottish actor who lives in Murrayfield. He has that lovely voice, and knows when to bring in a line and when not to speak at all. Yet a funeral commentary has to convey just as much detail as a wedding. Tom was master at that, controlling the tone and filling in the background. He still is, in fact, for you hear him from the Cenotaph on Remembrance Day. And of course various other commentators were positioned along the processional route, in the Abbey, and outside the main door to cover the departures. The overall director had pictures from forty different cameras, and from these he selected the one picture he wanted to transmit at any given time. He might want to stay on the scene in the Abbey or the approaching procession or, for variety, move to the crowd in the streets or pick up on some curious little incident. The permutations available for transmission are endless, and one director's finished product might be very different from another's. For many years Anthony Craxton was the director. Earlier he had worked in sport; in fact he was on the team during my first rugby commentary. But latterly he had done nothing but royal events. Now as there were fewer of these set-piece ceremonies and royal tours to cover, we could no longer afford this exclusive arrangement. Anthony had gone, and a new young man, Michael Lumley, took over for both the wedding and funeral.

Working in Royal Liaison was largely a matter of keeping in regular touch with the private secretaries – in particular Bill Heseltine, an affable Australian who had taken over from Philip Moore – and the people in the press office, who were a family in themselves. I'd go into Buckingham Palace at least once a week, and I would call at the Queen Mum's residence, Clarence House, on a Tuesday morning. Sometimes it wasn't much more than a courtesy call, a ten-minute chat and away. Other times there would be specific matters to discuss or vague possibilities to explore and I'd be there for an hour. It was the regular contact, however brief, which made sure that we didn't miss anything important.

I didn't have regular meetings with the Royal Family, but at various times I would meet one or other of them. For instance I went up to Scotland when we were filming a fantasy story the Prince of Wales had written called *The Old Man of Lochnagar*. We had a camera up on the hills outside Balmoral, and it was bitterly cold when we drove up there in a truck. It had been a lovely calm, warm autumn day when I left London, so I turned up in city shoes, lightweight trousers and a blazer. As soon as he saw me Prince Charles said, 'Come here, you'd better have these,' and he gave me a cap, a sweater and a jacket. Then he said, 'Try these wellingtons on,' so I wore those too. The cold didn't seem to trouble him too much because he insisted on going on with the filming.

Another time I met the Princess of Wales at a quarter to seven in the morning to take her to Lime Grove so that she could walk around the breakfast programme on television. I also took her to the set of 'EastEnders'. She gave me a bottle of champagne. I got lovely letters from Princess Diana's people afterwards. In fact, all I've ever had from the Royal

Family, I have to say, is honesty and a very decent sort of welcome.

I suppose the member of the family I came to know best, largely because she was a sports person, an Olympian in the eventing at Montreal, was the Princess Royal. I had the chance to do interviews with her, chat to her and meet her frequently, and I became very fond of her because she was forthright and upright, and had considerable warmth, though she didn't take nonsense from stupid people trying to do daft things. I admired the kind of work she did, and the energy she put into it. She had a sense of humour, too. She didn't take advantage of you, but you knew that you could share funny times with her. I quite liked her for that.

I think the only time I ever took advantage of my association with the Palace and Princess Anne was when it was my turn to be chairman of the Saints and Sinners Club in London. I wanted a guest speaker for my Christmas lunch at the Savoy, which is a big charity bash. After the meal all the money we have made during a golf day organised at Sunningdale by Nick Royds (that year it amounted to £60,000) is given away to a number of the little charities which are often overlooked. I'd asked the vicar of Swansea, Canon Don Lewis, a celebrated after-dinner speaker, especially in rugby circles; he'd accepted. And I'd also asked Princess Anne, which was breaking all traditions because the club had never invited a woman speaker before. They kept asking me at the meetings who I'd got. And I'd have to say I didn't know yet. Then I got a call to say Princess Anne would be delighted. It worked like a charm. She was terrific. Canon Lewis was in great form. And then Ned Sherrin wrote a poem for the lunch, which later I gave to Princess Anne with a Giles cartoon of her on a horse riding up to the hotel at Christmas with a red hood on. In the caption below, a policeman was saying to the doorman: 'This can't be the Princess, she doesn't ride side-saddle.'

Ned's poem began:

When we men grow old and our hearts grow cold and our
    sense of decorum fails,
We're too thick round the middle from too long on the
    fiddle, I can tell you some wonderful tales,
So push back your chairs and fill up your glass, and a story
    to you I'll tell
Of a clerical man and the Princess Anne, well known to
    Eskimo Nell.

It went on for ten or twelve more verses, which were very funny. Princess Anne lapped it all up, and stayed on talking for ages afterwards.

Just as memorable, in a very different way, was a meeting with the Queen Mother at Birk Hall, her Scottish home not far away from Balmoral. We had gone up from the BBC to present her with a videotape we had made of her eightieth birthday celebrations. The visit didn't start well for me. I was supposed to fly from Heathrow to Aberdeen early in the morning with Alasdair Milne, Director-General of the BBC. We'd then drive on to Birk House, where we were supposed to join Tom Fleming, who had come up from Edinburgh. At the airport I looked everywhere for Alasdair, but couldn't find him. A chap from British Airways took me into an office, gave me a cup of tea and went off to see whether he had already boarded the plane. Nobody could recall seeing him. I said that I couldn't go without him, and began ringing anyone who might know where he was. The plane left, and only then were we told he was on it. There was nothing for it but to catch the next flight, get a car to drive me to Birk Hall and hope to make the twelve o'clock appointment. I was twitching all the way, but I arrived only three minutes behind time.

By now they were having drinks and the Queen Mum was there. I can see her now, the lovely twin-set, the hat, the dogs and so on. For something to say, Alasdair remarked, 'The little Welshman's arrived.' She said hello, and welcomed me, not at all put out by my late arrival; then she added, 'I do hope that Lester doesn't win today at Leicester.' I said, 'So do I, ma'am,' without a clue what she was talking about. I found out later that she didn't want Lester to win in case it prevented Willie Carson becoming champion jockey. But racing wasn't all she knew about. She seemed very well read, and had a fund of local stories about Scottish country life and particularly the gillies who worked on the river. And without being at all sycophantic about it, we thoroughly enjoyed ourselves. As we were leaving, the Queen Mum said to us, 'I haven't shown you the political cartoons collected by the king.' This was George VI. They were right around the walls of a corridor, and as we finished looking at them, the doors opened and there was our car waiting for us outside. It showed us with perfect firmness and tact that this was the time to leave.

I was head of Outside Broadcasts for eleven years – from 1976 until I retired, or was asked to retire, on my fifty-seventh birthday in 1987. So it accounted for more than a third of the time I had spent in broadcasting. I was upset about leaving at the time; when they asked me if I would like to take early retirement, I knew it was just a posh way of saying, 'You're fired.' I understood that my attitude and my way of doing things was becoming old-fashioned. Just as I accepted that I couldn't go on doing rugby commentary at my age. I could comment on it. I could keep up an interest in the people who played. But I wasn't able to get inside the game as once I could. Still, it was one thing to acknowledge these things to yourself, another to be told them. So I did mind. It's no good pretending otherwise.

Now, on reflection, I'm convinced it was a good thing I left when I did. If I hadn't retired at an early age I would never have been able to return to radio. Never have had the chance to compile and present 'Sport on Four' on Saturday mornings, as I have for the past nine years. Never have done a series like 'Down the River'. I made it with Anthony Smith of Bristol who had, for many years, produced 'Down Your Way' with Brian Johnston. I absolutely adored my outings to follow the Tyne, the Tay, the Windrush, the Wye, the Dee and the Rhondda to the sea and meet the people who lived along their banks. The excitement of these radio programmes gave me a new lease of life. Apart from which I'd received a pay-off for my early departure, which I wouldn't have had if I'd left at sixty. It would have been a pension and not a penny more. So all in all the BBC probably did me a big favour.

I've said it about other phases of my life, I know, but I think I've enjoyed the last as much as any other. I've come to the conclusion that making programmes with a sympathetic producer is far more rewarding than sitting on committees. In fact it is the ultimate reward of broadcasting. What could be better than doing a series on Heroes with the incomparable and inventive producer from Cardiff, Peter Griffiths? How else would I have heard Alistair Cooke talking about Sir Arthur Quiller-Couch, his professor of English literature at Cambridge, the great American golfer, Bobby Jones, and the witty, scurrilous American writer, H.L. Mencken? Or Baroness Sear talking about Joe Grimond and her experiences in Berlin before the last war? Or Hugh McIlvanney telling of his belief in heroes and why we need them? These things have been a great boost to me.

And what has been an extra bonus is that they have all taken place on radio. As someone once said, I was too ugly for television. It's probably true. I haven't got the appearance of a television performer. For which I'm thankful. Ever since I was a child and heard the Light Programme and the Welsh Home Service brought home to us by the relay shed in the village, I have been fascinated by the wireless. I can't sit and watch television for too many hours, but I can listen to the voices and music on the radio for ever.

13

The state of the Union

I never thought that rugby would change so drastically or in such a short time. In the late 'sixties, when I was a freelance broadcaster at the BBC, John Player came to talk to me about a cup competition they wanted to sponsor. Obviously, they needed television support, and at that time it was the BBC which broadcast all the big rugby events. I said I wouldn't touch the idea with a barge-pole; the Rugby Union was thoroughly against inter-club competition and anyway it was all wrong for the game. A year later Peter West and Patrick Nally of the West Nally sports promotion agency had the thing all stitched up. The first final was played at Twickenham in 1972. Club merit tables followed in 1985, proper leagues two years later. And incidentally, to illustrate the effect of competitive rugby on club fortunes, the cup winners in 1972 were Gloucester and the runners-up Moseley, both now struggling to live with the leading clubs.

I was totally wrong about the way that rugby would move. I suppose I had too much faith in what the game had meant to me as a player. The change was inevitable, they tell me, though I'm still not certain whether cups and leagues have been such a great thing for the game. And the reason for my misgivings, to put it in its simplest terms, is that Cardiff no longer play Bristol, Bath, Coventry, Leicester, all those fixtures that enriched our seasons and gave them breadth and variety. Instead we have this endless series of internal battles in Wales and England which fail, I believe, to refresh the game in any way. They simply make it more introverted.

Then in 1984 a Mr Littlejohn from New Zealand and Sir Nicholas Shehadie from Australia, with whom I had played Barbarian rugby, came to my office at the BBC with a proposition for a World Cup. This idea I didn't flatly turn down. By now I felt that the momentum for change was unstoppable. Once you have established a little competition you want a bigger one, and eventually you want the world. I wasn't fully sympathetic to it, or convinced that it would succeed, but I went along with it as far as I could. What really stopped the BBC supporting it was that we couldn't reach an agreement with the World Cup Committe over cash. We didn't have the resources to compete with what others were prepared to offer for overseas television sales.

In the end West Nally again ran the show, and the BBC has basically been out of the World Cup ever since. Maybe we should have been more financially astute, gone with the tide, blown the expense, and shown more optimism about the future of the World Cup. I don't know. Perhaps I was a bit out of date even in those days. I was pretty certain that some good had to come of so many countries taking part, proving that the game wasn't the monopoly of the eight International Board members. That in itself was exciting. So was any event which would bring the world's best rugby players together. But I was concerned that, regardless of style, countries would want to win at all costs, with all the hardness and ruthlessness that goes with that attitude. Rugby would be dominated by commercial considerations. And as a result, the game would lose more than it gained. Which is how it turned out.

The 1995 World Cup in South Africa was a classic example. One team stood out like a beacon, playing rugby at its best.

That was New Zealand. They had terrific talent. They carried the ball with two hands, as all great backs do, and so they were able to pass it freely. Their basic forward play was tough but their support play on the move was not just impressive, it was inspired. It didn't win them the Cup. I don't know what part was played by the rumoured food poisoning at their hotel, but they came on in the final looking quite different from the side that had beaten England. The spark had died, the confidence was missing. Andrew Mehrtens, who looked to me the best fly-half in world rugby for a long time, took the wrong options, failed in his four attempts to drop a goal, kicked at the wrong time. There was something essential missing from their natural game, and in extra time they lost to a South African side which had marvellous commitment but little creative flair. You had to be pleased for the new South Africa, and in particular Nelson Mandela, whose very presence emphasised his statesmanship. I don't think the better team won, but the victory was marvellous for South Africa and mankind.

What people expect from cup competitions is little clubs beating big clubs, and little countries becoming giant-killers. But these are rare exceptions. World Cups are won by the great and powerful nations, whether or not they play the most thrilling rugby. As a result the tournament doesn't build up to a climax; the most memorable games are often played in the quarter- and semi-finals. In the first World Cup, in 1987, the semi-final between France and Australia at Sydney was one of the best rugby games I've seen. And not just because the incomparable Serge Blanco at full-back scored a record fifteenth international try to win the match for France in the final minute. The build-up to that try was just as exciting. The French began the move on their own line and developed it with spectacular inter-passing the length of the field. The unexpected, as in Blanco's try, is what you long to see. It was also there in 1995 in the kick-off by New Zealand which did for England in their semi-final at Cape Town. The All Blacks switched the direction of attack straight away, while the English backs were still talking to each other. Jonah Lomu burst through for a try and, psychologically, the game was over in sixty seconds.

Unfortunately, the more competitive the game becomes, the less often you are treated to these thrilling surprises. Instead of seeing backs run the ball at the defence, then swerve and side-step to create a scoring chance for the pace outside them, you see big forwards going willingly into the tackle with their shoulder down and knocking smaller backs over. It gets results, but to me it is exceedingly boring. In cup games you may see games which are exciting because there is very little between the two teams. Yet as you walk away you can't remember one moment of absolute brilliance. That is what scares me about these competitions, and I don't see much sign of improvement as the game goes professional.

I have no complaint against professionalism in principle. I turned down many offers to play for the Rugby League, but I never felt any hostility towards it. I have always enjoyed the game, admired many of its players, and found the officials decent and honourable. But you have to remember that professionalism in the League evolved gradually. The original split with the Union in 1893 was not about paying men for playing rugby, but compensating them for the Saturday shifts in mines and mills that they had to sacrifice to turn out for their clubs. It was another five years before pay-for-play was adopted, and even then it was only semi-professionalism: players had to have a regular weekday job so that they didn't become dependent on their rugby earnings. In this way the Northern Union, as it was then called, never lost touch with its local working-class origins.

I can well understand why players who attract the crowds who pay for the vast arenas, administrative blocks, shops, bars, restaurants and hospitality suites which have been built around their game should feel entitled to their share of the proceeds. In the 'fifties I would attend functions in London where I was meant to represent my sport and mix with celebrities from motor racing, horse racing, golf or boxing on equal terms. But I felt far from equal afterwards as I looked around for the nearest tube station and then travelled third-class back to Cardiff. Mind, any resentment I felt soon disappeared. There were plenty of other amateurs in the same boat – athletes, tennis players, swimmers. Even professional footballers were being paid only £20 a week in winter, and £17 in summer, and in 1956 their union was pressing for a bonus of £2–3 for appearing in televised matches. There were few objects of envy to spoil our fun. We didn't have as many commitments and expectations. The use of a sponsored car was unheard of. In fact, unless a car came with the job, you'd be in your late twenties before you thought of buying one of your own.

Nowadays rugby players have mortgages to pay, cars to run, a mass of new-found social and electronic 'necessities' to fund. So, since rugby is apparently awash with money, why should it be the only major sport not to support a professional class at the top? There's no question that leading players nowadays have to devote many more hours to the game than we did. And it isn't just a case of players being fairly rewarded for their skills. Some of them would have been justified in asking for those 'broken time' payments which first produced the rift with the northern clubs. Players who are in publicity-conscious jobs like marketing, sales promotion, publicity and even journalism probably find that their celebrity helps them in their jobs. This means that their absence at matches, at the four days of training in the week before internationals, and at routine squad sessions is readily excused. But for rugby-playing accountants, farmers and, especially, doctors, their sport is a professional liability which tries the patience of those they work with and damages their careers. They would have deserved some compensation anyway.

So it isn't the move to professional rugby in itself that bothers me, but the indecent speed at which it has been introduced. That, and the lack of any clear vision of what it's going to mean for the players and the clubs who turn pro – as well as those who don't. One thing has to be recognised: that rugby can be professional only at the very top. Whether we like it or not, rugby is not a world game. It isn't like soccer. Kids don't play it from the time they are weaned in the back streets of every country from Brazil to Bulgaria. So despite the sponsors' money coming into the game, rugby can't afford to be professional for everybody.

Nobody can yet guess exactly where the cut-off point will come. It's curious that although their game is less popular, grassroots rugby clubs tend to be more affluent than their equivalent in soccer. This is because they are more sociable, and members mean money over the clubhouse bar. But it's nothing like enough to pay the players. The smaller clubs don't draw casual spectators through their gates. This reduces their chance of attracting sponsorship, and in the end their only option is to stay amateur.

I really think the International Rugby Board was bounced into the decision to go professional – in part by the players and promoters, but even more by the newspapers and other media who had been criticising them for being hopelessly out of date and indecisive. So the IRB reacted with the surprise announcement that the game would immediately rewrite its first principle: 'The game is an amateur game. No-one is allowed to seek or receive payment or other reward for taking part in the game.' This was much to the glee of the papers, who had a big story to tell. But it came about a year sooner than it should have done, leaving all manner of questions unresolved. And this allowed the same papers to turn on the IRB because it didn't know where it was going.

One thing that bothers me is what professionalism means to the players. It isn't just about making money. I'm all for a professional attitude, but that implies playing the game well, presenting it attractively to the public, innovating, creating exciting stars, living dangerously. In theory being paid for their services should give players more time to apply themselves to training and developing the game. If they choose instead to be semi-professionals, spending no more time on rugby than they did as amateurs, and devoting the rest of the week to honing their images, they may blow their big opportunity. Rugby isn't irresistible as a spectator sport.

Twickenham matches are nowadays a sell-out, but nobody should assume that this is part of the natural order of things. What if England loses six matches in a row? The fans won't desert them in droves, perhaps, but they might lose a little of their old enthusiasm. Except on the biggest occasions there might be more seats than bums to put on them. Invitations to the hospitality boxes might not be accepted with such alacrity. And the sponsors will begin to wonder whether they should be investing their money here. In after-dinner speeches, this sponsor or that is often described as 'a great friend of the game'. But the fact is that sponsors are even more loyal to their shareholders and their balance sheets. They have certain marketing objectives; once these have been achieved they will move on to pastures new. I saw this happening in the negotiations for the first World Cup; expectations of vast sponsorships were soon cut down to a size that made sense in the market. Amateur rugby could get away with the old excuse that it was 'a game for players not spectators'. The new professionals, and their coaches, may not find the paying public so forgiving of a mechanical, stereotyped style of play.

I also worry whether the professional game will do enough to look after its amateur base. Clubs are already paying ludicrous amounts of money to attract key players without any assurance that they'll see any return on it. And Rugby Unions are vastly overspending on their national stadiums. I don't accept that bigger must be better, that a stadium for 75,000 people is an advance on one that holds 50,000; it lacks intimacy and puts a greater distance between the spectators and the play. I also have to confess that I'm against hospitality boxes at matches. I have a feeling that hospitality is one thing, and watching a rugby match is another. For the most part, anyway, the guests are looking at the telly in the box, with a gin and tonic in their hand. Good for them, but they might just as well be watching at home.

Decisions are increasingly being driven by marketing men who don't understand the loyalties and the amateur support systems that have been built up over the last century. The women who wash the kit and make the teas, the men who act as stewards and touch-judges, the so-called 'old farts' who sit on committees. Many of them have given their lives to providing facilities for the youngsters who, after all, provide the next generation of players from which the professionals will emerge. These unpaid officials have been the backbone of rugby, and the professional ranks can't afford to alienate them.

There is a great danger that the new set-up will get rid of those features which made rugby distinctive. That, for instance, by attracting players from Europe, Australia, New Zealand, clubs will weaken their local connections. They were immensely strong in my day. I couldn't have imagined not playing for Cardiff, and playing instead for Newport or Swansea. Cardiff was my nearest first-class club. I'm sure that if I'd come from the valleys of West Wales I would have felt equally drawn to Llanelli. The ambition to play for your village or your town has always been a big factor in rugby. Without these local ties and opportunities, we're going to lose players on the way up. The clubs benefit from them too. The presence of a French or All Blacks celebrity might bring in the crowds out of curiosity, but he wouldn't have the long-term impact of a genuine home-grown star.

Saddest of all, in my experience, is the suggestion that professional rugby will not be able to find room for the Lions and the Barbarians tours. These are where the lasting friendships are forged between players of different countries. They are the core of what has been unique in rugby; something money can't buy. If it just comes down to going out and winning matches, I don't envy the players of today and tomorrow. It offers no relaxation from daily life. It is part of the grind.

There's no question in my mind that, on the whole, the game is better now than it was when I was playing it forty years ago. Players are fitter, faster, bigger. They understand rugby far better than we ever did, because in our day we played it off the cuff and, in Tony O'Reilly's words, a coach was a posh bus. They also know the rules, which few of us ever read. I respect them for giving up so much time and making so many sacrifices for rugby.

Yet I also found it sad to hear one of the current England internationals predict that in five years' time, because of the level of professionalism required, there will be no doctors, no lawyers, no vets, no accountants playing at the top. That, for me, would make life immeasurably duller. I also worry that there will be so much year-round rugby – like cricket, like almost any sport – that players will not last so long or enjoy as many benefits as they do now.

On the other hand I see a future when there will be only five or six fully professional clubs in England, perhaps a dozen in the UK, meeting continental and world opposition. And at that point I suspect that if Wasps and Cardiff, for instance, are not among them, they will go back to what they have always done, getting players together at the weekend for no more reward than hard, competitive, uncommercial rugby in the afternoon and the enjoyment of each other's company in the evening.

Would I have wanted to turn professional if I had been playing for Cardiff and Wales today? I don't honestly know. The whole idea would have been unimaginable in the 'fifties. What I can say for certain is that it wouldn't have suited me. I don't think I could have given my life to a game where success was so important. I was too interested in the village, the chapel, the school orchestra, the singing. I could never have turned up for rugby training on a Wednesday evening. That was choir practice. I am grateful to have played rugby at a time when it was played for fun and friendship – when it demanded less and offered so much more.

Index